ARCHBISHOP LAMY:
IN HIS OWN WORDS

ARCHBISHOP LAMY: IN HIS OWN WORDS

EDITED & TRANSLATED BY
THOMAS J. STEELE, S.J.

FOREWORD BY JANICE SCHUETZ AND ANDREW BURGESS
AFTERWORD BY THE MOST REVEREND MICHAEL J. SHEEHAN

LPD PRESS
ALBUQUERQUE
2000

Copyright © 2000 by LPD Press
Albuquerque, New Mexico

All rights reserved
No part of this book may be reproduced or transmitted
in any form, or by any means, electronic or mechanical,
including photocopying, recording, or by any
information retrieval system,
without permission of the publisher.

Library of Congress Control Number 00-131080

ISBN 1-890689-04-1 (cloth)
ISBN 1-890689-10-6 (paper)
ISBN 1-890689-20-3 (CD-rom)

Printed on 250-year acid-free paper
Printed in the United States of America

First Edition
10 9 8 7 6 5 4 3 2 1

CONTENTS

ILLUSTRATIONS

Dedication

I dedicate this book to the
people, priests, and prelates
of New Mexico
who have kept alive
the traditional Hispanic culture.

I express my thanks to Barbe Awalt and Paul Rhetts of LPD Press; Archbishop Michael J. Sheehan, Marina Ochoa, and Loretta Medrano-Medina of the Archdiocese of Santa Fe; Sister Katherine Misbauer, S.L., of the Loretto Motherhouse Archives; Jesuit Fathers Frank Renfroe and Edmundo Rodríguez of Immaculate Conception Parish, Albuquerque; Jesuit Fathers David M. Clarke and Michael J. Sheeran of Regis University, Denver; the people of Immaculate Conception Parish and of the Catholic communities of Carnuel, Chililí, Escobosa, and Sedillo; Janice Schuetz, Andrew Burgess, E.A. "Tony" Mares, and Monique Durham of the University of New Mexico; Thomas Chávez of the Museum of New Mexico; Don Toomey; Bob Lewis; and especially Randolph F. Lumpp and Rowena A. Rivera-King, whose editing helped this book so greatly.

The research phase of this project was funded in part by the New Mexico Office of Cultural Affairs.

Foreword

For the researcher in early American religious history, sermons often best represent its intellectual and spiritual depth. The preaching of men such as Cotton Mather and Jonathan Edwards not only displays the ideas of the most educated men of their times but also sheds indirect light on their listeners.

These Puritan preachers are only part of the story, however. When the Mexican War altered the boundary of the United States in the mid-nineteenth century, the course of American religion changed as well. With the new territories the country inherited a new Spanish Catholic theological tradition that went back further than anything the English tradition of the Eastern seaboard could offer. The situation got still more complicated when Rome, to run the former Mexican territory, forthwith sent out a battalion of clerics, led by Bishop Jean Baptiste Lamy, whose native tradition was neither Anglo-American nor Spanish but distinctively French.

Lamy has been badly misunderstood, though not for the reasons one might expect. If any of his former parishioners in Ohio and Kentucky were upset by his French ideal of authority, their opinions have not survived, and the protests from New Mexico have not fared much better. No, the misunderstanding does not arise from his detractors but from someone who idolized him – Willa Cather ("that woman," as one person used to call her, between clenched teeth) – whose fictional work *Death Comes for the Archbishop* has clothed Lamy's heritage in unforgettable prose. The problem, as Steele acidly points out, is that the heritage Cather presents is just not true. Her book is not an historical novel, preserving the substance of the historical record, but a romance, with stereotyped characters drawn from the

imagination. The archbishop Cather paints is an introverted thinker and an intuitive visionary who feels deeply about his situation and empathizes with the people he serves. That picture, however, shows not the mind of Lamy but that of Cather herself. Her work is a classic of American literature, but as Steele says, it has "muddied the waters of New Mexican history" to this day.

In *Archbishop Lamy: In His Own Words*, Steele has provided abundant evidence for correcting the misunderstanding of Lamy, through the texts of 250 extant sermons and talks, fully a quarter of a million words. Steele's earlier volume of New Mexican sermons, *New Mexican Spanish Religious Oratory*, contains sermons from other writers of the period, including Lamy's great opponent, Padre Antonio José Martínez of Taos. Taken together, the two collections make up an historical treasure trove. Since sermons reflect the personality of the preacher and of the times, the reader can now listen to much of the testimony needed to appreciate the achievements and the struggles of Archbishop Lamy, almost as if one were sitting every Sunday and feast day in his cathedral.

The Lamy that emerges from these sermons is not the dreaming archbishop of Cather's book but a man of action. This Lamy is an extrovert, a pragmatic thinker, and an admonitor of those he comes to serve. In ways similar to politicians and traders who come to the frontier settlements, he is a progressive seeking to spread civilization to the uneducated and unsophisticated people of New Mexico. Like them he is an empire builder, but he sees the empire not as his own but as the Kingdom of God. To accomplish his goal of creating a respectable model of Roman Catholic life, Lamy builds churches, schools, and hospitals, and when need arises he removes priests and threatens excommunication to parishioners who do not tithe. He makes policy decisions without hesitation, and only when the work is already underway does he think of the steps necessary to carry them out. Perhaps he is the kind of leader the times required. Cather's archbishop could never have created a new archdiocese in the wilderness. The writer of these sermons could and did.

Even some of his weaknesses prove appropriate to the New Mexico of that era. Certainly this is true of the intellectual content of

his sermons and the rhetorical structure in which they are formed, as Steele shows. Lamy's rhetoric is typical of the preaching of the time, which turns scripture into "proof texts" or uses it in the service of allegory. The sermons are full of rhetorical questions and references to the virtues, weak on humor, but strong on moralizing. Moreover, the theology underlying the sermons allows an inconsistent mixture of Jansenism and Pelagianism, which are as far apart as two positions can be. Nonetheless, the preaching that emerges seems to have been surprisingly effective, perhaps because the Jansenism resonates with the Calvinism predominant in American culture, and the Pelagianism and moralism make him fit right in with the revivalistic spirit of his day.

Steele faces up to the accusation most commonly leveled at Lamy, that he is not willing to take seriously the values of another culture. Steele notes that Lamy's background did not provide him with the sensitivity to grasp some of the cultural traditions of New Mexico Hispanics, such as the Penitente Brotherhood and their rituals. Instead, the seminary training he received in France encouraged him to be suspicious of popular religious rites. Still, even here Lamy is neither as inflexible as he is sometimes portrayed, nor is he the most extreme case within the Roman Catholic hierarchy of the West.

Who was Lamy? Not the figure in Cather's novel. Who, then? Steele's introductory essays dispel a host of myths and then leave it up to the reader to decide by listening to Lamy himself – in his own words.

Janice Schuetz and Andrew Burgess
The University of New Mexico

Chapter 1
Lamy: Introduction and Chronology

French-born Jean Baptiste Lamy (1814-88), the first Bishop and Archbishop of Santa Fe, is a major New Mexican icon, and therefore he has served during the entire twentieth century as a movie-screen upon which a pair of very widely accepted interpretations, one positive and the other negative, have been projected.

Who was Lamy himself? This first chapter will present a "value-free" chronology that simply lists the events of the man's life without much interpretation; the rest of the answer to the question of Lamy's identity and character will occupy the remainder of the interpretative essay, and the sermons that follow will offer a small amount of the raw evidence.

What were and are the bases of the two popular views of Lamy? They were both based on the widespread "great-man" interpretation of history, that some individual made history happen and that he deserves all the praise or blame. The first view, which prevailed from the end of the nineteenth century until the 1960s, wrote the history of New Mexico as a positive tale of happy progress from less enlightened to more enlightened, culminating in suburbia, television, and the pre-Vatican-II Catholic Church. Lamy seemed during those years to be the greatest of New Mexico's children, whether native-born or adopted. The negative second view, in force from the 1960s until the present, has asked where the land-and-person-and-community-centered Hispanic culture of the olden days has gone and who is to blame for its disappearance. Because Lamy got so much of the credit for New Mexico's "Happy Days" projection, he has lately gotten the

lion's share of the blame that results from the sense of loss.

Why is a new "read" on Lamy needed? Well, for one thing, romanticism's "great-man" view of history no longer persuades historians. How many men, even the greatest, were accurately aware of the long-range *effects* of their deeds, were in control of the *outcomes* of their actions? "The best laid schemes o' mice an' men Gang aft a-gley," Burns told us, and his judgment was as keen about the schemes of men as it was about those of mice: the best leaders labored in semi-darkness doing what seems best, while the worst had an ideological plan that normally created disaster in short order. If as I suspect the era of Romanticism has already ended, the men and women of a new cultural era will demand a new interpretation of Lamy.

Where will this new view come from? I have located the original manuscripts of about 250 of Lamy's sermons, instructions, retreat talks, and other speeches, almost none of which have ever been examined. They comprise about 250,000 words of original English (from Lamy's Ohio and Kentucky years) and Spanish (from his time in New Mexico). Thirty-four talks appear in this book; all 250 of them are available on a CD-ROM, with all spelling standardized so that the texts are fully computer-searchable for any words and phrases that might interest the reader. A quarter of a million words provide a quite thorough self-revelation of a person's ideas, values, aims, and dislikes.

Lamy: A Short Chronology

1) Jean Baptiste Lamy was born 11 October 1814 in Lempdes, Auvergne, in the mountains of southern France. His parents, Jean Lamy and Marie Dié Lamy, had eleven children, only four of whom lived to adulthood. Jean was the town mayor for a term; Marie was very devout, and of her four surviving children two boys became priests and the one girl, Marguerite, became a nun; the other son married and had three children, one of whom became a priest and another a nun. Even as a young boy, Jean Baptiste was very devoted to Notre Dame de Bonne Nouvelle – Our Lady of Good Tidings, the patron of the parish church (Horgan, 12-15).

From age eight, Lamy boarded at a minor seminary in nearby

Billon which the Jesuits ran during the last three of his years there. He went on to the major seminaries at Clermont and Montferrand, where he met his lifelong friend Joseph Machebeuf, with whom he shared an interest in the foreign missions that stemmed both from reading and from recruiting visits to the seminary by bishops from America. Lamy received tonsure (making him a cleric) on 28 May 1836, minor orders (porter, lector, acolyte, and exorcist) on 17 December 1836, and subdiaconate on 20 May 1837; he was ordained a deacon on 28 December 1837 and a priest on 22 December 1838. His health was not the best, and it is recorded that he was bled twice by cutting a vein and fifteen times by leeches (Horgan 15-21; Warner 22; Chávez *AASF* 114; Bridgers 28).

2) In May 1839, Bishop John Baptist Purcell recruited Machebeuf and Lamy for work in his Diocese of Cincinnati, and they left (in a much-described "escape") from Riom on 21 May. They sailed from Le Havre on 9 July; after three weeks of sea-sickness, Lamy recovered, and the ship reached New York on 20 August. The party traveled through Baltimore and arrived at Cincinnati 10 September 1839, and Lamy was assigned to Danville in the middle of Ohio; he first preached in English on Easter Sunday, 19 April 1840. During his eight years there, Lamy built a number of churches, chapels, and rectories; he and Machebeuf visited each other when they could, but they were both busy and they were stationed about seventy-five miles apart (Howlett 40-44, 58, 67-68, 77, 84, 108, 122; Horgan 3, 22-24, 29-30, 56-59; Bridgers 34-44). On 26 January 1845 at Danville, Lamy wrote the earliest of his sermons to survive.

In September 1847, Lamy moved to Covington, Kentucky, across the Ohio River from Cincinnati. The next May he traveled to Europe, returning with his sister the nun and his niece Marie, who went to the Ursuline Convent in Brown County, Kentucky. In early 1849, Lamy talked Machebeuf out of volunteering for the missions of the Northern Plains, but on 11 May the Provincial Council of Baltimore asked Rome to establish a Vicariate-Apostolic – a diocese in the process of formation – in New Mexico, recently acquired by the Treaty of Guadalupe-Hidalgo, and nominated Lamy to head it.

Over a year later, Rome established the Vicariate on 19 July 1850 and named Lamy its Vicar on 23 July. He was consecrated on 24 November 1850 in Cincinnati and took Machebeuf along to be his Vicar-General (Howlett 150-52; Horgan 60-67, 73-81; Bridgers 43-45, 48, 62-63, 73; Chávez, *AASF* 114-16; Marc Simmons, "In the Shadow of the Miter: New Mexico's Quest for Diocesan Status," *Seeds of Struggle, Harvest of Faith* [Albuquerque: LPD Press, 1998], 207-18.)

3) Lamy left for New Mexico the following day, taking his ailing sister and his niece Marie with him to the Ursulines in New Orleans, where they arrived 4 December 1850. Lamy left for Texas on 6 January 1851 in a condemned ship, stopped for the day at Galveston and accepted the care of three towns in the El Paso area, Ysleta, Socorro, and San Elizario, from Bishop Odin; then in the evening of the next day, the ship sank at the edge of Matagorda Bay and the new bishop lost everything except the clothes on his back and one crate of books, vestments, and sermons. He traveled to San Antonio where he purchased a wagon and some mules, and when they ran away on 21 April, he severely sprained an ankle. The army caravan he and his four priests intended to accompany left without them, and since the spring rains did not fall, there was no grass in west Texas until mid-May. When Lamy finally arrived in El Paso, he visited Father Ramón Ortiz in Mexican El Paso and toured the three towns on the east side of the Rio Grande; while in Socorro del Sur on 24 June 1851, he first preached in Spanish. As the group traveled north toward Santa Fe, the townspeople along their route, alerted by Vicario Foraneo (Rural Dean) Juan Felipe Ortiz of Santa Fe, welcomed them with great delight (Chávez, *AASF,* loose documents 1851 # 7 and 8, p. 117; Horgan 81-110; Chávez, *But Time and Chance* 96; Bridgers 81-82).

Lamy and his party arrived in Santa Fe on 9 August 1851 to a splendid reception prepared by Vicar Ortiz, Ramón's cousin. A few weeks later Judge Grafton Baker got drunk and threatened the clerics if they tried to take possession of the Castrense Chapel. Lamy realized that he needed the acquiescence of Bishop Zubiría (Rome's notification had gone to Sonora instead of Durango), so he and Vicario

Foraneo Ortiz set out for Durango, 1400 miles away, leaving about 18 September 1851 and returning 10 January 1852; then Lamy left 1 April for the First Plenary Council of Baltimore, returning with some Loretto nuns who founded a school for girls upon their arrival in Santa Fe 26 September (Chávez, *AASF* 118; Horgan 114-64; Steele, "The Poet, the Archbishop, and the Heavenly Jerusalem," *Folk and Church* 104-20; Bridgers 89-93).

Lamy's and Machebeuf's next several moves were unfortunate. Lamy issued a pastoral letter at Christmas 1852 unilaterally changing the system of fees the priests received for their ministries. Machebeuf got too talkative about confessional matters and alienated one of the most powerful men in the territory. Lamy and Machebeuf relieved Padre José Manuel Gallegos of the Albuquerque parish, suspending him and losing a lawsuit over the ownership of the rectory. Nevertheless, the Vicariate-Apostolic of New Mexico became the Diocese of Santa Fe on 12 August 1853, and in early 1854 Lamy left for Europe to appear officially before the Pope; he returned 18 November 1854 (Horgan 156, 170-80, 183-84, 188, 190-213; Steele, "Padre Gallegos, Père Machebeuf, and the Albuquerque Rectory," *Folk and Church* 58-72; Bridgers 101-04, 109-17).

4) In the early months of 1856, Machebeuf prepared for his trip to Rome to defend himself against the charge of having violated the seal of confession, and he won his acquittal. Padre Martínez of Taos offered a conditional resignation, and Lamy replaced him with Padre Taladrid, a peninsular Spaniard who had little or no respect for the "colonials" of New Mexico; by 27 October 1856, Lamy suspended Martínez. Machebeuf returned to Santa Fe on 10 November 1856 with several more priests and priests-to-be. On 27 May 1857, Father Taladrid and Kit Carson summoned the U.S. Army from Cantonment Burgwin to save them from a non-existent plot by Father Martínez; Lamy removed Taladrid from Taos instantly. In May and June 1857, Machebeuf traveled to the eastern States and returned with Marie, Lamy's niece. The next spring, on 11 and 18 April 1858, Machebeuf read the excommunications of Fathers Martínez at Taos and Lucero at Arroyo Hondo (Horgan 220-46; Steele, "Kit Carson

and Padre Martínez," *Folk and Church* 73-80; Steele in Mares, ed., *Padre Martínez: New Perspectives* 99-100n30; Bridgers 130-37).

In the spring of 1858, Lamy founded the first Colorado parish, at Conejos. During the summer he traveled across the Santa Fe Trail to Kentucky to attend the Provincial Council of Saint Louis. On 27 October, Father Pierre Eguillon returned from Europe with several more priests and seminarians. On 16 January 1859, Machebeuf left for Arizona to begin to staff the new Gadsden Purchase region; a little over a year later, Lamy recalled him to Santa Fe, and when Northern Colorado was separated from the Vicariate-Apostolic of Kansas and added to Santa Fe, Machebeuf left for Denver on 27 September 1860 (Howlett 257-58, 285; Horgan 258-61, 267-80; Bridgers 150-53).

5) Lamy visited Machebeuf in Denver en route to another Saint Louis council; Machebeuf returned the courtesy in Santa Fe during the fall. On 10 March 1862, the Rebel army took Santa Fe en route (they hoped) to the Colorado gold fields; four weeks later they retreated southward. Machebeuf suffered a serious buggy accident on 14 June 1863, and Lamy rushed north to visit him; then when Lamy had returned to Santa Fe, he traveled to southern Arizona. On 14 September 1865, four Sisters of Charity of Cincinnati arrived in Santa Fe and used a bequest from Father Avel to start a hospital early the next year. On Christmas Eve 1864, a demented gunman accosted Bishop Lamy and wounded two of his priests in the Cathedral rectory (Howlett 300, 310-11; Horgan 287-313, 317, 321-24).

In February 1866, Lamy sent Jean Baptiste Salpointe to Tucson, then in May and June he traveled to Colorado to visit Machebeuf and try to settle a squabble in Central City. From the late summer of 1866 until a year later, Lamy traveled east to the Second Plenary Council of Baltimore, then set sail for Paris and Rome to recruit more priests and to deliver the proceedings of the Council to the Vatican; he returned through New York, Baltimore, and Saint Louis to Leavenworth, then set out with six Jesuits (one on temporary loan), five nuns (one of whom died en route), and several seminarians and young priests. They experienced grave troubles from cholera

and warring Indians, finally arriving in Santa Fe 15 August 1867 and learning that Padre Antonio José Martínez had died 27 July. The next year Lamy handed over Colorado to Machebeuf and Arizona to Salpointe, their new Vicars-Apostolic. Lamy laid the cornerstone of his new cathedral on 10 October 1868; it was stolen a week later and never recovered. Lamy traveled to the Ecumenical Council of the Vatican which opened 8 December 1869; he left six months before it ended, traveling homeward through Lempdes, his native village, to reconsecrate the newly renovated church (Howlett 326-27, 335-36, 364; Horgan 324-64; Bridgers 176-79).

6) In December 1872, jurisdiction over the Gadsden Purchase and the three Texas towns was still unsettled after twenty years. From the early till the late 1870s, the major news was the economic stagnation caused by the Panic of 1873, which stopped the progress of the railroad toward New Mexico. On 12 February 1875 Rome named Lamy Archbishop of Santa Fe, and Machebeuf preached when Salpointe bestowed the pallium – a liturgical neckpiece reserved to archbishops – on 16 June 1875. Lamy's nephew Antoine, pastor at Manzano, died on 7 February 1876; in 1876 and again in 1878, Lamy asked for a coadjutor, citing poor health. On 25 April 1878, Father Eguillon blessed the Loretto Chapel that still stands near the Plaza. Lamy was on a committee to bring a spur from the main Santa Fe line up to the capital city, and it was finished on 9 February 1880 (Howlett 380-81; Horgan 372-85, 392, 405-06; Bridgers 202-04).

7) Lamy traveled to Arizona by railroad to visit Salpointe; ex-priest José Manuel Gallegos died with Father Eguillon in attendance. Lamy continued to ask for a successor, hoping for Salpointe, and on 7 April 1884 Rome finally agreed. Lamy traveled from 21 July to 15 October 1884 through several Mexican dioceses, confirming about 35,000 persons and turning over the stipends to the cathedral fund, and the next month he departed for the Third Plenary Council of Baltimore. The following June Salpointe was installed as Archbishop on 1 May, and Lamy submitted his own resignation, turning the entire conduct of New Mexico over to Salpointe on 6 September.

On 7 March 1886, Lamy blessed the bells moved from the old adobe belfries to the Cathedral's new stone towers, and the following December he formally dedicated the finally-completed Loretto Chapel.

Since his retirement, the Archbishop had spent most of his time in his Tesuque rancho, and on 7 February 1888 he requested that a carriage come to bring him into Santa Fe. On 12 February Salpointe left for Las Vegas, where the Jesuits were giving him trouble, and early the next morning Lamy died; Machebeuf came down from Denver to sing the requiem Mass (Howlett 404-05; Horgan 386, 406-09, 421-39; Bridgers 222-23, 230-31).

Books Referenced

Bridgers, Lynn. *Death's Deceiver: The Life of Joseph P. Machebeuf.* Albuquerque: University of New Mexico Press, 1997.

Chávez, fray Angélico. *The Archives of the Archdiocese of Santa Fe.* Washington: Academy of American Franciscan History, 1957.

Horgan, Paul. *Lamy of Santa Fe: His Life and Times.* New York: Farrar, Straus, and Giroux, 1975.

Howlett, William J. *Life of Bishop Machebeuf.* Eds. Thomas J. Steele, S.J., and Ronald S. Brockway. Denver: Regis College, 1987 (orig. 1908).

Mares, E.A., ed. *Padre Martínez: New Perspectives from Taos.* Taos: Millicent Rogers Museum, 1988.

Steele, Awalt, and Rhetts, eds. *Seeds of Struggle, Harvest of Faith.* Albuquerque: LPD Press, 1998.

Steele, Thomas J., S.J. *Folk and Church in Nineteenth-Century New Mexico.* Colorado Springs: Hulbert Center for Southwest Studies of The Colorado College, 1993.

Warner, Louis. *Archbishop Lamy: An Epoch Maker.* Santa Fe: Santa Fe New Mexican Publishing, 1936.

Chapter 2
Willa Cather's Archbishop Latour vs. the Lamy of History

My friend E.A. "Tony" Mares used to perform a one-man play in which he portrayed – even *became* – Padre Antonio José Martínez, who was his great-great-grandfather's brother. Tony would often begin the play by coming on-stage muttering a phrase he often heard from his grandmother: "¡Esa mujer! – That woman!" His grandmother was referring, of course, to Willa Cather, who had stolen all the greatness that the famous Padre of Taos had earned in the long course of his remarkable life.

The problem we face is that *Death Comes for the Archbishop* is such a good novel (or more accurately, romance), so well written and so persuasive, that readers continually take it to be historically accurate. It is not. Willa Cather read all the readily available sources, especially Father William Howlett's biography of Bishop Joseph Machebeuf of Denver, but then she passed the historical data through the artistic crucible of her creative imagination and created a work of fiction, a work of creative writing. And since it was not a novel but a romance, the characters lack the three-dimensionality, the verisimilitude, and the solidity of the characters in a realistic novel. Most of the heroes are emblems of the seven great virtues, as many critics have pointed out, and most of the villains are allegories of the seven deadly sins, or they are American frontier versions of Odysseus' inhuman or semi-human adversaries, the souls in Dante's *Inferno* and *Purgatorio*, Christian's enemies in *Pilgrim's Progress*, fairy-tale ogres and goblins, or other stage-props suitable for a romance.[1]

The problem, perhaps, was that Cather did not alter enough of her source material. If she had believed less of what Fathers Salpointe and Howlett and historian Ralph Emerson Twitchell had told her and had changed both the names of Fathers Gallegos, Machebeuf, and Lucero and the names of the towns where they served their people, if in other words she had expunged absolutely everything factual from her work of fiction, it might not have been a better novel, but it would certainly not have muddied the waters of New Mexico's history as it has.

Cather "got some things wrong" in her novel because she was not very well acquainted with New Mexico, never having resided there and having visited only a handful of times. But much of what Cather changed when she transformed the prevailing version of history into literature was done for excellent *literary* reasons. She sends the aging Latour and the aging Vaillant westward from Santa Fe in the late afternoon so that the bishop can show his newfound treasure of golden stone to his vicar.[2] Cather wants the cathedral Latour will build to replace Father Vaillant in Bishop Latour's affections, and so Vaillant moves to northern Colorado and the novel skips quickly to a close. Cather makes Latour older than Vaillant in the novel and then kills Vaillant off so that Latour can attend his funeral in Denver and then die a few months later; a good novelist doesn't let her hero die first and make her story fizzle out with the anticlimax of a sidekick's burial.

Cather was a novelist, not a historian, so her reader should read her masterpiece as a novel — not an easy task, for even persons well-versed in New Mexican history must remember to tell themselves twice a page, "This is fiction; this is not history; beyond the pages of this novel, it wasn't like this at all." Cather biographer James Woodress accurately states that "what she didn't know about Lamy she made up,"[3] but it is equally true that much of what she *did* know she changed. Woodress sums up: "Latour's attitudes towards life, civilization, and culture are Cather's, not Lamy's, [because] Lamy's ideas on progress were the typical optimistic views of the nineteenth century."[4] Indeed, Latour's personality is for the most part Willa Cather's.

As I will show later in this book, the personality of the actual

historical Lamy is best described in terms of the Myers-Briggs Personality Inventory as **ESTJ** – Extravert, Sensor, Thinker, and Judger. By contrast, the fictional Archbishop Jean-Marie Latour is quite consistently described as **INT** – Introverted, iNtuitive, and a Thinker – but he performs not like a Thinker but like a Feeler when he ought to do so.

Latour's Introversion

The critics have described Cather's Latour as well-bred, fastidious, distinguished, aristocratic, urbane, refined, reserved, singular and solitary, so lacking in passion as to border on coldness, slow in making his few friends, reflective, introspective, and aloof.[5] The novel itself describes him as of gentle birth, courteous, and distinguished in manner (p. 19), and then it goes on to describe him as reserved (p. 13), possessed in the Indian guide Jacinto's eyes of "the right tone ... good manners" (p. 94), annoyed at having to meet a stranger (p. 227), being "a little cold – *un pédant*" (p. 262), and less inspiring of personal devotion than Vaillant (pp. 288-89); several times late in the book, Cather describes how her fictional hero fulfilled the Wordsworthian program of recollecting his emotions – his meaningful experiences – in tranquil solitude (pp. 265, 272, 283, 290, 299). And just as the silver medal he gives Sada is the physical, artistic, and religious image of human love (p. 219), so the cathedral is the physical and artistic "body" of Latour's religious aspirations to such a degree that it can even replace Father Joseph during Latour's life (pp. 175, 219).

These traits suggest introversion, the love of privacy, the tendency to set one's center within one's inner world of consciousness, to be energized by being alone, to listen well and then think in order to talk, to wish to understand the effects of living, and to tend to defend oneself against the intrusions of outer reality.

Latour's iNtuition

The critics see Latour as a man of large vision and aesthetic sensibility, and his aesthetic taste is of a piece with his detached visual observation of the life around him and the visual arts, most espe-

cially the Native Americans, the landscape, and his cathedral but also including santos and adobe architecture.[6] The novel shows him to be sensitive (p. 19), with severe and refined tastes (p. 13). On the positive side, he is appreciative of the Hispanic-made *santos* and adobe architecture (pp. 28, 33-35) and of an Indian-made wooden parrot (p. 86), and he is visually taken by the tamarisk tree (pp. 201-02). To his credit, he intuits that he doesn't and won't ever understand such native American mysteries as Jacinto's listening to the river and the turtle-like Ácoma parishioners; on the negative side, Latour instinctively loathes the mysterious cave, finding it terrifying and recalling it later with horror (pp. 127, 130, 133), and he has nearly as strong reactions of dismay to Cather's Father Martínez (p. 150) and to tacky Ohio architecture (p. 228).

Being introverted and intuitive both, Latour is hard to please, especially in the visual realm (p. 225), and a perceptive friend knows to please him by giving him as a gift "something good for the eye" (p. 179). Since the sacred and the beautiful, religion and art, belong together (pp. 241, 257), his cathedral, his physical, artistic, and religious creation and correlative, replaces Father Vaillant in his life (pp. 175, 271). Consequently, the golden stone from which he will build the architectural expression of the Kingdom of God is for him "the treasure hidden in a field, the pearl of great price" (p. 245; Matthew 13.44-46). Finally, in his last months and weeks of life, he recollects in the proper and prescribed Wordsworthian manner the deeds of his life that are most filled with emotional affect and successfully "reads" them to find the archetypal meanings and values by which he has lived his life and to achieve a good death, a happy death (pp. 265, 269, 272, 283); all his past was acceptable and accepted, comprehensible and comprehended, nothing needed to be discarded or outgrown, and so Archbishop Latour's life establishes a permanently valid paradigm (pp. 289-90).[7]

The characteristics noted above point to intuition, the trait of a visionary with an original mind and imagination. He is not fixed on the present so much as on the implications and consequences of the present for the future. He thinks in the patterns of metaphors, analogies, and models, and he possesses aesthetic imagination and appreciation.

Latour manifests one trait that is opposite to the first two letters (I and N) of his Myers-Briggs type: candor, having no agenda hidden from oneself or others (p. 94), a virtue typically associated most closely with Extraverted Sensors; but it is certainly suitable for a churchman to be open and guileless toward others and to have honest self-knowledge.

Now the Thinker, Now the Feeler

As he is described, the fictional archbishop shares Thinking with the real one, for Cather describes him as preferring, when faced with some task, *to make his decisions based more on objective standards* than on feelings of empathy with the other person or persons involved in the decision.

The literary critics, again, find a good deal of the Thinking function in Archbishop Latour. Because he is not very simpatico, he must live his life largely in his head; the critics describe him as thoughtful, scholarly, and intellectual, an aristocrat of cultivated, well-schooled mind; his visual emphasis draws him into a careful, disinterested contemplation, distances him from real persons and their warmth and tactility, and thereby impairs his compassion.[8] Strangely, the critics remark very rarely if at all about the Judging aspect of Latour's character; Skaggs alone breaks the silence by noting Latour's being an organizer and a disciplinarian who acts expeditiously to curb abuses.[9]

In the novel, we find Cather characterizing Latour as possessing a fine intelligence (pp. 8, 19) and being very visualist (pp. 18, 50, 179) – ideal for being detached and disinterested so as to reason from received principles to sure conclusions. As an introverted Thinker, Latour is cool and critical and hard to please (p. 225).

The cardinals and the American missionary bishop say what needs to be said here, that order is necessary to Latour and that "the French arrange!" (pp. 8, 9). As soon as Latour meets Father Gallegos, he starts arranging to defrock him (p. 83). Before Latour has been in Santa Fe more than two months he has already decided that he will oust Padre Antonio José Martínez (pp. 32; see also p. 141), and Martínez' scorn for clerical celibacy is so intolerable that the Bishop's

warnings and threats follow rapidly (pp. 145-46, 146, 147, 148). But
the history behind the plot demands these decisions and actions
more than Latour's character does.

In a more fictional vein, Latour's uncharacteristic feeling makes
him shrink from involvement in the Olivares lawsuit since getting
Doña Isabella to tell the truth will be so painful for all parties; but his
Thinking trait and the plot's need for Judging force him to say and to
do what he must say and do in order to secure justice (pp. 188, 190-
91, 193). He is sorry to send Vaillant to Tucson, but he sends him (pp.
208-09), and when he has recalled Vaillant for reasons of friendship
and soon discovers that he ought to send him to Denver to deal
with the gold rush in northern Colorado, he does so (pp. 248, 253-
54). And the cathedral, his alter ego, his substitute for Vaillant, gets
lengthy preparation (pp. 175, 243).

Thinkers are conscientious perfectionists, hard on others and even
harder on themselves, accomplishment-oriented, staunch in the face
of opposition, capable of figuring out a solution and arranging to
carry it through to successful closure. A Thinker who comes to judgment can face and state unpleasant conclusions, and he will tend to
be wholly intolerant of collaborators who are counter-productive.
Judgers are practical managers who control persons and processes
and delight in meeting deadlines but who tend unfortunately to
rush to premature judgments. Cather's hero Latour was never guilty
of such a mistake; would that we could say the same of Lamy.

Hermione Lee offers the best summary of my interpretation to
this point: "Latour becomes [Cather's] kind of hero: delicate and distinguished, chivalric, aesthetic, sympathetic (especially to the Indians …), nostalgic for France, in love with order and tradition, patient
to the point of passivity, vulnerable, self-doubting, and in need of
Vaillant's support."[10] Lee's remark about sympathy and her comment
that Latour is "in love with order" suggest that he was neither Feeler
nor Thinker as a abiding habit but effectively became whichever he
was called to be at the moment, fatherly listener or tough administrator, able by turns to sympathize with Doña Isabella and to get her
to say in court what he needed her to say.

In the final analysis, Latour is neither a real man in history nor a realistic character in a novel but an allegorical archetype in a romance, a deliberately idealized model of the aesthetic refinement that Cather's frontier needed so desperately and so rarely possessed.[11] And the problem is that readers consistently think that they are reading about the actual historical Archbishop Jean Baptiste Lamy.

Willa Cather as the Original of Bishop Latour

Willa Cather commented that she began wishing to write a book about Archbishop Lamy when she first saw Miguel Chávez and J. Jusko's bronze image of him in front of the Santa Fe Cathedral. So here we have it: Willa played Pygmalion to a statue – and here comes "My Fair Lamy."

"Willa Cather," John Charles Scott remarks, "has changed the very soul of the historical bishop and has recast the times and places in which he lived in such a way that her new creature, Bishop Jean Marie Latour, while resembling Lamy, in fact more closely reflects the image and likeness of Cather's own innermost being."[12] Cather's critics and biographers have discovered by induction some of her essential personality traits, some helpful clues to that "innermost being" of hers. James Woodress selects from her childhood worldview some essential values that she never relinquished: a proper world should be rural and it should possess a stable, traditional order and an aesthetic culture.[13]

I believe that by living the life she lived and by creating the fiction she created, Cather manifested traits that produce the Myers-Briggs schema INF – again, as with Latour, I do not find information that allows me to identify her as either Judger or Perceiver.

During her four high-school years in Red Cloud, Nebraska, Willa invented the extremely non-conformist William Cather, Jr., and William Cather, M.D., personas which she lived and dressed in a very public and extraverted manner. She dropped them when she moved to the University of Nebraska and never resumed them or anything like them, and as she aged she became more and more a private person until her quest for privacy amounted nearly to an obsession. She never married, and happy marriages are quite rare in her fic-

tion; she may well have idealized pre-sexual childhood, and she and Edith Lewis knew the prepubescent world of the Alice books extremely well.[14] It is hard to ignore her preference for close relationships to other women, but even if the preference arose from a sexual orientation, Cather probably did not act out her sexual desires; instant gratification – "Just Do It" – was neither the watchword of her era nor the watchword of her life.[15]

Her intuition hardly needs proof. Her preferred aesthetic was visual; we should recall that seeing the 1915 bronze statue was her great epiphany, an intuition about "the pioneer churchman who looked so well-bred and distinguished" which led shortly to the further insight that the "real story of the Southwest was the story of the missionary priests from France, with their cultivated minds, their large vision, and their noble purpose – the transference of European culture to the American landscape, the survival and reshaping of old orders in pioneer form."[16] While Germany enjoyed a top reputation for science and scholarship, France claimed preeminence in culture, and Cather loved everything French – except French grammar.[17] And finally, Willa Cather was a Feeler rather than a Thinker – she settled questions of choice more by her perception of mutual empathy between persons rather than by appeal to abstract, intellectual principles.[18]

Cather idealized Lamy to such a degree that she did not merely change him, she actually created him anew, and so Scott is right not only in saying that Archbishop Latour is "a composite personality whose sensitivities and emotions are portrayed as they have been contrived by Cather" but also in declaring that "both Lamy and Cather are Latour's parents, but the *Death Comes for the Archbishop* bishop more closely resembles the mother." Scott concludes, "Due to the immense popularity of *Death Comes for the Archbishop*, it is Cather's fictional creation and not the real man who is most remembered. Whatever greatness Archbishop Lamy earned during his life and deserved in history Willa Cather has stolen from him."[19]

"¡Esa mujer! ¡Esa mujer! – That woman! That woman!"

Endnotes

[1]   James Woodress, *Willa Cather: A Literary Life* (Lincoln: University of Nebraska Press, 1987), pp. 407-08 (in his earlier study [New York: Pegasus, 1970], pp. 223-24); Patricia Clark Smith, "Achaeans, Americanos, Prelates, and Monsters: Willa Cather's *Death Comes for the Archbishop*," in E.A. Mares, ed., *Padre Martínez: New Perspectives from Taos* (Taos: Millicent Rogers Museum, 1988), pp. 115-18; John J. Murphy, ed., in Willa Cather, *Death Comes for the Archbishop* (Lincoln: University of Nebraska Press, 1999), pp. 339-42.

[2]   West, where the sun sets, is a symbol of approaching death; during World War I, "to go west" was euphemism for dying. Actually, Cather probably got the idea for the quarry from James H. Defouri, *Historical Sketch of the Catholic Church in New Mexico* (San Francisco: McCormick Brothers, 1887), p. 145, where the stone for the outer walls comes from one unlocated quarry, that for the inner walls comes from a Lamy Junction quarry, and the "red volcanic lava, exceedingly light," for the ceiling comes from "immense quarries … on the summit of Cerro Mogino, a small mound twelve miles from Santa Fe."

[3]   Woodress, *Willa Cather*, p. 401.

[4]   James Woodress, "The Uses of Biography: The Case of Willa Cather," *Great Plains Quarterly* 2 (1982), 201; see also Frederick Turner, "Willa Cather's New Mexico," *New Mexico Magazine* 64 # 4 (March 1986), 33-34.

[5]   James M. Gaither, "A Return to the Village: A Study of Santa Fe and Taos, New Mexico, As Cultural Centers, 1900-1934," University of Minnesota dissertation, 1957, pp. 284; Edward A. and Lillian D. Bloom, *Willa Cather's Gift of Sympathy* (Carbondale: Southern Illinois University Press, 1962), p. 219; John J. Murphy, "Willa Cather's Archbishop: A Western and Classical Perspective," *Western American Literature* 13 (1978), 149; John Charles Scott, "Between Fiction and History: An Exploration into Willa Cather's *Death Comes for the Archbishop*," dissertation, University of New Mexico, 1980, pp. 26, 230; Woodress, *Willa Cather*, pp. 393, 397, 405.

      Edward and Lillian Bloom refer to Latour as "a philosopher" within a context that presents him as "an aristocrat [who] is strengthened by an introspective power of love" (p. 219), so I take that to point in Myers-Briggs terms to Introversion more than to Thinking.

[6]   Gaither, p. 284; Edward and Lillian Bloom, pp. 219, 231; Woodress, *Willa Cather*, pp. 392, 397, 405; Merrill Maguire Skaggs, "*Death Comes for the Archbishop*: Cather's Mystery and Manners," *American Literature* 57 (1985), 403; Bette S. Weidman in E.A. Mares, ed., *Padre Martínez: New Perspectives from Taos* (Taos: Millicent Rogers Museum, 1988), pp. 50, 54; Marilee Lindemann, *Willa Cather: The Queering of America* (New York: Columbia University Press, 1999), pp. 121-22.

[7]   Latour's landscapes begin with a frozen sea (p. 21) of near paralysis, then they are arenas for action, and finally, as memories, they become spaceless and timeless settings for recollection. Cather tells us that Latour "sat in the middle of his own consciousness" (p. 290) and remembered a life so well lived that he and it have

become archetypal (pp. 265, 283, 289-90). In quiet Wordsworthian recollection, the old man lives over the important emotional moments of his life without nostalgia or regret ("The mistakes of his life seemed unimportant" [p. 290]) until he completely understands his life and asserts it as the truth about his authentic self. See Weidman, p. 50.

On the romantic tendency to imagine the creative human as a priestly deity, see Michael Lind, "Defrocking the Artist," New York *Times* "Book Review" (14 March 1999), p. 39, and Murphy, pp. 338-39.

[8]   Murphy in Harold Bloom, ed., p. 168; Woodress, pp. 392, 397; Stouck and Stouck, p. 300; Skaggs, p. 403; Lindemann, pp. 121-22.

[9]   Skaggs, p. 403.

[10]   Hermione Lee, *Willa Cather: Double Lives* (New York: Pantheon, 1989), p. 268. In his defense, Howlett "had no time" for the Indians because he had no experience of them; Latour's preference for them is mainly Tony Luhan's contribution. –Lee seems to think that during the nineteenth century all the French or French-educated priests in fictional and historical New Mexico were Jesuits (pp. 274, 262, 266, and 279).

[11]   Edward and Lillian Bloom, p. 219. David Stouck, *Willa Cather's Imagination* (Lincoln: University of Nebraska Press, 1975), p. 141, notes that the characters in *Death Comes* are quite medieval in being based on moral strength or weakness and that Cather did not construct them either in the alternate medieval manner of psychology (four humors) or in the modern psychology of Freud, Jung, and so forth.

[12]   Scott, p. 184. My friend Don Toomey called my attention to fray Angélico Chávez's poem "A Caballero Recalls Lamy," where the caballero attributes more Cather traits to Lamy than historical-Lamy traits.

[13]   Woodress, *Willa Cather*, pp. 24-26.

[14]   Woodress, *Willa Cather*, pp. 55, 475; 127, 416.

[15]   Woodress, *Willa Cather*, p. 141.

[16]   Lee, pp. 262, 60-61; Woodress, *Willa Cather*, p. 392-93. The non-quote about the "real story" is from Cather's October 1946 letter to E.K. Brown, the scholar she chose to write her authorized biography; the letter is in the Newberry Library and may not be quoted verbatim.

[17]   Woodress, *Willa Cather*, p. 80.

[18]   Edward A. and Lillian D. Bloom, pp. 165, 236; Cather indeed defined her world more by emotion than by analysis, and "Sympathetic Imagination" is the title of Chapter Five in the Blooms' *Willa Cather: Gift of Sympathy*. They might rightly have added, "and the best novel to date about New Mexico."

[19]   Scott, pp. 34-35, 184-85.

Chapter 3
The Background of Lamy's Preaching

Introduction

Jean Baptiste Lamy retained a few truly archaic traits from his birth in a small town of rural France in 1814, such as references to the four elements – fire, air, water, and earth – and to the four humors – choleric, sanguine, phlegmatic, and melancholic. Lamy seems to have spoken literally rather than metaphorically of the four elements when he stated in his sermon for Pentecost 1849 that "of all elements, fire is the most noble" and that "the iron put into the fire takes the nature of the fire, becomes fire itself" (L052).

As to the humors, Lamy was, after all, "bled twice and treated fifteen times with leeches on the abdomen" during his younger years; both treatments were predicated on the theory of the four humors.[1] It is not impossible that Lamy had ceased to believe in the four-element-and-four-humor theory and that his later remarks about such nonentities were therefore merely convenient verbal summaries (as when we say "the sun rose" rather than "the earth turned in such a manner that I was carried to where I could see the sun"). But Lamy certainly made statements in his sermons that suggested his belief in the humors. In 1848: "Unless you love the cross, unless you love sufferings, you will never be satisfied, never find rest nor peace, for in many things you must mortify your humor, bring your passions under subjection, resist temptations, avoid evil, and do good" (L037); six months later he added, "Do we truly listen to Jesus Christ? Do we not rather listen to the world and to our own will and humor?" (L044). Here is humor in the archaic sense: our individual psychological tilt, our idiosyncratic "emotion *du jour.*"

One of Lamy's Kentucky sermons mentions the culture of honor
– another archaic survival from tribalism and the classical era which
endured and still endures in such groups as peasants, aristocrats,
teenagers, and the military. In the first paragraph of sermon L063,
pronounced on 14 October 1849 in Covington, Kentucky (where
the population doubtless thought they knew a thing or two about
honor), Lamy announced his topic and his division of it:

> As we are bound to honor God, so also we are bound to
> honor true religion, for God must be our last end and true
> religion the very means to attain this end. Faith or religion
> is a precious estate which we have received from our fore-
> fathers. We are under the obligation to keep and maintain
> it with honor. As Christians we must acknowledge in our
> religion two essential qualities, truth and sanctity, truth in
> its doctrine and sanctity in its moral. If then our religion is
> true we should honor it by the profession of our faith. If
> our religion is holy we should honor it by the purity of
> our morals.

The 2100-word sermon contains 27 uses of the word "honor" in
its various forms, a rate about twenty times Lamy's average; his focus
on the topic and his insistence on Christianizing honor were evidently conscious and deliberate.[2]

Lamy was in some ways truly a child of the Romantic period, at
least in his relatively free-form sermons – unstructured by contrast
to the set structures of sermons during the previous cultural period,
the Neoclassical. But I have caught no hint of the developmental
world-view that began in France in the middle of the eighteenth
century and developed from Turgot and Condorcet through Hegel,
Schleiermacher, and Erasmus Darwin, through Comte, Marx, and
Charles Darwin (Erasmus' grandson), and finally to Newman, Freud,
and Piaget. Lamy was an essentialist without a trace of the phenom-
enological or the existential; his world was static and non-develop-
ing.

Moralist that he was, Lamy posited so strong a distinction between the human mind and the human will that it practically

amounted to a separation; human beings had little need for mind, but their wills had better be strong in all trials. An attentive reading of sermon L021, from 13 June 1847, will suggest that Lamy was a voluntarist and not an intellectualist at all.

The minor seminary in Billom that Lamy attended was run by the Society of Jesus from 1826 to 1829, while Lamy was twelve to fifteen years of age, and his Jesuit teachers almost certainly exposed him to a very positive view of the classical authors of Rome (and perhaps Greece) which were the principal subjects of study. Since the Society of Jesus was founded during the Renaissance, Jesuits have tended to view human nature more positively than have the members of older religious orders; the Jesuit "spin" has typically been to affirm the fact of human liberty and to view salvation as normally requiring free human cooperation. Consequently, Jesuits usually insist on a realm of natural goodness and natural evil in between the realm of supernatural goodness (God, revelation, salvation, and so forth) and that of preternatural evil (devil, diabolical temptation, damnation, and so forth).

I must admit that if the Jesuits taught Lamy anything in this area, he completely got over it during his nine years in the major seminary at Montferrand. Lamy's hand-sewn commonplace book from his seminary days in the late 1830s contains an essay in his own hand on faith, which he describes as "the first of the virtues, for without it we have no other virtue – la première des vertus, sans laquelle nous n'en avons point d'autres."[3] Without Christian faith Aristotle and the Stoics did pretty well at understanding, defining, and practicing such virtues as prudence, justice, temperance, and fortitude.

Jean Baptiste Lamy's theology of the Church was very much centered on Rome and papal primacy, as was very normal for a nineteenth-century French Catholic, especially a cleric. With the disappearance of the hapless Bourbons and the end of church establishment, there was no immediate possibility of help from Paris, so the only thing to do was to look "beyond the mountains – beyond

the Alps" to Roman primacy:

> The Church, figured by the bark [fishing boat] and gov-
> erned by the successors of Peter, should be until the con-
> summation of the world the seat and the center of truth,
> its pillar and foundation. It is from this bark we must re-
> ceive all our teaching concerning the true doctrine of Christ.
> The instructions we hear, the books we read must have
> the stamp and the seal of that authority (L056).

Pseudo-Dionysius' various hierarchies, which were enduring para-
digms for all existence both heavenly and earthly, and the Great
Chain of Being, which survived from the Medieval and Renaissance
periods into the nineteenth century, induced in Lamy an extreme
respect for authority – and something of a tilt toward authoritarianism.
In commenting on the miraculous draught of fish in the same 1
July 1849 sermon, Lamy says:

> Could there be a greater obedience than that of Simon by
> which he sacrifices his own knowledge? He knew better
> than anybody else that the great daylight was not a time
> as favorable for fishing [as] the night. He had just had the
> experience that there was no fish in that place, but there
> should be no reasoning when we should obey. Obedi-
> ence is not perfect unless we sacrifice to it our own knowl-
> edge. … Without a moment's delay he and those who
> were with him cast their nets. They did not wait for an
> answer nor explanation nor new orders nor a new pledge
> of success from our Saviour. It is in this manner that we
> obey our superiors who hold the place of Jesus Christ on
> earth.

And eight and a half years later he adds, "We see then obedience, the hidden life or the humility of our Lord Jesus Christ, and
from this consideration we should realize the obligation we have to
imitate this obedience and the humility of the Lord" (L149). Talks
L175 and L176, from 1861, reaffirm blind or nearly-blind obedience
to authority.

Lamy and Scripture

Lamy's Bibles were many in number. At times he doubtless recollected passages from the French translation of scripture he had
been familiar with from childhood, and he seems to have made
offhand translations into English or Spanish as needed. Since he
read Mass and his divine office daily, a total of about an hour's reading in Latin largely drawn from scripture passages from the Latin
Vulgate version of Saint Jerome (c345-c419), Lamy sometimes wrote
impromptu translations.

When he quoted at some length during his time in Ohio and
Kentucky, Lamy used the Douay English translation of the New
Testament (1582) and the Rheims Old Testament (1609). Bishop Richard Challoner edited both parts down from fine Elizabethan English into eminently forgettable mid-eighteenth-century prose. For a
little variety or by accident, Lamy used one quotation from the King
James Version: "The Spirit of truth was promised to be forever with
the pastors of God's Church to guide them into all truth in teaching
God's people and to be forever with the sheep of Christ to guide
them into all truth in their belief and life."[4] After he had moved to
New Mexico, Lamy seems to have used two Spanish translations of
the Bible by turns, that of Felipe Scio de San Miguel (1792) and that
of Félix Torres Amat (1825); there may have been another which I
cannot identify, or he may have translated French, Latin, and perhaps English texts that he knew by heart. I usually used the Douay-
Rheims English when I translated Lamy's Spanish.

Like the vast majority of Christian clergymen of the middle of
the nineteenth century, Lamy approached sacred scripture in a manner that would seem to us extremely naive, but we have to recall
that during his lifetime there were only about ten scholars doing
what has come to be called higher criticism, and not a one of them
lived in Ohio, Kentucky, or New Mexico, for nearly all of them were
in Germany, a few others in France or Holland.[5]

Modern scripture scholars frown on any interpretation of scripture that the text does not at least imply. *Ex*egesis – reading a meaning out of the text – is fine; *eis*egesis – reading a meaning *in* – is bad

form. The literal meaning of scripture – what God wrote and means, what the human author wrote and means, and what the text says – is very rich in meaning because it includes whatever is expressed in so many words *and* whatever is expressed in simile, metaphor, symbol, irony, parable, hyperbole, or any other figure of speech.

For ancient and medieval students of Holy Writ, by contrast, three "spiritual" senses lay beyond the literal: the allegorical sense served as the source of doctrine in which to believe, the moral or tropological pertained to the pursuit of Christian moral goodness, and the anagogic pertained to hopes for the afterlife.[6] Contemporary scholars tend to be suspicious of these three "spiritual" senses since they often lapse into *eis*egesis. "The allegorical *interpretation* of the Bible first appears in Jewish interpreters and was widely practiced by many of the Fathers of the Church. In this view the entire Old Testament signifies by allegory the entire Christian revelation; since the presupposition is false, allegorical interpretation is usually fanciful."[7] Much the same must be said for the other two "spiritual" senses, the moral and the anagogical.

Lamy frequently turned Christ's actions, teachings, and parables into allegories – what the seventeenth century could have called "anatomies," what the twentieth might call "autopsies." For instance, in L040 "The different hours represent the different ages of the world: Adam, Noe, Abram, Moses, Christ"; in L070 "'Then the devil left him, and behold, angels came and ministered to him,' that is, gave him to eat. There is no food so delicious as the consolation that a soul feels after having resisted the temptation." In L110, right after quoting Christ's "The field is the world," Lamy states, "God sowed good seed in the field of the Church."

Lamy constantly skipped at random from one book of the Bible to another, decontextualizing nearly everything he quoted and thereby turning the whole of Holy Writ into a vast homogenized grab-bag of proof-texts or jumping-off points for allegorizing. In other words, Lamy was a typical preacher of his day, normal in any Christian church and in all Christendom.

Lamy and the Fathers of the Church

The Reformation and the Catholic Counterreformation, which occurred during the Renaissance, looked to the Jewish and Christian writings of the Classical period as normative of belief and church practice. Three centuries later, Catholics of the Romantic period became especially interested in the largely early-medieval writings of Fathers of the Church; though not so authoritative as the Hebrew and Greek scriptures, they were a record of the Church tradition which, according to Trent, began oral (as did much if not all of the New Testament) but was written down here and there as the centuries succeeded one another, so in France from 1838 to 1868 the Abbé Jacques-Paul Migne published his *Patrologia* of the works of Greek and Latin fathers and doctors.[8]

For this reason, surely, Lamy quotes from the Fathers of the Church surprisingly often. It is inconceivable that he owned the hundreds of Migne folios, but brief passages from the writings of the Fathers occurred daily in the priest's breviary, and there were doubtless "trots" – books of selected excerpts – to decorate a sermon with the borrowed plumage of someone else's erudition.

What Jesus Christ Knew with His Human Mind

A study of scripture will reveal that various writers of the New Testament had emphases or "programs" which were usually difficult and sometimes impossible to reconcile among themselves; at times one part of a book of the New Testament might contradict another part or at least seem to do so. As mentioned above, the Enlightenment invented the criterion of internal consistency of the text.

Early Christological heresies led to the first six general councils, from Nicaea I (325) through Ephesus and Chalcedon to Constantinople III (680), which progressively defined what Christ was and is: a unified composite of the unique divine nature, the second Person of the Trinity, and a complete human nature. The Alexandrine fathers from the late second to the mid-fifth centuries – Clement of Alexandria, Origen, Athanasius, Didymus the Blind, Epiphanius, and Cyril of Alexandria – formed the center-line of the developing doctrinal orthodoxy.

The medieval Christology of the fathers and the schoolmen be-gan with Christ's "components" and perfections, deduced his various attributes, faculties, and powers from the councils' decrees, and predi-cated them of the Savior. As with the communication of cultural traits between a colonizing power and its colonials, the street ran pretty much one way only, from the superordinate to the subordi-nate; and furthermore, being heavily Platonic in their theology, the theologians turned the humanity of Christ into a world-creating ar-chetype by exaggerating its perfections, thereby diminishing every-thing in Christ that we would recognize as the experience of being human and living a human life.[9]

The medieval theologians attributed three sorts of knowledge to Christ's human mind even from the first moment of his incarnation in Mary's womb:

1. *The Beatific Vision,* a direct, non-conceptual, non-verbal knowl-edge of the divine nature and hence of the Word and of the Father and the Spirit. Saint Thomas Aquinas asserts that Christ knew every real thing in the Divine Word, though in a non-comprehensive manner (*ST* III, 9, 2; 10, 1-3). The beatific vision is as close as the human mind will ever come to possessing divine knowledge.

2. *Infused intellection,* which God directly implanted. Christ's soul was perfected so that "he knew whatever humans could know by virtue of the light of the *intellectus agens,* whatever pertained to human learning and … whatever humans could know by divine revela-tion" – and this "without turning to phantasms." It was, in other words, angelic knowledge.

3. *Acquired or experiential knowledge.* The fact that Christ knew expe-rientially all that was or is or ever will be real provided no further content beyond Christ's infused knowledge; Christ merely checked his infused knowledge against his sensory, experiential knowledge (*ST* III, 12, 2). He never learned anything from any human person or any angel, but at least in his human mind he could be said to have known things in a human manner to go along with his beatific and infused knowledge.

These purely theoretical claims about Christ's human knowledge are incompatible with the Christ we meet in scripture, nor do they resemble the experience of any human person who has ever lived. Everything that Jesus experienced in his time on earth would have been totally redundant, for his infused knowledge would have anticipated everything that he might have learned by living in the world and by communicating with other human beings. From the time that Jesus (supposedly) lay in his mother's womb thinking about nuclear physics, the NFL playoffs of 2009, the number, velocity, and location of all the electrons in the moon, and other such interesting topics, he knew everything – except mental growth. From the very start, he knew absolutely every least thing that was going to happen to him in his life and passion and death, and the result was that his life was nothing like human life, for it was instead a constant string of "*deja-vu*-all-over-again."

Such was the standard doctrine not only in the Roman Church but in every Christian communion of the nineteenth century, and so of course Jean Baptiste Lamy subscribed to it and preached accordingly. For example, L060 tells us of "Jesus Christ, with his wisdom infinitely superior to any human craftiness."[10] In L068, Father Lamy notes:

> It is written of our Lord with relation to this private part of his life that "he increased in wisdom and age and grace with God and men" [Luke 2.52]. Our God from the first moment of his conception was full of all heavenly wisdom and divine grace, but as the sun though equally luminous in itself yet shines with more splendor according as he rises and advances, so Jesus Christ the true Sun of Justice who enlightens every man coming into the world [John 1.9] was pleased in proportion to his advancing in age to show forth every glory more than other in his words and actions.

Indeed, the Christ Child comes off looking like a make-believe human youngster. And when Sermon L173 tells us that "as Jesus continued asking, the woman [with the hemorrhage] came up, fell

at his feet, and confessed the whole truth. Our Lord knew well who had touched him, but on this occasion he wanted the person herself to declare what had happened," Christ appears to be a make-believe human adult. The divinity of Lamy's Christ appears nearly to have absorbed his humanity – just as the Monophysites claimed.

With the support of the Holy See, Catholic scripture scholars of the last half-century have been instrumental in fostering a development of doctrine that will get us in better touch with the human Jesus of the first century – the Jesus whom the gospel writers (Matthew, Mark, and Luke especially) proclaimed, a man who experienced his human awareness within the context of time and space and matter. His human mind was limited somewhat as ours is, and so the great Alexandrine Cyril said of him, "We ought rather to wonder at [Christ's] philanthropy, by which he was moved in his love for us to lower himself to such a humble condition that he donned all our characteristics, one of which is ignorance." Christ was a wayfarer, a pilgrim in this world, and although he always knew what to do and say when the time came, he did not necessarily know what might be the thing to do or say thereafter – thereby resembling the *viator* of Cardinal Newman's "Lead, Kindly Light" who prays, "I do not ask to see The distant scene; One step enough for me."[11]

Pelagianism and Jansenism as Rhetorical Excesses

Jean Baptise Lamy had done well in the seminary studies, but he was not cut out to be an academic or a scholar, and he was by no means a professional theologian. In his sermons, he makes a few minor doctrinal errors of no consequence and betrays one odd but consistent flaw: an illogical juxtaposition of two diametrically opposed heresies, Pelagianism and Jansenism. Pelagianism denied original sin, so it had no need of the order of grace and the supernatural; thus Jesus came to earth not to save us but only to tell us and show us how to save ourselves by our own good will and good works.

Jansenism was, by contrast, a tinge, a trickle, an underground river of Calvinism within the French Catholic Church. It was Pelagianism's polar-opposite heterodoxy, for it insisted that original

sin was so destructive of human nature that God had to perform the absolute entirety of our salvation. Lamy quite often puts on his Jansenist hat and talks Jansenist talk. He maintains Calvin's and Jansenius' maximalist view of original sin, frequently and throughout his whole career describing it as having corrupted and depraved our nature. Now if humans are so depraved and corrupt by birth that the human intellect seeks error and human freedom seeks evil, the human mind and will must never play even the least part in the process of salvation, which it would inevitably thwart and prevent; and therefore God must do absolutely everything, the human will must do absolutely nothing, and the human soul must remain utterly passive to divine redemption.

But the next thing you know, Lamy could don his Pelagian hat and talk Pelagian talk, continually encouraging his congregations to assert their free will and "save their souls" both by choosing to live a good life and then by following through and actually living one.[12] True, he sometimes mentions God's grace, but like most preachers he lays the majority of the burden on his listeners' shoulders and consciences; Lamy the preacher is far more concerned with strength of will than with strength of intellect. He is above all the moralist; the principal purpose of his sermons is to *form* character and will, not to *inform* the mind.

Faith and grace seem unnecessary for doing good works: "The angels say, 'Peace to men of good will.' If our will is good, we need do no more than to begin, to the extent that we are well disposed, to align our will completely with God's supreme will, trying to achieve this good will, something that we all can do if we really wish it, then we have the right to possess this peace that our newborn God has established on earth" (L205).

In sermon L026, Lamy overemphasizes Christ's example and seems to neglect his passion and death: "Our eternal salvation, even our temporal happiness, depend upon imitating and faithfully copying the actions of our divine model Jesus Christ." Ten years later, in 1858, Lamy is still at it: "Our Lord Jesus Christ was tempted in order to teach us how to resist temptations" (L151); and nearing the end of his long career, he informs the nuns in an instruction on prayer that

"After having labored all day in preaching the Gospel, Jesus Christ 'spent the night in prayer — *pernoctans in oratione Dei*' not because he needed to for himself; he did so to give us an example" (L233).

Pelagianism tended to reduce Christianity to a mere moralism and to reduce Christ to a mere model rather than proclaiming him as redeemer and liberator. The great foe of Pelagianism, Saint Augustine of Hippo, noted that "Christ did not say 'without me it will be hard' but 'without me you can do nothing.'"[13]

But Augustine also said, "God who made us without us will not save us without us," and so Jansenism is not the right answer either. Jansenism survived in the nineteenth-century French church less as doctrine than as moral rigidity. But in Lamy's preaching we find much more than mere moral rigorism; for instance, one of the great Jansenist slogans was "God owes us nothing," and we can hear it echoing in Lamy's statement in sermon L059, "A great number [of persons] seem to rely upon their own merits and in the prayers ask God's grace not as a grace but as a debt."[14]

Because Jansenists take a maximalist view of original sin and hold that human nature became corrupt and depraved, we find Lamy saying in sermon L030, "Two things were necessary for our salvation: to satisfy an offended God, to reform corrupt man"; in L046, "[God] sees the desire of our corrupt nature for abundance and superfluity, he then first restrains this desire to your mere wants and necessaries"; in L046 the excuse that we fear need "comes from the depravity of our nature, the corruption of our hearts"; in L091, "[The apostles] have a depraved will, for like the rest of men the readily believe whatever favors their inclinations"; in L104, "This pretext comes from the depravity of an ungrateful heart that forgets the benefits it has received from God, the miracles of his providence."

Jansenism also tends to view sex as the archetypal sin of sins, and on several occasion Lamy appears to agree. Jansenism held that a penitent must have perfect contrition (focused on God's lovableness and his almighty will) and not merely "imperfect" (focused on fear of punishment), and Lamy states in sermon L114 that "contrition ought to be supernatural. We ought to abhor sin not because of

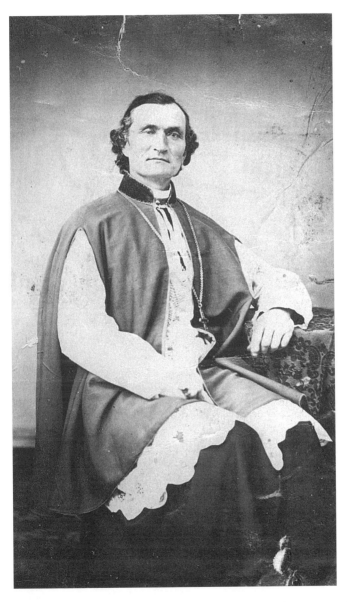

Bishop Jean Baptiste Lamy, ca. 1860. Photograph courtesy of the Museum of New Mexico, Santa Fe, NM. Neg. no. 35878.

Bishop Jean Baptiste Lamy, 1870s. Photograph courtesy of the Archdiocese of Santa Fe, Santa Fe, NM.

Bishop Jean Baptiste Lamy, 1880s. Photograph courtesy of the University of Notre Dame Archives, Notre Dame, IN.

Bishop Jean Baptiste Salpointe, Archbishop Jean Baptiste Lamy, and Bishop Joseph Machebeuf, 1870s. Photograph courtesy of the University of Notre Dame Archives, Notre Dame, IN.

The old bells and clock from La Parroquia as the new cathedral was being built, ca. June 1880. Photograph by Ben Wittick, courtesy of the Museum of New Mexico, Santa Fe, NM. Neg. no. 149374.

[God's] vengeance and because it increases the punishment we humans must suffer; this sorrow ought to arise instead from God's grace, and sin must be detested solely because it is an offence against God's law and against his divine will – *pecado ha de ser detestado solamente porque es una ofensa contra la ley de Dios y contra su voluntad divina.* This contrition, this contrite and humbled heart which the Lord will never scorn [Psalm 50.19], we can achieve by begging God by means of humility and by frequent examination of our consciences, asking him to assist us with the help of his divine grace so that we will never against fall into those sins which we have come to abhor and still hate"; Lamy's implied corollary is that mixed, merely natural motives (fear of having to endure God's vengeance), even with the help of a priest's absolution in the Sacrament of Penance, avail nothing. And he repeats this doctrine in the positive form while speaking of the Prodigal Son in L123: ""I will go to my father and say to him, 'Father, I have sinned against heaven and before thee.' He might be able to excuse himself because of his youth and the bad company. He says nothing, nothing of this, for he has confessed his fault. 'I have sinned.' His offense saddens him more than his unfortunate condition. Such must be our sorrow for our sins, and this true sorrow never fails to be accompanied by sincere humility." Jansenism taught further that frequent communion was to be avoided because human beings were habitually unworthy, and Lamy certainly thought that even Catholics who regularly practiced their religion consistently committed mortal sins.[15]

To his credit, Lamy seems never to have voiced one elitist tenet of Jansenism, that Christ died only for the elect.

The Common Threads of Pelagianism and Jansenism

Pelagianism and Jansenism agreed on two points: the small number of the saved (implying an elitist view of justification) and rigorism in moral theology. More to the point at issue for ourselves, Lamy agreed with them both.

In an early instruction entitled "The Small Number of the Elect" (L012) – the title of the best-known sermon of Bishop Jean Baptiste Massillon of Clermont – Lamy stated that "though this be a frightful

truth that the number of the just is small, no Christian can doubt of it." In 1849 he added, "They may lose faith, the grace of God, their soul; and though having been first called they might not only be among the last but also be excluded from the Kingdom. Many called, few elected" (L040), and one week later he interpreted the parable of sower in such a manner that three quarters of the seed perishes — and that three quarters of human beings go to hell (L041). This is a Jansenist and a Calvinist thesis, elitist if there was ever such, and yet the contrast between heroes' innate greatness and common men's meanness is an elitist Pelagian tenet as well.[16]

Whether Jansenist or Pelagian, rigorism teaches that there is no merit if it doesn't hurt, and so in L051 we read, "However rough and hard this way may be, we have to go by it and bear its roughness to the end. If we had nothing to suffer it would be a loss to us, for what recompense could we expect? Recompense is only given to merit, and where would be merit be if there were no trials, no difficulty? All the saints have suffered and rejoiced in sufferings."

And so Jansenism and Pelagianism, like right-wing anarchism and left-wing anarchism, converge at a bleak antipodes, at the farthest possible point from Christian doctrine, actual experience, and common sense. The mystery of grace and the mystery of free will become more mysterious rather than less when they are brought together. The saving trick is to affirm them both, to state boldly that grace works so powerfully yet so subtly in human persons that it makes us more free rather than less, and that grace, which is a mode of God's omnipotence, perfects the freedom of human free will. And as regards theology, the best advice is to trust that history is real, that God is the Lord of history, that real change really happens, and that doctrine develops indeed.

Lamy rarely has any good to say of the world; the world as cosmos is a system of meaning and order and beauty, but it pretends to be self-enclosed and thereby denies its creator, denies its redeemer, and denies God as its purpose and goal. John Charles Scott speaks of the "authoritarian, traditionalistic, rigoristic heritage of Jansenism," but Pelagianism had an "authoritarian, traditionalistic, rigoristic heritage" as well. But fortunately for Lamy, the Inquisition was usually

quite aware that "preachers' failings were more apt to come from oratorical passion than willful heresy."[17]

The French Church and Its Seminary Education

The changes mandated by the Council of Trent (Tridentum) took about a century and a quarter to come to fruition, so by the latter decades of the seventeenth century there was a new sort of French priest at work in a new sort of diocese. The Tridentine-seminary-educated priests, directed and supported by stronger bishops and at work in parishes that were undergoing socieconomic transformation, were sent as strangers to the people of the towns where they were to work; no longer was clerical education an apprenticing of a boy to his uncle the priest, who educated him as best he could and eventually presented him to the bishop for priestly ordination so that he could become his uncle's successor.[18]

The new priests were educated well beyond the norm of their society, and so they felt themselves to be capable leaders and set about with considerable skill and even greater paternalism implementing in their parishes and in their towns the goals of the Council of Trent: standardization of belief, cult, and mores (of which more later); eradication of local folkways (the eighteenth century loathed the survivals of medievalism and of paganism about equally much); and a rigid morality which could be expressed as "more Puritan than thou" both vis-a-vis the Calvinists outside the Catholic Church and the Jansenists within. In addition, the priests were not just religious specialists; they were major social, civil, and cultural functionaries in the towns and villages of their parish.[19]

The Mexican "lowerarchy" of the 1810 "Rebellion of the Clergy" sided with the Indians and the mestizos because as pastors they knew their parishioners' pain first hand; similarly, the French parish priests of 1789 had thrown in their lot with the Third Estate – what the English called "the Commons" – and blindly helped to pull down the temple on their own surprised heads.[20] When the twin tornadoes of the Reign of Terror and Napoleon had finally passed, French Catholicism found itself organizationally and intellectually dead – seminaries closed for ten years and much of its academic and hier-

archical leadership vanished. Into the vacuum came two forces, Chateaubriand's romantic, aesthetic, and poetic traditionalism of a Church creatrix of incomparable beauties and de Maistre's and Bonald's theoretical traditionalism, reactionary and authoritarian, whose slogan was "More Faith and More Police" – or in its no-more-mister-nice-guy form, "The Pope and the Executioner."[21]

In this context, the Romantic reaction against the Enlightenment and Neoclassical rationalism and secularism reached backwards in time for medieval subjects – the Fathers of the Church, the religious orders, Marian devotions, and the modes of feeling and intuition (which provide great emotional excitement but have little staying power for the mind and will) that led to various forms of fideism ("blind faith") and traditionalism.[22]

The French clergy of the Restoration era (1815-1848), especially the seminary professors and their students, were largely out of touch with the socioeconomic realities of their actual world, and so they tended to drift off into an unworldly and next-worldly eschatology.[23] They therefore created a Catholicism that suffered from a sentimentalization of piety, a ghetto mentality, and a world-view that emphasized the strange inverse power of poverty, simplicity, and humility – the weapons of traditional rural innocence.[24]

The Tradition of Sermons

The disciplinary decrees of the sixteenth-century Council of Trent about public preaching still had the force of law in the nineteenth-century Catholic Church. The decree on reform passed in the fifth session placed preachers and preaching under the direct guidance of the bishops, who composed the center of gravity of the Church that the Council of Trent mandated. All priests with the care of souls were obliged to preach at least on Sundays and solemn feasts, taking as their subjects what is necessary for salvation, such as a knowledge of virtues to pursue and vices to avoid. A similar decree from the twenty-fourth session commanded pastors also to preach daily – or at the very least three times a week – during Advent and Lent, announcing the sacred scriptures, the divine law, and other topics as needed. The people were bound to attend and so learn the rudi-

ments of faith and obedience to God and their parents.[25]

When the eight-year-old Jean Baptiste Lamy began to attend the minor seminary – *petit séminaire* of Billom in 1823, he was a fellow student of many boys who had not the slightest intention of becoming priests but whose parents wanted them to have the benefit of a private education under the auspices of the Church. The college, founded by the Jesuits in 1558 as their first college in France, actually belonged to the municipality, but the municipality entrusted it to the bishop of Clermont, who in turn entrusted it to the Jesuits in 1826, when Lamy was twelve. Under their care, Lamy probably received a very positive slant on human nature in the course of reading the classical authors who made up much of the subject-matter of the school. The Jesuits had been founded in the Renaissance and tended to retain Saint Ignatius Loyola's positive view of classical culture: though it was neither explicitly supernatural nor capable of being part of the process of salvation, it was nevertheless good and not evil, for both the persons and the culture of Greece and Rome were marked both by original sin and by grace. The Jesuits only taught there until 1829, about the time Lamy finished Billom and moved on to the major seminary.

A former bishop of Clermont was Jean Baptiste Massillon (1663-1742), well known as a preacher and especially renowned for a 1704 masterpiece "On the Small Number of the Elect," a favorite Jansenist subject. Massillon had been both a student and a teacher in Oratorian schools, so he had learned a few apparently Jansenist traits. He was a good bishop and a very rigid moralist in his preaching, but many of his dogmatic utterances were driven more by rhetorical than by theological impulses. At any rate, Lamy might have felt some kinship with a former prelate of his diocese who shared his first name with him, and he may well have read his "Small Number of the Elect," for he later preached on the topic six different times in Ohio, Kentucky, and New Mexico between circa 1846 and circa 1880.

The little handsewn booklet mentioned above contains twenty essays on religious topics,[26] a list of passages from scripture and *The Imitation of Christ* for a six-day retreat, and the lyrics of a short song.[27]

There are in addition two items related to preaching, a very brief division of a sermon on the Holy Virgin[28] and a five-page outline of François de Salignac de la Mothe Fénelon's sermon for Epiphany 1685 before the ambassadors of the King of Siam, who had just decided to permit the preaching of Christianity in his kingdom; it is a pleasant surprise to find our seminarian choosing a sermon of the great French preacher which indicates his abiding interest in the foreign missions. Fénelon's sermon is an oration in full Renaissance form – the Bible text in Latin with a vernacular translation, an exordium, a statement of the *propositio*, which is like a thesis statement, a division of the topic into two parts, a prayer to Mary recited by priest and people, and a repetition of the scripture text. Then comes the body: narration (or history) and the confirmation or proof, followed by a refutation to rebut real or imagined objections. The discourse ends with the peroration or conclusion which contains a highly rhetorical recapitulation and an attempt to get the congregation to make some practical resolutions-to-action.[29] Though Lamy was evidently drawn to Fénelon's matter, his form seems to have left the young man cold; such is the distance from Renaissance to Romanticism.

Lamy probably began to learn English shortly after ordination when he offered himself to Bishop Purcell of Cincinnati. He must have started with a British book, because he learned the *-our* spellings of words like ardour, honour, neighbour, and so forth; by about 1849 he had dropped all the *-our* spellings except one, "Saviour," which I have retained as a reminder of the nineteenth-century tone of Lamy's writing. The most difficult set of idioms for our Frenchman were verb-preposition or noun-preposition pairs, for he more often than not put the wrong preposition with his verbs and nouns: "to feel loathsome of this divine word," "my soul loathes upon this food," "firm belief to all the truths that God reveals," and "to instruct us of some deep truths."

In Spanish, which he began to learn after he had been named as the Vicar for New Mexico, Lamy similarly retained one word in an archaic spelling which I have retained, "Yglesia."

Persons who heard him preach say that both in English and in Spanish, Lamy spoke with a good clear voice and with a slight and pleasant French accent. He worked out a structure that he thought suitable for each of his sermons, but in the Romantic manner each structure was designed only for the sermon at hand, quite unlike the set and predictable sermon form sketched above that had prevailed during the Renaissance era. One Lamy sermon with this structure survives, L028, but he labeled it with a cryptic "B. tr." which I take to mean that he translated it into English from the French of some master preacher as Bossuet, Bourdaloue, or Besançon. Though Lamy stayed much closer to the scriptural text of the Mass than I had expected, his reverence and respect for the inspired Word of God did not prevent him from interpolating his own commentary into his quotations from the Bible, and his manner of handling scriptural passages was of course not according to the hermeneutic canons of the twentieth or twenty-first century. Lamy tended to moralize in the manner of nearly all American clergymen of his own day, as James Brown said to Alexis de Tocqueville: "I think that for the majority [of Americans] religion is something respected and useful rather than a proved truth. In the depth of their souls they have a pretty decided indifference to dogma. One never talks about that in the churches. It is morality with which they are concerned."[30]

One of Lamy's favorite stylistic "ploys," "tricks," or "devices" was to ask numerous rhetorical questions not only for their rhetorical but also for their accusatory effect. Especially in Ohio and Kentucky, Lamy deluged his parishioners with such rhetorical questions as if he blamed them for the sad state of Catholicism; in New Mexico, by comparison, he rarely used that figure of speech, perhaps blaming not his parishioners but their former priests of the Durango Diocese for the religious troubles of the Southwest. Another trait of Lamy's literary style was Ciceronian triplets without any conjunction: "pride, vanity, revenge"; "Your religion, virtue, justice must be entire, disinterested, interior"; "[the sheep] sticks close to the shepherd, hears his voice, follows him"; "We understand that he is wise, that there is a providence, that this world is governed by him." In Spanish, Lamy pulls off a conjunctionless Ciceronian quintuplet: "Esta palabra es

un espejo en donde se ve la verdadera figura del siglo, sus promesas inciertas, sus bienes perecederos, sus placeres mezclados de tantas amarguras, sus honores con todas sus vanidades," but he was also into triplets: "hemos de considerar con el evangelista la salida de los reyes, su llegada a Jerusalem, su vuelta en su patria"; "perdiendo en este mundo su reputación, sus bienes, su salud"; "Por eso nuestra gloria, nuestro interés, todo nuestro ser debe perderse en la gloria, en el ser de Dios."

Lamy never inserted any topical reference into his sermons such as "two weeks after I excommunicated Padre Gallegos" or "ten days after I suspended Padre Martínez"; instead, it was always just "the Second Sunday in Advent" or "the Sixteenth Sunday after Pentecost." In his margins or in spaces at the end of his pages Lamy occasionally wrote notes for announcements, but these were given before or after the sermon, not as observations during it.

Lamy tells one real story, a sort of exemplum, in all the 250 or so surviving sermons:

A missionary had converted an Indian: after he had been well instructed, the Indian received the sacraments. The Father went away and returned in a year. The Christian convert very earnestly requested Communion. The Father replied that he would very gladly give him Communion but only after having heard his confession. The Indian was very astonished and replied, "Can anyone sin after having been baptized and having received the Eucharist? Thanks be to God that I have no sins."[31]

There is no example of humor, though when he wasn't preaching Lamy had at least a "passive" sense of humor, an ability to see the incongruity of some situation. Instead of comedy, Lamy satisfied his nineteenth-century auditors' hunger and thirst for the sublime, a culturally induced desire for the ultimate and transcendent of which Edmund Burke and every eighteenth-century romancer, poet, and painter was master. Death, judgment, heaven, and hell serve as the standard scenery for the full-contact industrial-strength "good bawling out" that Americans of the era – both Spanish-speaking and Anglophone – expected and felt was good for them, like a weekly

draught of some particularly bitter medicine.[32] Lamy was by all accounts well received as a preacher; though nobody every claimed that he was a great orator, his sermons were, if prosaic and unimaginative for the most part, at least consistently thoughtful, judicious, moderate, and workmanlike.

The American Religious Scene, 1840-80

In the first half of the nineteenth century, American Catholicism spent most of its energy searching for disciplined uniformity in doctrine, in ritual practices, and in behavior. External discipline would bind the parishes into proper dioceses, the dioceses into the unified American Church, and the American Church into the universal Church. As an unfortunate result, nearly all activity and all power passed into clerical hands.[33]

The nineteenth-century Catholic Church in the United States got a triple dose of Calvinism: from the dominance of French and French-trained clergy and especially bishops in the first two thirds of the century who brought with them at least a tinge of Jansenism, from French seminary professors, Oratorians especially, who had fled to Ireland during the French Revolution and imparted their Jansenism to Irish seminarians who came to the States, and from American Protestants of the Calvinist sort, especially Dutch Reformed, French Calvinists, Congregationalists, Presbyterians, and Baptists.

A Catholic phenomenon that resembled the Protestant practice of revivals was the parish mission.[34] But despite the common practices and even the many doctrines and practices common to Protestant and Catholics, there was serious trouble at times, trouble that peaked in the period of the Mexican-American War (1846-48). Ray Allen Billington notes,

> The mere fact that the Mexican War was fought against a Catholic power was sufficient to provide grist for the mills of prejudice. The East heard repeated rumors of Catholic desertion to the enemy and popish plots to poison [U.S.] soldiers. ... Polk's attempted use of Bishop John Hughes of New York as a peace mediator stirred such a hornet's nest of criticism that Hughes reluctantly refused to act.

Even the successful conclusion of the war failed to quiet nativists' fears, for they professed to see in the acquisition of a Catholic-populated domain only a new plot to surround the United States toward eventual papal subjugation.

And of course all of this was socio-cultural baggage that Lamy acquired in the Middle West and took with him to New Mexico in 1851.[35]

Endnotes

[1] Paul Horgan, *Lamy of Santa Fe* (New York: Farrar, Straus, and Giroux, 1975), p. 21. Since the different humors were aligned to different quarters of the day, days of the week and prevailing planets, signs of the zodiac, and so forth, there were right times and wrong times to bleed; and since the parts of the body were aligned to different signs of the zodiac and so forth, there was a right part and a wrong part to make the cut or place the leech so as to draw off some blood and the offending humor with it.

[2] See Thomas J. Steele, S.J., "The Code of Honor in Western Culture," Working Paper # 124, Southwest Hispanic Research Institute, 1998. By elevating honor into a specifically Christian context, Lamy separates it from its tribal and classical origins.

[3] AASF ld 1876-15a, pp. 10-12.

[4] The translation "will guide [persons] into all truth," which Lamy uses twice here, is a King James Version of John 16.13 and a word-for-word translation of the Greek *"hodēgēsei humas eis tēn alētheian pasan,"* whereas the Douay, which translates Saint Jerome's Latin, has "will teach you all truth — *docebit vos omnem veritatem."*

[5] Richard Simon (1638-1712), Oratorian and Molinist, is often termed "The Father of Biblical Criticism"; as a Molinist, he probably had a sense that God and the inspired writer could simultaneously be authors of the same piece of writing — that inspiration, like grace in general, does not manipulate but instead liberates. The Oratorians kicked Simon out of their congregation both because he was a Molinist (they tended to Jansenism) and because of his conclusions about scripture, and they got most if not all of his important writings put on the Index of Forbidden Books.

It was not until the nineteenth century that there were enough scholars doing scholarly criticism of scripture to have a conversation around a pot of coffee.

[6] In the following example of the supposed anagogic meaning of a passage, Lamy has too quickly identified entering into the Kingdom of Heaven with going to heaven, thereby getting too eschatological too soon: after quoting the text for the

Fifth Sunday after Pentecost, "Except your justice exceed that of the scribes and Pharisees you shall not enter into the Kingdom of heaven" (Matthew 5.20), Lamy begins, "The justice of the scribes and Pharisees must have been a false and deceitful justice, since our Saviour condemns it and declares to us that to go to heaven our justice must have a different character from theirs" (L023).

[7]   John L. McKenzie, S.J., *Dictionary of the Bible* (New York: Macmillan, 1965), pp. 393-95. The rare and brief allegorizing by the authors of scripture is one thing (see Galatians 4.24), while allegorizing by subsequent readers is quite something else.

A thirteenth-century couplet goes, *"Littera gesta docet, quid credis allegoria, Quid agis moralis, quo tendis anagogia* – The literal teaches what happened, allegory what you believe, The moral what to do, the anagogical whither you are going."

[8]   R. Howard Bloch, *God's Plagiarist: Being an Account of the Fabulous Industry and Irregular Commerce of the Abbé Migne* (Chicago: University of Chicago Press, 1994). Since copyright hardly existed anywhere in the world in the mid-nineteenth century, "plagiarist" is not quite the correct word.

[9]   Karl Rahner and Herbert Vorgrimler, *Theological Dictionary* (New York: Herder and Herder, 1965), p. 990, gives the scholastic ground rules for speaking correctly of the *communicatio idiomatum*.

[10]   If Lamy means "infinitely" in the literal sense of the word, this is an example of the "maximalist-human-intelligence" Christological doctrine that was prevalent throughout Christianity up to the nineteenth and early twentieth centuries. Scripture scholars and theologians today would tend to say, by contrast, that "becoming flesh" (John 1.14) – taking on the human condition of being immersed in time, space, and matter – meant that while Christ always knew in his human mind what to do or say next, he did not normally know what might come thereafter. Putting the same view negatively, he was not provided with all possible infused knowledge.

[11]   Cyril of Jerusalem, *Thesaurus*, PG 75.369; my translation.

A very recent and very impressive technical article of interest is David Coffey, "The Theandric [Human] Nature of Christ," *Theological Studies* 60 (1999), 405-31. Coffey preserves the unity of Christ without suppressing his human nature by a sort of *perichoresis* of the divine Person and the human nature, each "supposited" within the other so as to take advantage of the *actiones-sunt-suppositi* principle; Coffey thus avoids the *a priori* application of Ephesus' *communicatio idiomatum* which scholastic theology used so heavy-handedly.

[12]   Karl Rahner, *Sacramentum Mundi* (New York: Herder and Herder, 1969), 4:383-85. Pelagianism was and is a throwback to the pre-Christian dispensation, especially Stoicism; it generates less friction with the synoptics, especially Matthew, than with Paul and John and their emphasis on faith, but it is very non-Christian. Jerome's Latin translation of Paul is pretty incomprehensible, but Paul goes well with Augustinian Jansenism; people who undergo conversions need to be watched carefully.

[13]   Quoted in Rahner, 4:383, from *PL* 35:1841, *In Joannis Evangelio Tractatus* 81.3: "Cum dixisset [Jesus], 'His fert fructum multum', non ait quia sine me parum potestis facere sed 'Nihil potestis facere.'" —Is it Pelagianism or technology that brings us to view Christian saints as mere models rather than as active patrons and protectors of their devotees?

[14]   Augustine, Sermon 169, Chapter 11, Section 13, in *PL* 38:923: "Qui ergo fecit te sine te non te justificat sine te."

Leszek Kolakowski, *God Owes Us Nothing* (Chicago: University of Chicago, 1998), tries to prove in the first half of his book (pp. 3-110) that Jansenism is nothing more or less than an Augustinianism that was perfectly orthodox until the Catholic Church, for various reasons that Kolakowski deems inadequate, chose to swing from Augustine to Thomas Aquinas. He does not seem to suspect that there is such a thing as development of doctrine.

[15]   Noted both by Joseph P. Chinnici, O.F.M., "Organization of the Spiritual Life: American Catholic Devotional Works, 1791-1866," *Theological Studies* 40 (1979), 241, and by Jay P. Dolan, *The American Catholic Experience* (Garden City: Doubleday, 1985), pp. 225-29.

[16]   Rahner, *Sacramentum Mundi* 4:383-85.

[17]   John Charles Scott, "Between Fiction and History: An Exploration into Willa Cather's *Death Comes for the Archbishop*, University of New Mexico dissertation, 1980, p. 80; Manuel Morán and José Andrés-Gallego, "The Preacher," in Rosario Villani, ed., *Baroque Personae* (Chicago: University of Chicago Press, 1995), p. 146.

[18]   Morán and Andrés-Gallego, pp. 137-38.

[19]   Philip T. Hoffman, *Church and Community in the Diocese of Lyon, 1500-1789* (New Haven: Yale University Press, 1984), pp. 164, 169-70.

[20]   Hoffman, p. 165.

[21]   Louis Foucher, *La Philosophie catholique aux xix siecle* (Paris: Librarie Philosophique J. Vrin, 1955), pp. 11-27.

[22]   Kenneth Scott Latourette, *The Nineteenth Century in Europe* (New York: Harper and Brothers, 1958), 1:374-76. The happily resolved stalemate on the question of Marian May devotions between young Father Machebeuf and the old pastor (Howlett, pp. 32-35; Bridgers, pp. 31-33) could better be interpreted as Romantic-versus-Neoclassicist rather than True-Catholic-versus-Jansenist. —In its "other" document, the First Vatican Council had to try to strike a better balance between faith and reason.

[23]   Latourette, p. 400; John Charles Scott, "Between Fiction and History: An Exploration into Willa Cather's *Death Comes for the Archbishop*, University of New Mexico dissertation, 1980, p. 80.

[24]   Thomas A. Kselman, *Miracles and Prophecies in Nineteenth-Century France* (New Brunswick: Rutgers University Press, 1983), pp. 94-112; see also Steven Sharbrough, "El Ciclo de los Pastores," *History of Religions at UCLA Newsletter* 3 (1975), 7-11, for a description of the discoveries, apparitions, and miracles the age demanded.

[25] *Canones et Decreta Sacrosancti Concilii Tridentini* (Rome: City College of the Propagation of the Faith, 1834), Session 5, *De Reformatione*, Chapter 2, pp. 29-32, and Session 24, *De Reformatione*, Chapter 4, pp. 232-33. See also Morán and Andrés-Gallego, pp. 127-28; William B. Taylor, *Magistrates of the Sacred: Priests and Parishioners in Eighteenth-Century Mexico* (Stanford: Stanford University Press, 1996), pp. 160-61.

[26] The more positive topics: three on prayer, two on sanctification, one each on faith, mortification, chastity, good example, study, and the Holy Virgin, plus two from the first purgative period of Saint Ignatius' *Spiritual Exercises*, death and judgment. The more negative: human respect, delay of conversion, abuse of grace, idleness, scandal, and three more from the *Exercises*, one on mortal sin and two on hell.

[27] The song, made up of a two-line chorus and four four-line stanzas, is sentimental "greeting-card" verse wishing the recipient best wishes on New Year's Day.

[28] The whole text in my translation:

  1. Mary the object of our devotion due to her prerogatives. The devotion consists of honor because she is the most perfect creature, love because she is our mother, and placing all our confidence in her because she is filled with goodness to us.

  2. Mary the object of our imitation. The best manner of proving to Mary our love and our devotedness is to imitate her virtues of which she has given us the example.

[29] Fénelon, *Oeuvres Complètes* (Geneva: Slatkine Reprints, 1971 [orig. 1851-52]), 5:616-24; Lamy's precis is a fifth to a quarter the size of the original. Fénelon quotes two other passages of scripture, echoes many others, and refers to Irenaeus, Tertullian, Augustine, and Ignatius Loyola.

[30] George Wilson Payne, *Tocqueville in America* (Garden City: Doubleday, 1959), p. 313. Brown was born in Virginia in 1776, moved to Kentucky around 1790 and married Henry Clay's sister, moved to Louisiana in about 1805, and served twice as senator from Louisiana and later as Minister to France; he died in Philadelphia shortly after the interview with Tocqueville.

[31] Lamy concludes the little tale with the legalistic remark, "Doubtless he confessed in order to comply with the precept of the Church." The obligation to confess annually is binding only on those who have committed a serious (mortal) sin during the interval, for it derives from the obligation to be in the state of grace so as to receive the Eucharist at least once a year between the First Sunday of Lent and Trinity Sunday (the first after Pentecost).

[32] Consider Gray's "Elegy in a Country Churchyard," Goethe's *Sorrows of Young Werther*, Fuseli, Turner, the Gothic novel (or better, romance), Charles Brockden Brown, Cooper, Melville, Hawthorne, and the Hudson River School of American painting.

[33] Jay P. Dolan, *Catholic Revivalism: The American Experience, 1830-1900* (Notre Dame: University of Notre Dame Press, 1978), pp. xvi-xvii, 196-97; Joseph P. Chinnici,

O.F.M., "Organization of the Spiritual Life: American Catholic Devotional Works, 1791-1866," *Theological Studies* 40 (1979), 229-33, 255; on pp. 233-34 and 253, Chinnici gives fascinating lists of things and rituals to be micromanaged.

34   Much like the Puritan "Great Awakenings" in New England, Catholic parish-missioners had special sermons "On Delay of Conversion" (Lamy himself had an essay by that title on page 64 of his commonplace book); see Dolan, pp. 79-80, 95-97. Dolan, pp. 82-83, 100, notes special mission music; for New Mexico, see also Father Jean Baptiste Rallière's "Pecador el tiempo santo," "A misión os llama," and "En estos dias de gracia," ## 231-33 in any edition of *Cánticos Espirituales.* – Chinnici, p. 237, notes that the original prayer-book tradition switched from mainstream Catholic to Jansenist after 1815.

35   Ray Allen Billington, *The Protestant Crusade, 1800-1860* (Chicago: Quadrangle Books, 1964 [orig. 1938]), pp. 238-39. Hughes counter-threatened at one threatening moment to "see to it personally that this whole town [New York City] is burned to the ground."

MYERS-BRIGGS TYPES

Lamy

GUARDIAN: SUMMARY OF ESTJ
Adventuresome; spreader of the lifeways of cities (civilization); preserve and extend rather than create; strong ethical commitments; practical common sense; loyal and obedient and demand loyalty and obedience from subordinates; consistent, conservative, perserving; principled reasoning; achieve closure.

EXTRAVERT
Has to talk in order to think; energized by being with people; easy to meet and work with; ready to accept challenges; accessible, companionable.

SENSOR
Trusts present realities; prefers traditional procedures; patiently tames, organizes, makes productive.

THINKER
Principled reasoning from maxims/proverbs; dutiful in advising and reprimanding others; guardian of the past; cool, visualist, and scholarly; outcome-oriented.

JUDGER
Getting closure through step-by-step planning; good at delegating authority; perfectionist, but willing to cut his losses; a legalistic disciplinarian.

Cather

INTROVERT
Thinks in order to talk; refined, reserved, solitary, aloof; makes few friends; introspective; private.

INTUITIVE
Visionary; aesthetic, artistic; sensitive to the beautiful and the sacred; imaginative and creative; future-oriented.

FEELER
Empathetic, compassionate; sensitive to others' feelings; simpatico; warm, process-oriented.

PERCEIVER
Waits for more data, more information, more insight, whatever; never rushes to judgment.

Latour

Note: For Latour, the plot, not the character, determines both T or F and J or P. For Cather, there is no evidence for choosing J or P.

Chapter 4
Lamy's Psychological Profile

Joseph Wood Krutch remarked, apropos of an early novel of Willa Cather's, that "she can evoke by a few characteristic touches and by subtle suggestion a scene and a society without producing merely a 'document,' she can present a character without writing a psychological treatise, …and hence she is a novelist."[1]

Well I am not a novelist, and so I *will* attempt a psychological treatise. I have chosen one of the sixteen options presented by the familiar Myers-Briggs Type Indicator as the best description of Jean Baptiste Lamy: Extravert-Sensor-Thinker-Judger. It has been, incidentally, the most common profile among twentieth-century American males.

The Myers-Briggs says nothing about right or wrong, better or worse, much less sane or crazy; it speaks only about *de facto* habitual manners of interacting, gathering information, deciding, and doing. And far from claiming to be at all deterministic in the "Character Is Fate" mode, the Myers-Briggs is an invitation to round out one's personality and break free not so much from habits as from their limitations.

David Keirsey describes the ESTJ as a person with many administrative skills who seems to have been born to be a guardian. Guardians cooperate with others in keeping watch over persons and organizations, supplying needs, protecting against dangers without, and putting an end to misbehavior within. Their moral bent leads them to generate laws, regulations, and rules, and they evaluate their subordinates more in terms of method than outcome; they readily ad-

monish, discipline, and terminate uncooperative subordinates. "Their business is to mind others' business."

ESTJs are adventuresome, so they take on the challenge of spreading civilization – the ways of cities – into the less-developed realms of towns and villages. They preserve and extend rather than create, transplanting the approved pattern into new territories; they idealize but do not fantasize the past, admitting its hardships in a stoical manner, and their pessimism about the future makes them chronically sad.

Guardians respect authority and quote scripture verses, proverbs, and other such maxims, merely citing the texts without rehearsing the reasoning that lay behind them because they hold them as self-evident truths. The ESTJs' approved moral beliefs and practical common sense make them successful and effective in reaching their goals.

Guardians are loyal and obedient and insist on the loyalty and obedience of their subordinates mainly because they value the security and continuity of civilization, which they wish to carry, in their consistent, conservative, and dogged manner, from the past into the present and on into the future, from established cities into a developing frontier and then into further areas beyond.[2]

The following sections discuss each of the ESTJ's "letters."

LAMY THE EXTRAVERT

The way I read Lamy from his public biography, he was a natural *extravert* who donned a veneer of introversion when he became a priest, a bishop, and finally an archbishop and had to learn the dignified and reserved demeanor – and even some of the sternness, aloofness, and "higher seriousness" – that was expected of nineteenth-century clergymen and especially of bishops, who strode through life in impregnable fortresses of red satin and white lace. But Lamy had the whole run of the extravert's traits, for he was by nature friendly, easy to meet, very candid, self-confident, and ready to accept new challenges. When he had been only a year and a half in this country, Lamy described facing the test of preaching on Eas-

ter Sunday in English to about a thousand persons, "the most part of whom was no-Catholic, and many nothing at all, how earnestly have I desired that I could be able to speak the English well? because they are all very desirous of instructions. However, I did not get scared."[3]

Taking phrases and statements from his biographers and later historians, we find Lamy described in this manner: "He was naturally so kind, so innocent, that his little companions [in the minor seminary] had named him The Lamb'"; at the end of his life, when he lived at Bishop's Lodge in Tesuque, "he was glad to see visitors"; he had an "affable simplicity"; "he was a genuine friend of marvelous capacity for removing harshness; calm, peaceful, amiable, achieving goodness." And fray Angélico Chávez titled a chapter of his biography of Padre Martínez "A Friendly French Bishop."[4]

Historians describe Lamy's being easy to meet and work with by saying that he was "always accessible" and "generally companionable … easy with his colleagues." Their perceptions of Lamy's candor take these forms: "scrupulous sincerity"; "not eloquent save in the directness and simplicity of his utterances"; "It took a certain stalwartness to know oneself in honesty and still go forward with affairs in the world for the sake of others."[5]

Defouri sees Lamy as a self-confident "take-charge" man, especially during an all-night rainstorm along the Santa Fe Trail:

> The Bishop, regardless of the storm, was everywhere, with his usual and untiring energy, now encouraging the frightened Sisters, then giving directions to the muleteers, saving the party from another dreaded accident, the stampede of the animals; visiting the traveling party, never taking any rest until everyone was as comfortable as possible, thus acting the part of a father with all;

and on another crossing of the plains, "The Bishop had his hands full buying animals, wagons, and provisions and perfecting all arrangements for a speedy departure." Later, at home among the troubles of Santa Fe, Lamy "kept his head; he entrenched himself ever deeper in the minds of right-thinking men, and in the end he came out triumphant. And the secret of it all lay in the fact that he made and

held sincere friendships by virtue of his own intrinsic worth."[6]

The extravert is ready to accept new challenges, and Lamy was "always kind and even gay under trying circumstances"; en route to Denver after Machebeuf's accident in 1863, Lamy just took what little food was available at each stopping point, confident that he could control whatever situation might arise. Salpointe further describes him as "unmindful of his own safety," Warner points out that Lamy "headed the petition for an election to pass upon a bond issue" for a spur line from the main railroad up to Santa Fe, and Bridgers notes that Lamy's life encompassed "the adventures of the explorer [and] the beckoning call of the unknown."[7]

LAMY THE SENSOR

Being a *sensor*, Lamy gathered information by trusting present realities. For a Catholic priest, the paramount realities were those of faith: the Triune God, Jesus the Word Incarnate who came to save us, the order of grace and sacraments, church authority and duty, and the "four last things," death, judgment, heaven, and hell. Lamy approached the challenges mentioned above with practical common sense, relying mainly on traditional procedures and rarely going beyond what was approved and authorized. He civilized the places where he lived with the mainstream European-American lifeways and the Catholic religion he knew in Auvergne and Ohio, organizing them, civilizing them, and making them productive.

That Lamy trusted present realities, including such present and eternal realities as those of the afterlife, appears from Scott's remark about the strong "'unworldly' (that is, spiritual) … inclinations of seminary staff and students." Bridgers identifies one trait of a call to the foreign missions as "the spirituality of the priesthood," the priest's sense of the validity and value of his baptizing, absolving, marrying, saying Mass, and giving Communion. Horgan remarks on Lamy's self-knowledge in humility – for candor is a trait that grows from being both an extravert and a sensor.[8]

Lamy's practical common sense – including his preference for deeds rather than theory or empty talk – shows in Warner's comment that "he was not eloquent save in the directness and simplic-

ity of his utterances," and Horgan adds a quote from a casual acquaintance of Lamy's that depicts him as "a man of works rather than words, whose field of work is an empire, his diocese stretching from Denver to Mexico, from the Rio Grande to the Colorado."

Lamy was unmistakably a spreader of civilization — that is to say, of the ways of the cities, things like mass manufacturing, mass transportation such as railroads, mass media and advertising such as newspapers, and all the seemingly innocent components of consumerism and mass society. Horgan speaks of Lamy's energy "as he saw civilization spreading under his hand," Warner quotes Lamy as writing about how "we will be able to construct houses and churches as in the East" (quite a contrast to Cather's Latour, who cringes when ugly Ohio architecture hunts him down in the Southwest), and Warner quotes Tom Catron as terming Lamy "a leader in the community for better things," adding that "he was for enterprise, progress, and advancement." Horgan states that in 1882 "Lamy 'heartily' endorsed the growing manufacturing interests of Santa Fe." Woodress provides us a summary up to this point:

> Jean Latour is quite a different person from Archbishop Lamy in his attitudes toward the social and economic development of his diocese. Lamy, who was one of the prime movers in getting the railroad to come to New Mexico, viewed it, as did most of the settlers in the West before the railroad, as a blessing. It would bring New Mexico closer to the East, carry supplies more cheaply and abundantly than the wagon trains that crawled over the old Santa Fe Trail, and it would draw new settlers to fill in the empty spaces and help pacify the marauding Navajos and Comanches. Lamy supported the government's treatment of the Indians and held a typically optimistic nineteenth-century view of progress and civilization. Cather's Archbishop deplores the changes that are overtaking Santa Fe and opposes Federal efforts to relocate the Navajos.[9]

Lamy certainly did try to make New Mexico better in ways other than strictly religious, as Salpointe pointed out: "He did not neglect, when opportunity presented itself, to do what he could to better the

condition of his people," and after stating that Lamy, like another Ben Franklin, encouraged work and thriftiness, Salpointe refers to Lamy's gardening – as it happens, a favorite pastime of Guardians – which added so many trees, vegetables, and flowers to New Mexico.[10]

Lamy's sermons suggest that he was very much the sensor – a Christian sensor, we must add. In sermon L034, he tells us that "Since then the time we have to remain in this world is so short, the sorrows, the troubles of this life should not disturb a Christian because they will soon pass away, and also they are not worthy to be compared with the glory of eternity which we can acquire by bearing them with resignation to the will of God; neither should the enjoyments and comforts of this life take our affections and hinder us from minding and seeking the things of heaven, the spiritual interest of our souls, because these temporal enjoyments will soon have an end." In another early sermon, L038, Lamy embeds a reference to the next life so as to contextualize what he has had to say in the biggest of big pictures: "Finally, beloved friends, we should all be at the conclusion of this year in the strong determination never to commit any mortal sin but to spend all our time in such a manner as to secure to our souls the grace of God here and a happy eternity hereafter." In L091 he tells the faithful of Santa Fe,

> Given the reality of paradise, let us set ourselves to work.
> … In tribulations, in difficulties, in our crosses let us imitate the penitent who died on the cross next to Our Lord Jesus Christ. By our patient sufferings we can merit the pardon of our faults, and we might console ourselves with the words of Our Lord to this penitent sinner, "Today thou shalt be with me in paradise" (Luke 23.43). Today – how sudden! With me – what a companion! In paradise – what a resting-place! With the same patience, the same resignation, we might merit the same consolation. Amen.

"Given the reality of paradise": for Lamy, paradise is a given far more real than a curbstone or a Euclidean axiom.

The great, bizarre poet Arthur Rimbaud stated that every little cleric in France had a notebook of poems which he hoped to get published, but Rimbaud never met Jean Baptiste Lamy. Padre Martínez is known to have written poetry of the neoclassical, satiric sort, and I can easily imagine Machebeuf trying to write poems. But not Lamy, not Lamy. Civilization is one thing, Lamy was perfectly adapted to spreading it, and he did so; culture, however, is something quite different, and Lamy possessed little of the psychological equipment needed to create it, though he actively supported culture that he approved.

Architecture as Reminiscences

The Romanesque architecture of round arches and barrel vaults prevailed in Europe, most especially in southern France, from the tenth to the twelfth centuries. The first New Mexican church to be built in the Romanesque style was Nuestra Señora de los Dolores in Las Vegas (1867), and it was much admired in the Territory. Lamy sought architects for his cathedral in Auvergne, and whether it was he or they who suggested the idea, the building as it existed in 1895 – after Jean Baptiste Lamy's and Pierre Eguillon's deaths, when work ceased for three quarters of a century – seems to have been an eclectic gathering of parts of buildings, not all of them Romanesque, from several cities that Lamy fondly recalled: the rose window may well be a knockoff from the early Gothic Church of Saint Francis in Assisi, and aspects of the Santa Fe towers derive from the fine Romanesque Church of Notre-Dame-du-Port in Clermont, the Baroque Chihuahua Cathedral, Viollet-le-Duc's neo-Gothic plans for finishing the Clermont-Ferrand Cathedral, and the spire of Cincinnati's Saint Peter in Chains Cathedral.

While the new Santa Fe Cathedral was under construction, people universally liked it. In recent years, architectural historian Carl Sheppard, who made more sense of its design-motifs than anyone else, referred to it as "an anomaly," which translates equally easily into "a triumph of the eclectic order" or into "a hodge-podge." It cannot quite be described as something that Mussolini might have or-

dered by telephone, but it has certainly not endured in the eyes and hearts of most contemporary viewers as the triumph of aesthetic intuition that Willa Cather designed her Latour to be capable of.[11]

LAMY THE THINKER

In the world of Myers-Briggs, "thinking" does not refer to rarefied intellectual activity but to data-evaluation by means of principled reasoning which is unemotional and impersonal. As a *thinker*, then, Lamy felt obliged both to be obedient himself and to tell his subordinates what they were doing wrong; and even if he knew that he would cause the person pain in the short run, he had a duty to scold, suspend, or excommunicate someone if he had decided he ought to do so.

A perhaps surprising example of Lamy's principled reasoning was his guardian's wish to retain "the best of [Santa Fe's] historic past" such as the Castrense altar screen and the various other items in the museum in the Cathedral sacristy, and he also "opposed the destruction of the Old Palace and the erection of the capital." One of his contemporaries described Lamy as "determined [about building the cathedral] as the rock in it is hard," and an army officer stated that "when he believed himself to be right, he could be as firm as a rock."[12]

Weidman mentions Latour's "detached observation," and we can think of Lamy's – with the fundamental difference that Latour's detached observation is that of the intuitive introvert, Lamy's that of the thinking sensor. The impersonality could make it appear that rules were primary and persons secondary, and when Weidman remarks about Latour that in the novel "he meets the challenge mounted by Martínez and Lucero not personally but by the weight of church discipline and tradition," I suspect that in history Lamy reacted in the same manner. Warner described Lamy as "stern, perhaps severe at times. He was serious-minded. He was sometimes sad." Scott wrote of his "shrewdness as an ecclesiastical manager and politician," and Bridgers speculated about his having a "strategic, carefully analytical approach to problem-solving and a sophisticated, albeit sometimes highhanded, approach to administration" and a

reliance on the "familiar structures of the Catholic Church."[13]

Warner thought of Lamy as being generally "able, intelligent, just, and conscientious," and Scott added that like the other priests and bishops of his day in the United States, Lamy consistently tried to get his parishioners to be respectable in the eyes of their Protestant neighbors by avoiding alcohol, dancing, and Sunday frivolity. Many a Lamy sermon whether in the Midwest or in the Southwest was "a good bawling out," but the faithful of that age seemed to think that tough truths delivered with tough love might be good for them. Lamy was himself obedient to his superiors and to Church regulations, for even in his youth "he was loved both by his superiors and companions for his strict obedience and kind disposition of heart; … he was a scrupulous and yet cheerful seminarian [who] followed all the rules with religious scrupulousness"; and as a bishop he dealt with emergencies "without neglecting a single one of his many episcopal duties." John Gilmary Shea summed him up as possessing "zeal, piety, devotedness, and endurance which shrank from no toil," and Twitchell termed him "a noble and lofty character, of heroic spirit, capable and just in all his dealings." In conclusion, certainly Lamy did not spare the rod of justice in dealing with the priests in his jurisdiction, for he fulminated suspensions and excommunications lavishly.[14]

The sermons suggest that Lamy was a thinker. Sermon L093 suggests, by way of a horrible-example description of the hireling shepherd, how essential principled commitment is:

> The mercenary, who has no real concern for the sheep, abandons them in time of danger because he does not do his duty either for the glory of God or out of zeal for the salvation of those immortal souls but acts only for his own benefit. This hireling wants only his own profit, getting rich. He will not fail to flatter his sheep so as to please them, shut his eyes to their faults, never talk about their duties, never instruct them about virtues, and leave them in crass ignorance. When they are on the road to perdition, he will not warn them of the danger, and since it takes some effort and sacrifice to safeguard the eternal in-

terests of his sheep, he will abandon them, he will quit
them rather than run any risk.

The young Bishop exemplifies the principle stated in the sermon
about the parable quoted just above with a two-paragraph adden-
dum to his Sunday sermon on 17 July 1853 (L101):

A word about respect for our churches – "My house is a
house of prayer, but you have turned it into a den of
thieves" [Luke 19.46]. Here we see how criminal is the
lack of respect for God's house. It is an outrage against
God.

The church is a place where we come to humble ourselves, to seek pardon and mercy; and if we lack respect,
we emerge from church more guilty, and achieve our condemnation where we should have found grace. Your respectful behavior would render our churches respectable
to all.

This is a perfect example of the nineteenth-century push to get American Catholics to earn respectability in the eyes of the non-Catholic
majority.

I suspect that L182, delivered on 24 June 1863, provides us with
Jean Baptiste's candid self-portrait under the guise of a little panegy-
ric on his patron saint, John the Baptist; Lamy describes John's

zeal to advance the glory of God, to maintain justice and
truth without respect of persons. Toward humble sinners
who truly wished to change he was full of gentleness and
goodness. He told them that the privilege of being sons of
Abraham could not save them, only their obedience to
God's law. He spoke to all men, with the freedom of a
prophet, about their duties and obligations. He did not
know how to flatter the rich and famous despite their
power and influence. When they failed in their duties,
the man of God fearlessly told them, *Non licet* – It is not
lawful" [Mark 6.18].

I think we can see here Lamy's zeal for the Catholic faith, his
dislike of favoritism, and his gentleness to the sincerely repentant.

LAMY THE JUDGER

As a *judger*, Lamy organized his life and his tasks by making step-by-step plans that led to closure. He was an early starter, deciding on a plan, implementing it by giving appropriate orders, and delegating authority well. When he was in his thinking and judging mode, Lamy empathized poorly and doubtless seemed cold and aloof. He had high ethical standards approaching perfectionism and tended to be a strict disciplinarian. He seldom discerned the signs of the times, and he tended at times to force both himself and others into a single ideal – or ideological – mold.

His Judger characteristics made Lamy shrewd in the business and political realms of matters ecclesiastical; he was a typical bricks-and-mortar bishop of his epoch, and he was a focal point for the railroad-spur bond issue and various other civic "booster" projects. Bridgers associates his stubborn, tenacious character with the Auvergnat slogan *"Latsin pas* – Never give up." Because he was an early starter on projects that he felt obliged to undertake, his step-by-step plans were sometimes invented as he went along; he started right away with the goal clearly in mind and figured out the means as he went along, as when he got news of Machebeuf's summer 1863 accident and set out for Colorado with hardly a moment's preparation. He delegated authority as a matter of course, placing priests in parishes and not trying to be everybody's pastor.[15]

Lamy's lack of empathy and his apparent coldness led to Warner's statements "He was stern, perhaps severe at times. He was serious-minded. He was sometimes sad"; fray Angélico Chávez remarked that Lamy was "depressed in moments of indecision," when circumstances kept him from closure. Warner mentioned that "he was able, intelligent, just, and conscientious," and Chávez summarized his high ethical standards by stating that Lamy was "a fair-minded man at base, as well as most charitable." His sophisticated if high-handed approach to administration led to his dependence less on personal understanding than on the weight of church discipline and tradition – "the familiar structure of the Catholic Church." The astute passage from Bridgers' *Death's Deceiver* from which I took the previous phrase can serve as a summary of Jean Baptiste Lamy's ESTJ person-

ality from his seminary years to the end of his life: "Missionary life combined the spirituality of the priesthood, the adventure of the explorer, the familiar structure of the Catholic Church, and the beckoning call of the unknown."[16]

Such is the profile of Jean Baptiste Lamy's ESTJ type as drawn theoretically from half a dozen books on the Myers-Briggs Personality Inventory and as drawn from episodes in Lamy's public biography and from statements in his writings. To sum up with a few negatives, Lamy the Guardian was an introvert only by comparison with the raging extravert Machebeuf; since Lamy was short on intuition, he had little or none of the strong aesthetic turn that Cather gives Jean-Marie Latour; Lamy possessed an administrator's efficient tilt toward legalism rather than interpersonal sympathy; and he put little value on keeping his options open as long as possible.

To mention a trait that does not come up on the Myers-Briggs, Lamy did have a passive sense of humor. He may not have had the intuitive knack of creating jokes, but he could recognize the funny dimension of a situation that arose. Salpointe tells of Lamy ordering a group of newly arrived priests and seminarians to speak either Spanish or English, whereupon "a perfect silence ensued," which Lamy quickly ended "by bursting into laughter and reopening the conversation in French." Again, toward the end of Lamy's life, the historic La Conquistadora statue (now officially known as Nuestra Señora de la Paz) went out on procession one May afternoon only to be kidnapped en route by the youngest daughter of Willi and Flora Spiegelberg, who lived at the northwest corner of Palace Avenue and Paseo de Peralta. Only when Flora tucked her child into bed did she discover the figure and rush with it to her good friend the Archbishop to explain and apologize. Lamy reacted "with roars of laughter" and soon replaced the irreplaceable little Nuestra Señora by giving the little girl a lovely French doll.[17]

Concrete Applications To Problems

Especially as bishop and archbishop, Jean Baptiste Lamy had to deal with innumerable problems, some of them major and some of

them minor, some of them simple (and often quite protracted) and others of them complex (and rather interesting). I will begin by naming and dismissing five problems that I would term simple, then go on to interpret another five complex problems that will serve as proving grounds – test cases – for my hypothesis about Lamy's ESTJ personality profile.

(1) Rome sent the notice that it had erected the Vicariate-Apostolic of New Mexico not to Durango but to Sonora, and so when Lamy arrived in Santa Fe, he learned that the most recent Roman instructions told Bishop Zubiría of Durango to continue to administer that northern part of his sprawling diocese. The solution required a 2700-mile round trip with an entourage that included Vicario Forane (Rural Dean) Juan Felipe Ortiz – a simple solution that took about five months of hard travel.[18]

(2) Fray Angélico Chávez comments that Father José Manuel Gallegos' September 1852 trip to Durango was "something most indiscreet for him to do under the current conditions, but it goes with his character." Gallegos had been engaged in a scandalous and flagrantly public affair with the widow María de Jesús Trujillo de Hinojos for five years when Antonio José Martínez told Bishop Zubiría about it in a letter of 1844; eight years later it still continued. Principally for that reason Lamy suspended Gallegos, who went into politics.[19]

(3 and 4) The church at Belén sat too low in the valley to be safe from spring runoffs, and in the 1840s and 1850s it became a continuing concern. When it finally collapsed in June 1855, Father Antoine Juillard and some people who owned higher ground to the west wished to build the new church there, while most of the people preferred the old site. With some help from Machebeuf, Juillard managed to alienate the maximum number of parishioners, and the next spring when he was touring the smaller villages in the parish and got into a fracas with an Hispanic convert to Protestantism, a justice of the peace (alcalde) summoned him to his court and perhaps took out on the priest his disappointment over the church site. The solution to both problems was to move Juillard first to Sandía Pueblo and then to Arroyo Hondo, which at that time was the Santa

Fe Diocese parish closest to the North Pole.[20]

(5) For twenty long years Lamy pursued the Gadsden Purchase areas, the southern counties in New Mexico and Arizona, and the three Indo-Hispanic towns near Juárez that Odin had given him, until finally Rome acted on his behalf; he just stayed with the issue in the "*Latsin pas* – Never give up" manner of Auvergne and outlasted even the Roman Curia.[21]

Five further problems were not just major but also complex. They will bring out Lamy's personality in concrete and revealing circumstances.

1. The Christmas Pastoral

The main income of the New Mexican priests of the Durango Diocese had come from the fees they required for sacramental rituals. Lamy unilaterally decided to cut those fees sharply and to enforce the ancient traditions of first-fruits and tithing with threats of *de facto* excommunication.

As early as 1842, when he worked in Ohio, Lamy had written Bishop Purcell that he wished all the families in his parish could

> help toward the church [and also] contribute a little according to their abilities for the support of the clergyman. In regard to this last point I do not know what to do with a number of them. I wish you would advise me some means to make them do. Could I not tell them that if they do not help [a] little, [even] if they are not able to do much, they have no right to the services of the priest? I could not, to scare some of them, refuse to hear their confessions once or twice? You will oblige me very much if you suggest me what I could do in such a case.

There is neither any record of Purcell's reply nor any hint that he permitted Father Lamy to do as he wished.

But at Christmas 1852, when he had become the Vicar-Apostolic of New Mexico, Lamy announced his transformation of the fee structure and threatened to withhold the sacraments from all members of any family that did not pay up. Since the proceeds of tithing

went mainly to the Bishop himself, New Mexicans might have heard echoes of the Mexican government's centralization in the mid-1830s which led to Governor Albino Pérez' assassination. Lamy sued in justice-of-the-peace courts for his due – and amazingly, he won. Early the next year later he made the arrangement even more stringent:

> The faithful of this Territory … should know that we have taken from the pastors every faculty of administering the sacraments and giving church burial to the heads of families who refuse to yield up faithfully what they owe in tithes. They should be clear about this, that insofar as they can they should give grain or animals and not the price in cash. The collectors will accept the value in cash only when the number of animals is less than ten. After 1 February 1854, triple fees will be charged for administering Baptism, Matrimony, and church burial for members of families that do not comply.

Such threats ought to have bothered the priests of the new Vicariate more than they apparently did.

Lamy's ploy certainly seems mercenary, and his threat to withdraw priestly faculties conditionally was probably invalid. Granted that he desperately needed the money and that there is no record of anyone actually dying without the sacraments; but if it is wrong to shoot someone it is also wrong to wave a gun and threaten to do so.[22]

Then why did Lamy do what he did? As an Extravert, he was a self-confident take-charge man who was always ready to accept a challenge. As a Sensor and Thinker, he had a strong sense of duty and relied on the authority and the traditional structures and procedures of the Church. As a Judger, he felt obliged to solve problems as soon as possible. Uncharacteristically he went well beyond the approved and authorized procedures – at least as New Mexicans understood them.

2. Father Juan Felipe Ortiz

Padre Juan Felipe Ortiz came from a very wealthy and promi-
nent family of Galisteo and Santa Fe; his granduncle, Antonio José
Ortiz, rebuilt and enlarged the Santa Fe parish church in the 1790s.
After seminary studies in Durango and ordination, Juan Felipe returned to New Mexico, becoming *cura propio* (irremovable pastor) of
the Santa Fe parish and in 1832 Zubiría's *vicario forane* (rural dean) for
all of New Mexico, and so he presided over the various troubles of
the next twenty years.

Ortiz arranged the welcomes along the Rio Grande and in Santa
Fe in July and early August of 1851, when Lamy and his party
arrived. Lamy and Ortiz traveled to Durango together with a sub-
stantial entourage for safety. For many months they remained friendly,
even despite Ortiz's claim to own the Santa Fe rectory; diocesans
preferred to own and maintain their residences, whereas during the
Franciscan era the civil government probably held title to all church
property. Lamy eventually purchased the *convento* and much later
allowed Ortiz to occupy it during the last months of his life.

Ortiz is said to have ordered Lamy out of his house after having
heard not only of the change in fees discussed above but of Lamy's
new plan to divide the Santa Fe parish, all of which Ortiz had a life
claim to. Since the United States Catholic Church did not recognize
irremovable pastors, when Ortiz remained adamant about being the
rightful pastor of San Francisco de Asís the Bishop ousted him, and
when he appealed to Rome Lamy suspended him.[23]

Lamy dealt as he did with Ortiz because the Sensor in him relied
on the rightness and effectiveness of church authority and the Thinker
and Judger in him perceived a strict duty to reprimand and discipline an uncooperative subject and moved as soon as possible to
closure.

3. The Seal of Confession

One day when Machebeuf was serving as parish priest in the
small community of Peña Blanca, he got to talking from the altar
about unnamed persons who had repented of certain sins — and
nearly everyone in church knew who the culprits were. Don Fran-

cisco Tomás Cabeza de Baca, a brother-in-law of Father Juan Felipe Ortiz, jumped to his feet and objected strenuously to having been one of the persons so described. When it came to any question of violating the secrecy of the confessional, William Taylor remarks, "Priests who violated the seal of secrecy or the decorum of the occasion could expect harsher punishment than for almost any kind of personal immorality."

Machebeuf's defense for breaking the seal was that he knew what he had spoken of from other sources than the persons' confessions, and over the next several years Bishop Lamy certainly did all he could to get Machebeuf exonerated (Machebeuf himself had to make a trip to Rome and do a lot of fast writing and talking). I suspect that this was one of the few times when the Thinker in Lamy yielded to the Feeler — when his longtime friendship for Father Machebeuf and his TJ loyalty to loyal subordinates overcame his normal recourse to unemotional, impersonal, principled reasoning. I imagine that Lamy told Machebeuf something like "I am sure you are innocent. Now, never do it again, and never even *seem* to do it again." For indeed, it is not only the substance of breaking the seal of confession but even the appearance of doing so undermines the parishioners' confidence in the confidentiality of the sacrament.[24]

The Extravert Lamy solved Father Machebeuf's confessional-secrecy problem by staying with his loyal and sincere friendship, and he suppressed his Thinker's penchant for principled, impersonal, unemotional reasoning.

4. Father Antonio José Martínez

Although Horgan claimed that the New Mexican pastors' rejection of Lamy's 1852 Christmas pastoral on tithing was the main cause of all the problems that followed, Chávez is probably right in seeing the Spanish Father Taladrid as the main cause of Padre Antonio José Martínez' difficulties; after all, Martínez remained friendly and acquiescent to Lamy until the early summer of 1856. Doubtless the penalties that Lamy added to his demands pained Martínez because in 1832 he had initiated the law that stopped the civil government from forcing the people to tithe to the church, and it surely

pained Martínez to read in the Santa Fe *Gazette* that the Bishop had
hauled his parishioners into the alcalde courts. Due to a combination of age, frustration at Lamy's failure to understand and assent to
his defensive arguments, and anger at the increasing insults to his
honor, Martínez lost his vaunted ability to think straight, and he
became subject to confusions that would never have occurred six or
eight years earlier.[25]

Taladrid had been the main problem. A former chaplain for the
reactionary Carlist army and an arrogant peninsular, Taladrid looked
down his nose at what he doubtless considered the mongrel colonials
of New Mexico. He seems to have challenged one of the Padre's
brothers to a duel, though fortunately nothing came of his proposal.
In May 1857, a fiasco of Taladrid's making led Kit Carson and the
U.S. Army into embarrassing itself, and Lamy removed Taladrid from
Taos as soon as he learned of it. Lamy sent Taladrid to Isleta and then
to Mora, where he proved himself incompetent, for Archbishop
Salpointe commented very pointedly on the mess he made of the
Mora parish in the brief time he had been there. There is good evi-
dence that he was a drunkard and a compulsive gambler, for these
twin problems forced his resignation from the U.S. Army.[26]

A partial trail of letters that leaves an immense amount to an
historian's imagination suggests a painful and protracted sequence
of alienations between Lamy and Martínez. In retrospect, it is a tale
of self-destruction, and what a great disaster that arguably the two
most impressive persons in nineteenth century New Mexico, when
brought together in difficult circumstances, could do no better than
to tarnish their own reputations, the one as badly as the other.

Lamy dealt with Padre Martínez almost exactly as he had dealt
with Ortiz four or five years earlier (see above). Being a Sensor, Lamy
failed to perceive the old man's oblique signals of helplessness and
confusion; as Thinker he applied the abstract principles of canon
law in a circumstance where sympathetic feeling would have been
more appropriate; as Judger he hurried to closure when much of the
evidence was still undiscovered. Lamy admitted in a letter to Purcell
that he was not in the habit of observing the formal niceties of judi-
cial procedure: "They [suspended priests] have submitted but have

said that I did not observe the rules prescribed by the canon law in inflicting these censures. The fact is that if I would comply with all the formalities they want, I could never stop abuses."[27] Like a lynching in the old West, it may not have been legal but it certainly worked.

5. Lamy and the Brotherhood.

An unpublished paper by Robert Lewis of Santa Fe adopts a business-management methodology to study the relationship of the three main bishops of nineteenth-century New Mexico, Zubiría, Lamy, and Salpointe, to the penitential Brotherhood of Our Father Jesus the Nazarene. Lewis begins by suggesting that the Catholic Church's objectives were to help the Catholic peoples of nineteenth-century New Mexico maintain their practice of their religion and to provide the parishioners with the advice and leadership that the clergy could give them. "In business metaphor, one can describe this Church-membership relationship as a resource-management issue of how leadership can accomplish the organization's goals, given the various environmental conditions and constraints that might exist."

Chief among the numerous challenges were that proportionally fewer priests were available to advise and lead the widespread and burgeoning Hispanic population and that the infrastructure of churches, schools, and hospitals was sadly lacking. On the plus side, "a grass-roots support organization, the Penitentes, had emerged to provide complementary religious guidance and nurture (as well as social support) to resident Catholics who sought to practice their faith." On a day-to-day basis and on a town-and-village level, the Brothers were the sole actual Church.[28]

Bishop Zubiría of Durango learned about the Brotherhoods in 1833 and reacted altogether negatively; Lewis comments,

> A more effective process would have involved his learning more about the Penitentes, their role in the parish community, and their practices before offering such unilateral leadership direction. By not doing so, Zubiría missed an opportunity to reinforce positively the leader-member part-

nership that must exist for any organization, including
the Catholic Church, to be successful.

And Lewis comments further that a proper relationship between
clerical, especially episcopal, leadership and lay initiative is a critical
success factor – a necessary requisite.[29]

Bishop Lamy came to New Mexico with attitudes, convictions,
and programs which he did not always adjust to New Mexican
reality; he expected instead that New Mexico would adjust to him
and his ways. As a result, the infrastructures he built tended to
marginalize rather than incorporate the "little churches" of village
Catholicism, especially the Brotherhoods. Lamy made overtures to
the Brothers several times as did the Brothers to Lamy, but no real
progress resulted; Lamy seems to have been satisfied with a truce
rather than a partnership. There were two exceptions: in 1879, the
railroad finally arrived, and so Lamy drafted a damage-control letter,
a very understandable move in a century when one of the bishops'
greatest concerns was to make Catholicism respectable; then in 1884,
Archbishop Salpointe had arrived, and on his way out the door
Lamy did his successor the favor of signing a letter that expressed
his successor's mind and that Salpointe had doubtless largely composed.

Lamy was confident that he could take on the challenge of dealing with a rural, grass-roots, vernacular confraternity of a pre-Re-
naissance cast which, being an outsider, he did not understand very
well. He was uniquely disqualified by being the chief executive
officer of the Latin-speaking level of the Church and at the same
time a spreader of civilization – of city values – embodied in the
conventional wisdom of his day: enterprise, progress, advancement,
and respectability in the eyes of the WASPs.

Lamy was much easier on the Brothers than Zubiría and very
much easier than Salpointe, but Lamy has had the popular name
(whereas few besides scholars can name the names of the other
two), and so Lamy gets all the praise *and* all the blame. Unfortunately
for him, there is more blame than praise available for the bishops'
dealing with the Brothers, since from the first episcopal awareness
of the Brotherhood in 1833 until nearly the end of the nineteenth

century, the dioceses of Durango and Santa Fe suffered an unfortunate lapse of managerial skills, underutilization of a major available resource – the Brotherhood, and some unfortunate pastoral losses.[30]

Endnotes

[1] Review of *A Lost Lady* (1923), *Nation* (28 November 1923), from James Schroeter, ed., *Willa Cather and Her Critics* (Ithaca: Cornell University Press, 1967), pp. 52-53.

[2] David Keirsey, *Please Understand Me II* (Del Mar: Prometheus Nemesis Book Company, 1998), 75-107; the quotation is from p. 84.

Besides Keirsey, I used Isabel Briggs Myers and Mary H. McCauley, *A Guide to the Development and Use of the MBTI* (Palo Alto: Consulting Psychologists Press, 1985); Robert Benfari, *Understanding Your Management Style* (Lexington: Lexington Books, 1991); Paul D. Tieger and Barbara B. Tieger, *Do What You Are: Discover the Perfect Career* (Boston: Little, Brown, 1992); Rowan Bayne, *The Myers-Briggs Type Indicator* (London: Chapman and Hall, 1995); Isabel Briggs Myers and Peter B. Myers, *Gifts Differing* (Palo Alto: Consulting Psychologists Press, 1990); Angelo Spoto, *Jung's Typology in Perspective* (Wilmette: Chiron Publications, 1995); Jean M. Kummerow et al., *Worktypes* (New York: Warner, 1997).

Lamy must be credited with building the organizational structure of diocesan parishes, schools, and hospitals. See especially Nancy Hanks, "Lamy's Legacy: Catholic Institutions of New Mexico Territory," *Seeds of Struggle, Harvest of Faith* (Albuquerque: LPD Press, 1998). pp. 385-414.

[3] Lamy to Purcell, 11 April 1841, AASF l.d. 1850 # 7.

[4] James H. Defouri, *Historical Sketch of the Catholic Church in New Mexico* (San Francisco: McCormick Brothers, 1887), 30; J.B. Salpointe, *Soldiers of the Cross* (Banning: St. Boniface Industrial School, 1898), p. 275; Salpointe, p. 44; Thomas Benton Catron, quoted in Louis H. Warner, *Archbishop Lamy: An Epoch Maker* (Santa Fe: Santa Fe: Santa Fe New Mexican Publishing, 1936), p. 245; fray Angélico Chávez, *But Time and Chance: The Story of Padre Martínez of Taos, 1793-1867* (Santa Fe: Sunstone Press, 1981), pp. 92-100.

[5] Salpointe, p. 276; Paul Horgan, *Lamy of Santa Fe: His Life and Times* (New York: Farrar, Straus, and Giroux, 1975), p. 416; Salpointe, p. 19; Warner, p. 275; Horgan, p. 41.

[6] Defouri, p. 39; Defouri, p. 46; John Charles Scott, "Between Fiction and History: An Exploration into Willa Cather's *Death Comes for the Archbishop*," dissertation, University of New Mexico, 1980, p. 76; Warner, p. 259.

[7] Defouri, p. 88; Salpointe, pp. 236 and 276 twice; Warner, pp. 154-55 and 276; Lynn Bridgers, *Death's Deceiver: The Life of Joseph P. Machebeuf* (Albuquerque: University of New Mexico Press, 1997), p. 28.

[8] Scott, p. 80; Bridgers, p. 28; Horgan, p. 41.

[9]   Horgan, p. 419; Warner, pp. 179, 245 (quoting Catron), and 276; Horgan, p. 397; Woodress, *Willa Cather*, p. 401.

The spur line to Santa Fe, mentioned under the heading "Extravert," is of course pertinent here as well (Warner, pp. 154-55), and William A. Keleher mentions Lamy's key role in *Fabulous Frontier* (Santa Fe: Rydal Press, 1945), pp. 23, 133. The bonds were in two groups, and the $79,000 sum passed 192-72 and the $71,000 sum passed 192-67; see Dudley M. Lynch, "Lamy – Railroad Junction," *New Mexico Magazine* 44 # 10 (October 1966), 3.

Lamy's acquiescence in the Navajo Long Walk is corroborated in Jacqueline Dorgan Meketa, tr., ed., *Legacy of Honor: The Life of Rafael Chacón* (Albuquerque University of New Mexico Press, 1986), pp. 240-41, but Marc Simmons declares that when Lamy later visited Bosque Redondo, he was appalled by the Navajos' misery – *New Mexico: A History* (New York: W.W. Norton, 1977), p. 152.

[10]   Salpointe, pp. 276-77. Warner, pp. 147-51, 256, and Horgan, p. 410, agree.

[11]   An anonymous Jesuit writer was lavish in his praises; *Revista Católica* 9 # 28 (2 July 1883), 341-42, and so was Paul Horgan, "In Search of the Archbishop," *The Catholic Historical Review* 46 (1961), 411, 413, 419.

Bruce Ellis, *Bishop Lamy's Santa Fe Cathedral* (Albuquerque: University of New Mexico Press, 1985), pp. 1-2; John J. Murphy, ed., *Death Comes for the Archbishop* (Lincoln: University of Nebraska Press, 1999), illustration 20 and pp. 482-83; Carl Sheppard, *The Archbishop's Cathedral* (Santa Fe: Cimarron Press, 1995), passim. In regard to Saint Peter in Chains Cathedral, Lamy made a point when in Rome in 1867 to get permission to see and venerate the chains; Finbar Kenneally, O.F.M., *United States Documents in the Propaganda Fide Archives: A Calendar* (Washington: Academy of American Franciscan History, 1966-87), 8:383, 2314.

[12]   Warner, pp. 135, 279, 145, and 271; Horgan, p. 419. In "Santos 1948," *Saints of the Land* (Santa Fe: St. Vincent Foundation, 1948), p. 6, Willard Hougland noted that there was no Lamy document suggesting that he disliked the New Mexican santos; in the half-century since then, no such document has come to light. By contrast, Bishop Zubiría disliked them intensely.

[13]   Bette S. Weidman, "Willa Cather's Art in Historical Perspective: Reconsidering *Death Comes for the Archbishop*," in Mares, ed., p. 50; Weidman, p. 53; Warner, p. 275; Scott, p. 76; Bridgers, pp. 27, 28.

[14]   Warner, p. 276; Scott, pp. 84, 159; Defouri, pp. 30, 31, 49; Shea, *History of the Catholic Church in the United States from 1843 to 1866* (New York: John G. Shea, 1892), p. 307 (volume 4); Twitchell, 2:331; Horgan, pp. 150, 175, 178, 191-92, 195, 212, 228-29, 235-36, and 241-42 (suspensions); 242-45 (excommunications).

[15]   Scott, pp. 76, 77; Warner, pp. 154-55, 276; Bridgers, p. 27; Salpointe, pp. 236-37. When he faced the thousand Easter worshipers with his faltering English, Lamy had at least the consolation of knowing that "I had before[hand] prepared *mon petit mot*," and so he did his best to deliver it; Lamy to Purcell, 11 April 1841, AASF l.d. 1850 # 7.

[16]   Warner, p. 275; Chávez, *Très Macho – He Said* (Santa Fe: William Gannon, 1985), p. 37; Shea, 2:329; Warner, p. 276; Chávez, *But Time and Chance*, p. 99; Bridgers, p. 27; Weidman, p. 53; Bridgers, p. 28.

[17]   J.B. Salpointe, *Soldiers of the Cross* (Banning: Saint Boniface Industrial School, 1898), p. 219; Horgan, pp. 272, 415-16. The second story is implausible because the statue is nearly a yard tall and too heavy for an innocent young child to carry, but perhaps it is "true" in the sense that it should have happened and unaccountably did not – but that it remains true to the character of the Archbishop.

The Spiegelbergs were close friends of the Archbishop because he took Levi Spiegelberg into his Santa Fe Trail caravan and nursed him through a bout of cholera.

[18]   Howlett, pp. 178-79, Horgan, pp. 131-46; the Congregation of the Propagation of the Faith misdirected its letter to Sonora where the Bishop did not forward it largely because he was dead: Kenneally, 2:504, 4:1398, and 4:1405.

[19]   Chávez, *Très Macho*, p. 52; Thomas J. Steele, S.J., "Padre Gallegos, Père Machebeuf, and the Albuquerque Rectory," pp. 61-63, 65-69; Rev. W.G. Kephart's *Santa Fe Weekly Gazette* (27 August 1853), p. 2, stated "The Bishop does not think the possession of a mistress [in the Spanish translation on p. 3, "una querida"] to be necessary or becoming to a priest in the discharge of his ecclesiastical duties. If the truth must out, there is the truth, the whole truth, and nothing but the truth; and we defy the defenders of Padre Gallegos to prove us false in what we say." There were no challengers.

When Machebeuf sued to recover the Albuquerque rectory he lost, and Lamy paid Gallegos $1501 for the building and the land it stood on.

[20]   On the church location, see George B. Anderson, *History of New Mexico: Its Resources and People* (Los Angeles: Pacific States Publishing, 1907), p. 485; and Margaret Espinosa McDonald, "'Vamos Todos a Belén': Cultural Transformations of the Hispanic Community in the Rio Abajo Community of Belén, New Mexico, from 1850 to 1950," dissertation, University of New Mexico, 1997, pp. 124-26. On the Protestant and the J.P., see Jammes Project F03455a; Steele, "Father Juillard and the Belated Reformation," unpublished paper, 1999. On both, see AASF loose document 1857 # 24: recantations by Bernardino Torres (the J.P.) and Juan Domingo Valencia (who sued the Bishop).

[21]   Finbar Kenneally, O.F.M., et al., *United States Documents in the Propaganda Fide Archives: A Calendar* (Washington: Academy of American Franciscan History, 1966-87), 10:261.

[22]   AASF 1850 # 10 (Lamy to Purcell, 24 June 1842), p. 2; Horgan, pp. 42-43; *Gaceta Seminaria de Santa Fe* (Christmas Pastoral text, 1 January 1853), p. 4; AASF l.d. 1854 # 3 (Circular to Clergy, 14 January 1854); AASF 1853 l.d. # 6 (Lamy to Purcell, 10 April 1853).

Regarding similar situations in New Spain, William Taylor remarks, "By withholding the sacraments, the priest could jeopardize their salvation," and he offers a

pair of examples from further south in New Spain, one from 1767 which failed because the viceregal *audiencia* stopped it and the other from 1777 which was not so financially motivated as Lamy's action; William B. Taylor, *Magistrates of the Sacred* (Stanford: Stanford University Press, 1996), pp. 222-23. Analogously, Jay Dolan describes a measure from certain Polish-American parishes in the 1920s which did not prevent the non-practicing parishioners from getting the sacraments necessary for salvation; Dolan, *The American Catholic Experience*, pp. 223-24, referring to Mary Cygan, "Ethnic Parish as Compromise: Spheres of Authority in a Polish American Parish, 1911-1930," Cushwa Center for the Study of American Catholicism, University of Notre Dame, Working Paper 13 # 1, (Spring 1983), pp. 5-6.

²³   Demetrio Pérez manuscript "Il Ilustrísimo y Reveredísimo Señor Don Juan B. Lamy – Rasgo Histórico," Ellis Collection, fray Angélico Chávez Library, Palace of the Governors, with partial translation by Bruce T. Ellis, "New Notes on Bishop Lamy's First Years in New Mexico," *El Palacio* 65 (1958), 28-29; Howlett, pp. 153-59, 163; Horgan, pp. 74, 105-10, 173, 202-03; Chávez, *But Time and Chance*, pp. 115-18; Chávez, *Très Macho*, p. 56; Bruce T. Ellis, *Bishop Lamy's Santa Fe Cathedral* (Albuquerque: University of New Mexico Press, 1985), pp. 61-80 (Antonio José), 84-88, 98 (Juan Felipe); Steele, "The Poet, the Archbishop, and the Heavenly Jerusalem: Romanticizing Lamy's 1851 Arrival in Santa Fe," *Folk and Church in Nineteenth-Century New Mexico* (Colorado Springs: Hulbert Center for Southwest Studies, 1993), pp. 104-20; Bridgers, pp. 73, 86-89, 103, 119.

Regarding the convento-rectory, neither as individuals (because of their vows of poverty) nor as an order (because of their Franciscan calling to absolute poverty) could the Observant Franciscans own any property of any sort.

²⁴   Horgan, pp. 176-80, 184; Chávez, *But Time and Chance*, pp. 108-13; Bridgers, pp. 109-12; Taylor, p. 165.

²⁵   Chávez, *But Time and Chance*, pp. 133-34; Bridgers, pp. 132, 134. The various "sermons" published by José Vicente Ferrer Romero on his father's printing press in Martínez's name (1859-61) might be proof of the Padre's failure of mental faculties, assuming that Vicente did not compose them himself.

²⁶   See Steele, *Folk and Church*, pp. 73-80; Bridgers, p. 133; Salpointe, p. 223; Nancy Hanks, *Priests and Parishes of New Mexico Territory*, April 1993, pp. 101-02.

²⁷   Lamy to Purcell, 10 April 1853, AASF, loose document # 6.

²⁸   Robert F. Lewis II, "Catholic Leadership and the Penitentes: A Lesson in Resource Management," unpublished paper, University of New Mexico-Santa Fe, Summer 1999, pp. 1-4, citing Alice Corbin Henderson, *Brothers of Light* (New York: Harcourt, Brace, 1937), p. 108; E. Boyd, *Popular Arts of Spanish New Mexico* (Santa Fe: Museum of New Mexico Press, 1974), p. 451; Thomas J. Steele, S.J., and Rowena A. Rivera, *Penitente Self-Government* (Santa Fe: Ancient City Press, 1985), pp. 6-7: "The origination of the New Mexico Penitente movement was a perfect example of a vital culture's activating its own internal forces and bringing about the adaptive changes which allowed it a continued vitality."

²⁹   Lewis, pp. 6-8; he cites Marta Weigle, *Brothers of Light, Brothers of Blood* (Albuquerque: University of New Mexico Press, 1976), p. 24, and Joseph A. Bator, "Authority and Community in Nineteenth-Century American Catholicism: John Baptist Lamy in New Mexico," dissertation, Northwestern University, 1994, p. 12.

³⁰   Machebeuf in Colorado did better even than Lamy because from the Denver viewpoint the Colorado Hermanos were geographically marginalized and far less noticeable than the New Mexico Hermanos

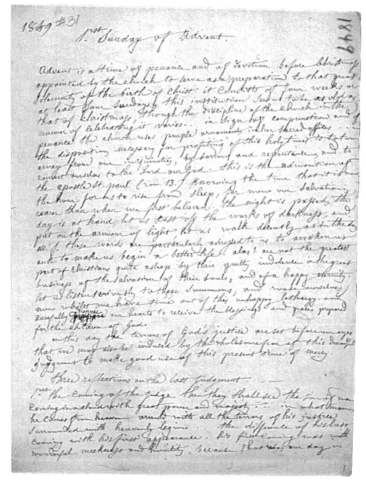

Example of Lamy's handwriting in one of his sermons in English. Sermon for 1st Sunday of Advent, 1849 (L066).

Chapter 5
Spirituality

The section on scripture in Chapter Two noted the three spiritual senses that for medieval scholars lay behind the literal: the allegorical, which reveals what we are to believe and which feeds theology; the anagogical, which leads us to hope for an afterlife and to work toward it by prayer; and the moral or tropological, which instructs us how to live a Christlike life and which provides the stuff of homilies.

These three spiritual senses continue to serve well to divide spirituality into its three great components, and spiritual theology may be defined as *a phenomenology of dogmatic and moral theology*; more simply put, any Christian spiritual theology – especially the Catholic – is a study of the personal human experience of believing in what some Christian community holds and teaches, the experience of praying, especially in a group, so as to get in regular conscious touch with the sacred personalities, and the experience of living by what the community demands and practices.[1]

Christian spirituality has nearly always tended to be mystical in interpreting scriptures – looking for the "hidden meanings" beyond the visible and literal, to be conservative in staying in live contact with the tradition even while growing beyond it, and to be practical in witnessing to faith, praying, and living a life where Christian charity is the form of all other virtues. There are numerous rich traditions of Roman Catholic spirituality, and French spirituality is outstanding among them, espeically that of the founder of the French Oratorians, Pierre de Bérulle (1575-1620). His world-view and theol-

ogy seem to have been traditional and Augustinian, Neo-Platonic and Pauline, viewing each individual as proceeding from God, emphasizing original and personal sin and the need of a Savior, and making Christ our model for returning to the Father.[2]

The first identifiable Catholic spirituality in the United States was marked by the new democratic milieu and the cool and reasonable mindset it flowed from. But when French and other European priests came to join the few ex-Jesuits (including John Carroll) and small number of other priests, they soon became dominant and introduced a revival of the baroque spirituality of the pre-Enlightenment past which included a great number of revived devotions – Christ in the Blessed Sacrament and Corpus Christi, the Sacred Heart and the First Fridays, Mary, May devotions, and the rosary in October, various devotions to angels and saints, the cult of papal authority then growing toward the Vatican I declaration of infallibility, and the cult of miracles and apparitions.[3]

The Allegorical: Faith and Doctrine

At the core of Christian faith are the birth and crucifixion of the God-man Jesus; Lamy firmly grasps the doctrine and presents it very effectively (L029): "We should admire and adore the circumstances of divine providence which was pleased that the glory of our Saviour's birth should be hidden in the obscurity of a poor stable in little Bethlehem, whilst he chose for the ignominy of his passion the great theater of Jerusalem and the pascal time, which the whole nation of the Jews was assembled in the holy city. 'Learn of me that I am meek and humble of heart' [Matthew 11.29], had he said to us, and to teach us humility himself, he would hide before men the glory of his divinity and make public on the contrary the ignominy of his passion and the scandal of the cross, as Saint Paul expresses it [Galatians 5.11]." The mystery of the *kénōsis* (emptying) which leads to our divinization – an insight more often found in the spirituality of the Orthodox churches – also occurs in Lamy's presentation at Christmas 1855 (L122): "God deigned to take our nature so as to raise it up. Due to sin we were far from God, but God in heaven had pity on us. He manifested 'his goodness and kindness' toward man-

kind, and 'he saved us not by reason of the works of justice which we have done but according to his great mercy' [Titus 3.4-5]. The Son of God became man; this Son has been given to us; it is for us that this little child has been born. An Incarnate God is a God who gives himself to us. *Parvulus natus est nobis* – A son is born to us' [Isaias 9.6]. God has loved us so that in taking on our nature he has abundantly given us that which he is in himself, so that we might adopt nobler and more worthy attitudes from God. In this mystery of the Incarnate Word, God loses nothing of his grandeur, of his majesty, but he lifts us from our miseries. God loses nothing, he remains what he is, but he makes us rich, and in this manner he teaches us his liberality and love." And ten years later, Lamy's Christmas sermon (L199) repeats the same truth of the faith: "In this adorable mystery all the strength, all the virtue of the Son of God was changed into debility, infirmity, and weakness. And if our divine Saviour submitted himself to all those humiliations and labors, it was not to acquire a sterile, vain glory; but being a God of mercy, he became man, that man might become like God."[4]

The Anagogic: Hope and Eschatology

In the formal sermon of the Renaissance, a prayer at end of introduction asked that the preacher receive the grace to preach the truth well and that all the members of the congregation receive the grace to hear it. As Romanticism took hold, the old oratorical format fell away, but many preachers continued to use prayers in their freeform sermons; Lamy fairly often set impromptu prayers anyplace in his sermons where they could be effective – for instance, in the middle of L060: "When will it be, o my God, that we will love only you and everything else for you and according to your divine pleasure, that my heart, my soul, my body, and my mind will be perfectly submitted to you, and that I will be able to say with Saint Peter, 'You know, o Lord, that I love you'?" [John 21.15-17]. In L129, Christmas 1856, the two prayers that follow were among four scattered throughout the homily: "Oh my God, I am resolved to place my heart at your disposal, to prepare it to receive your grace, rejecting from my soul whatever can diminish your divine majesty in

my heart, my loveable Saviour, so as to be adored as my God, as the author of the grace to destroy sin, as my Protector to defend me from the enemies of my salvation, as my Master to teach me virtue, as the treasure to enrich me with all good things."

"Most holy Mary, mother of my Lord, teach me to adore your divine Son with the same attitude and the same reverence with which you adore him and to offer him all the faculties of my soul; pray that he might be indeed my Saviour."

But he usually set his prayers (or at least good wishes) at the sermon's end, as with L067: "O my divine Saviour, so far from being scandalized in you, grant I may adore, love, and obey you and put all my trust in you. Enlighten my mind, make me walk in the practice of your holy law, purify my soul from its sins, open my heart to your sacred word that I may taste and practice its divine maxims which will procure my happiness in time and eternity." Very similar is the ending of L153, delivered on Trinity Sunday 1858: "Most holy Trinity, Father, Son, and Holy Ghost, one sole God in three distinct Persons, grant me the grace to look with gratitude upon the benefits you have made in creating us, in redeeming us, and in calling us to the faith, and help us so to live in conformity with your holy will that we will deserve to possess you forever in heaven." The majority of Lamy's terminal prayers voice eschatological hope for an afterlife in heaven, but he explored other ways of helping his congregation remember their last end such as the fear of hell (L066) and the brevity and value of time (L034 – with a few Jonathan Edwards motifs).

The Moral: Charity and the Homily

Lamy yokes each of Christ's Seven Last Words from the cross to one of seven rather pedestrian virtues (L030):

> Our Saviour dying on the cross teaches us all virtues by his last words:
> - *perfect charity*: "Father, forgive them" [Luke 23.24]
> - *mercy* and *compassion* by the plenary indulgence he grants to the thief: "I say to thee, this day thou shalt be with me in paradise" [Luke 23.43]

- *duty to our parents* in recommending his mother to Saint
  John: "Behold thy mother" [John 19.26-27]
- *thirst for the conversion of sinners*: "I thirst" [John 19.28]
- *fervent prayer to God*: "My God, my God, why hast thou
  forsaken me?" [Mark 15.34; Matthew 27.46]
- *persistence* till we have completed our salvation: "It is con-
  summated" [John 19.30]
- *resignation to God* in life and death: "Father, into thy hands
  I commend my Spirit" [Luke 23.46].

And Lamy is long and strong on lists of virtues and vices. He
instructs us in L040 how to work in the Lord's vineyard: "*with fidelity*
since all our time belongs to God; *with perseverance* since those alone
shall receive a reward who labor until evening, i.e., unto the end;
with courage to repair time lost; *with humility* to avoid the danger to be
excluded from the wages for pride would put me among the last,
while humility will bring me up among the first; *with fervor* since the
recompense is measured not so much upon the time as upon the
diligence, fervor, and good will." Doubtless to the great relief of his
congregation, Lamy practiced restraint: "The holy scripture says of
Saint Joseph that he was a just man, that is, possessing all virtues.
We will consider only three virtues in this great Saint Joseph, which
constitute the character of a just man: simplicity, disinterestedness,
[and] the love of interior life" (L076). Lists of vices might be more
entertaining, such as this one from L120: "I will merely mention the
temptations to sin. We can reduce them to three classes,
concupiscence, pride, and avarice. To comfort us and also to teach us
the manner of overcoming temptations, Our Lord Jesus Christ
deigned to undergo these three temptations" [Matthew 4.1-11]. And
in L156, Lamy's New Year's Day homily of 1859 pointed Santa Feans
toward "Renouncing godlessness, rejecting worldly desires. ... There
will be no scandals, which are the dishonor and the infamy of families as of society. Thus restraining ourselves within the limits of sobriety and temperance, families and the individual members who
make them up will not witness such injustices, frauds, robberies,
swindles, and evil deeds."[5]

Conclusion

A really incarnational spirituality ought to enable a Christian to state with equal conviction "I am my soul" and "I am my body." I suspect that Lamy would have said that he was his soul and that he presently and temporarily possessed his body. First of all, that self-definition would hint at Augustinian Manichaeanism – human nature is corrupt and depraved less on the side of soul than on the side of body, where sex is the sin of sins; and secondly, it would lead inevitably to an excessively other-worldly attitude.

Endnotes

[1]   As a phenomenology of dogmatic and moral theology, spirituality will embrace both *myth*, the group's sacred story which each member of the group believes so that he or she can "live in a world that fits the description," and *ritual*, the group's sacred action by which each member of the group cooperates in living "the right way of life." Further, moral theology strictly speaking will develop only after a development of individual self-consciousness sufficient to verify an ethics as a branch of philosophy. Finally, the person's getting into "conscious touch" with the numinosum need not be (and perhaps ideally will not be) self-conscious and reflective.

The first paragraph of "The American Religious Scene, 1840-80" in Chapter Two uses the same three-part structure of belief, prayer, and moral living.

[2]   Joseph P. Chinnici, O.F.M., "Organization of the Spiritual Life: American Catholic Devotional Works, 1791-1866" *Theological Studies* 40 (1979), 236-45; Jay P. Dolan, *The American Catholic Experience* (Garden City: Doubleday, 1985), pp. 33-34; *Bérulle and the French School* (New York: Paulist Press, 1989), pp. 5-16, 32-47.

[3]   Dolan, pp. 112-14, 117-23, 211-40.

[4]   For the associated Neo-Platonic doctrine of participation, *méthexis*, the sharing in the divine that comes with being in the state of sanctifying grace, see L037 and L137.

[5]   For sex as the archetypal sin, see L052, L053 (where Lamy barely allows marriage), and L156 (where virginity seems to be the only real virtue); the Jansenism section of Chapter Two dealt with this issue.

Lamy also played very occasionally with his auditors' guilt feelings; see L070, L078 (twice), and L116.

A Selection of Sermons
by Archbishop Jean Baptiste Lamy

In choosing these sermons, I tried to create a facsimile of the liturgical cycle within which Father, Bishop, and Archbishop Lamy did the majority of his preaching – on Sunday mornings during the Catholic Church's sacred times of Advent, Christmas, Lent, Easter, and Pentecost. Since Lamy spent eleven years in Ohio and Kentucky before he left for New Mexico, English sermons begin: six from Advent, Christmas, and Lent, one saint's-day talk from January, and two instructions, one an 1848 marriage talk and the other a talk to nuns on perseverance. Then eighteen Spanish sermons take over, running from Lent through Easter and Pentecost and overlapping into Advent and Christmas since there was not a very good selection of English sermons from that period. Then the program concludes with three saints'-day talks and four instructions.

As noted above, since Jean Baptiste Lamy was French-born and bred, there is nothing normative about his use either of English or of Spanish, and so I have normalized and modernized the paragraphing, punctuation, and spelling to give the reader an easier time[1] and standardized the spelling to enable the scholar to use the companion CD-ROM to search for any word or phrase.

A slash mark (/) indicates the end of one manuscript page and the start of another.

Endnote

[1]   I have completed all abbreviations and translated all Latin, and I have added in square brackets any lacking words and any scripture references Lamy did not himself provide. The two non-standard spellings I preserved as a token of Lamy's use of the languages are "Saviour" and "Yglesia."

Sermons in English

L066 – First Sunday of Advent, 2 December 1849, Covington, Kentucky; about 1300 words on Romans 13.11-14 and Luke 21.25-33; from AASF loose documents 1849 # 31. Advent is the mildly penitential period that begins the annual liturgical cycle.

Father Lamy goes quite far beyond the intrinsic meaning of his scripture passages, but this sermon must have kept his congregation's attention, for they as well as he believed literally and unquestioningly in the various parts of his subject matter. The sermon probes only four of the five senses at the end of the second-last paragraph; perhaps Lamy did not trust his restraint in exploring the tactile pains of hell.

First Sunday of Advent

Advent is a time of penance and of devotion before Christmas, appointed by the Church to serve as a preparation to that great solemnity of the Birth of Christ. It consists of four weeks or at least of four Sundays. This institution seems to be as old as that of Christmas, though the discipline of the Church in the manner of celebrating it varies. In sign of compunction and penance the Church uses purple vestments in her sacred offices.

The dispositions necessary for profiting of this holy time is to turn from our iniquities by sorrow and repentance and to convert ourselves to the Lord our God. This is the admonition of the apostle Saint Paul (Romans 13.11-14): "Knowing the time, that it is now the hour for us to rise from sleep, for now our salvation is nearer than when we first believed. The night is passed, the day is at hand; let us cast off the works of darkness and put on the armor of light, let us walk decently as in the day."

My friends, these words are particularly addressed to us to awaken us and make us begin a better life. Alas! Are not the greatest part of Christians quite asleep by their guilty indolence in the great business of the salvation of their souls and of a happy eternity? Let us listen seriously to these summons and rouse ourselves, now whilst we have time, out of this unhappy lethargy and carefully dispose

our hearts to receive the blessings and graces prepared for the children of God.

On this day the terrors of God's justice are set before our eyes that we may also be induced by the wholesome fear of this dreadful judgment to make good use of this present time of mercy. Three reflections on the last judgment:

1° The coming of the judge. "Then they shall see the Son of Man coming in a cloud with great power and majesty." In what manner he comes from heaven armed with all the terrors of his justice, surrounded with heavenly legions. The difference of his last coming with his first appearance: his first coming was with wonderful meekness and humility because that was our day in / which he came to redeem us by his mercy. He came then as a Saviour without any marks of power and terror, but at his second coming it shall be his day, in which his justice will take place.

What a happy day for the just, when they will see the heavens opened, the angels coming down to assist at the general judgment. When the terms of the judgment spoken of in the gospel [Luke 21.25-33] shall come [to] pass, they will remember the words of our Saviour, "Look up and lift up your heads because your redemption is at hand."

But if the just find any consolation in the thought of their deliverance, sinners shall weep at the sight of the cross, for the nails of the cross will complain of them, the wounds and the cross of Jesus Christ will speak against them, the presence of this Judge will give the reprobate more pain than hell itself. Hence according to Saint John, the wicked shall call on the mountains to fall on them and to hide them from the sight of the Judge [Apocalypse 6.16].

2° The separation of the good and of the bad. The sovereign Judge being seated on his throne, millions of angels and of heavenly spirits around him, he commands them to make a separation of the good from the bad, which separation shall be instantly made, after which these two companies shall never meet. The true servants of God shall be placed with honor on his right hand, and we, my brethren, where do we expect to stand at that day? In which these two companies shall we be numbered? We have it now in our choice,

but we shall not have it then. Let us choose now in this our day that better part that shall never be taken from us.

What will be the thoughts and sentiments of the wicked on this occasion when they shall [see] the poor in spirit, the meek, the humble that were so contemptible in their eyes, now honored and exalted and crowned with immortal glory, but themselves depressed to the lowest extremity of disgrace. Their sentiments are expressed by the Spirit of God in the Book of / Wisdom (5.2): "These seeing it shall be troubled with terrible fear and shall be amazed, … saying within themselves, repenting and groaning for anguish of spirit, 'These are they whom we had sometimes in derision, and for a parable of reproach. We fools esteemed their life madness and their end without honor; behold how they are numbered among the children of God, and their lot is among the saints. Therefore we have erred from the way of truth, and the light of justice has not shined upon us, and the sun of understanding hath not risen upon us. We wearied ourselves in the way of iniquity and destruction and have walked through hard ways, but the way of the Lord we have not known.'"

3° This great judgment shall be concluded by a definitive sentence by which the just shall be called to eternity, up where sorrows never enter and joys never end, and the wicked shall be condemned to everlasting fire. Give ear, beloved friends, to that sincere and amiable invitation by which our Saviour shall call all his servants, friends, and children into the glorious mansions of eternal life: "Come, ye blessed of my Father, possess the kingdom prepared for you" [Matthew 25.34]. Come from the vale of tears to the blissful regions of never-ending joy, from a tedious banishment to your heavenly country, from your mortal pilgrimage in the midst of crosses [and] sufferings to your blessed home.

Then turning himself toward the wicked on his left hand, with fire in his eyes and terror in his countenance, he shall thunder out the dreadful sentence of their irrevocable doom, "Depart from me, ye cursed, into everlasting fire" [Matthew 25.41]. Depart, begone forever from me, far from the joys of my kingdom, into the place you have chosen and preferred before heaven. You shall go from me, but you shall take my curse along with you. I would have given you /

my blessing, but you would not receive it. A curse you have chosen, and a curse shall be your everlasting lot. It shall stick close to you like a garment which you shall never put off: a curse upon your eyes never to see the light of heaven, a curse upon your ears to hear for all eternity [nothing but] groans, blasphemies, and maledictions, a curse upon your taste to be embittered with gall, upon your smell to be always tormented with the stench of the bottomless pit.

O accursed sin, to what unhappy end will you one day conduct so many souls redeemed by the blood of Jesus Christ? O unhappy souls, for whom is prepared such unhappy end. My friends, it is in your power now to avoid such misfortune. Put off the works of darkness, the works of sin, be reconciled with your God, have confidence in him. Jesus Christ is now a father,[1] not a judge; he is ready to pardon all who repent. Let your repentance and sincere conversion induce him to show you mercy.

L067 – Second Sunday of Advent, 9 December 1849, Covington, Kentucky; about 1635 words on Romans 15.4-13 and Matthew 11.2-10; from AASF 1849 loose document # 32.

John the Baptist disappears from the sermon a third of the way through, but Jean Baptiste Lamy was always fond of his patron saint, the culminating figure of the Old Covenant who appears in the New. Since John preached repentance, Father Lamy takes the occasion to preach in favor of the good example that good works give and against the scandal that comes from evil-doing. The nineteenth-century Catholic clergy in the United States were extremely afraid of their parishioners making the Church look bad in Protestant eyes.

Second Sunday of Advent

The relation of the wonderful works of Jesus Christ, of the doctrine he preached, and of the great reputation he had acquired gave occasion to Saint John the Baptist to send two of his disciples to Jesus Christ. The holy precursor was then in prison. Everyone knows the reason for which he was a prisoner; it was for having done his duty and maintained truth, but he received a sensible consolation

in his captivity from hearing the wonders and miracles Jesus Christ was working though Palestine. Though persecuted he wishes to fulfill his office of precursor and to instruct his disciples.

He had told the Jews in their presence that he was not the Messias, that he was not even worthy to loose the strings of his shoes, that Christ must increase but himself must decrease, that he was only an empty sound, a voice in the wilderness; yet the disciples of Saint John had so great an idea of him that they could hardly believe that Jesus Christ could be his superior. Prevented by such prejudices, they could not see without some sentiments of jealousy the reputation of our Lord increase and the number of his disciples multiply.

To cure them from their prejudices, John profited of the relation they had made concerning the miracles of our Lord. He called two of them and sent them to Jesus Christ that they might [be] convinced by themselves of the truth. Thus Saint John in his prison found the means to exercise his ministry and to labor for the glory of his Master, to make him known, to correct with mildness the defects of his disciples, and to turn to their edification what had been a scandal to others. If we had the same zeal for the glory of God and the salvation of our neighbor, how many occasions would we not find to procure both?

Now the subject of this embassy was to ask our Saviour if he was the Messias. "When John had heard in prison," says the gospel, "the works of Christ, sending two of his disciples, he said to them, 'Art thou he that art to come, or look we for another?'" Saint John believed it, but for the sake of his disciples he sent this question to Jesus Christ. As Christians / we ought to make this same question to ourselves. Has Jesus Christ come to save the world? Will he come to judge it? Or do we look for another? To judge from our indifference for him, from our want of faith to his word, from our want of hope in his promises, want of obedience to his laws, want of conformity to his examples, would not anyone have the right of asking us if we look for another one, another who favors our inclinations, our ambition, avarice, self-love, another who will have regard for riches, honors, pleasures, and cunning in deceiving others. Or if we believe that Jesus Christ our Saviour will come also to be our judge, how

does it come then that we do not love him, serve him, and fear him as our judge?

Jesus Christ in his answer gave the proofs of his divine mission: "Go," said our Saviour, "and relate to John what you have heard and seen: the blind see, the lame walk, the lepers are cleansed, the deaf hear, the dead rise again, the poor have the Gospel preached to them" – an answer worthy of God and which proved the divine mission of our Saviour. Would to God, beloved Christians, we could answer those who ask what we are by our good works. This is the true way to make ourselves known and to know ourselves also. The words, the exterior appearance, the outward profession of religion – all these marks may deceive, but the actions and the conduct never deceive. Can we say that our conduct, our actions, prove us to be good Christians, children of God, saints? There is nothing more efficacious than good works to bring others to the practice of virtue, nothing stronger than good examples. This is a sensible proof that we can practice good works and also how it can be done. It puts to shame those who don't practice virtue. Everyone can preach in this manner by his own good works, by his exemplary conduct. If good example brings others to the practice of virtue, bad example also has but too much power, too much influence, to bring others to evil. Such conduct teaches vice to those who don't know it, causes others to flatter themselves in their disorders, and to put down virtue. There is no temptation more violent, more dangerous than that of examples. See, beloved friends, how you behave, and be careful / that you may not tempt others by bad examples and draw them in vice. And also, if you see bad examples, turn away your eyes that you may not follow them.

The sin of scandal is so great that our Saviour says (Matthew 18.6-9) that "it were better for him that shall scandalize one of the little ones that believe in him that a millstone were hanged around his neck and that he were drowned in the depth of the sea. Woe to the world because of scandals. It must needs be that scandals come; nevertheless, woe to that man by whom the scandal cometh. If thy hand," adds our Saviour on the same subject, "or thy foot scandalize thee, cut it off and cast it from thee. It is better for thee to enter into

life maimed or lame than having two hands or two feet to be cast into everlasting fire. And if thy eye scandalize thee, pluck it out and cast if from thee. It is better for thee with one eye to enter into life than having two eyes to be cast into hell-fire. Woe to the man by whom scandal comes." The reason of this anathema of our Saviour against such is that they not only murder their own souls but also before God they murder all the souls of those whom they scandalize and will answer to God for the sins of those they shall have scandalized. Saint John [the Evangelist] says of the devil that he was a murderer from the beginning (John 8.44) because he caused souls to perish in seducing them. Now whoever scandalizes his neighbor carries on the work of Satan by drawing them into vice. Our Saviour came to save what had perished [Matthew 11.11], but he who gives scandal puts every opposition to the work of our redemption. Let those who give bad example by drinking, by swearing, cursing, using unbecoming language reflect upon the enormity of the sin of scandal. If you caused your neighbor to fall off from the practice of his religion, if from your society and bad example he is become wicked, his blood will cry louder at the tribunal of God than that of Abel, it will demand justice and vengeance against you. "I will require his blood at thy hand" (Ezechiel 3.20), says the almighty God.

May God remove from you so great a misfortune as the sin of scandal, but on the contrary "let / every one of you," as says Saint Paul [Romans 15.2], "please his neighbor for good works unto edification," that is, by his good example, Christian conduct, thus bringing others to the practice of virtue, specially when you are under the obligation to edify as parents are in regard with their children.

"Blessed is he that shall not be scandalized in me," said our divine Saviour [Matthew 11.6]. After so many miracles, Jesus Christ had [a] right to expect that so far from being scandalized of his Gospel, men would glorify themselves to embrace it. The wonders of every kind which he wrought ought certainly to have merited for him the veneration and adoration of the whole world, yet he says, "Blessed is he that shall not be scandalized in me." Who can find a subject of scandal in this model of all perfection, yet he has been a subject of scandal to the Jews, and he is even nowadays to many Christians. The

occasion of this scandal is the sublimity of the mysteries of the Christian religion, and the incomprehensibility of the ways of providence. Man is not able to understand his own nature, and he would have the presumption to comprehend his God, to penetrate the secrets of his counsels, to know the reasons of his providence. What gives occasion to this scandal is the sanctity and purity of Christian morality. The sensual and voluptuous man believes the practice impossible or too hard to submit himself to it.

Another occasion of scandal is the weak appearance of Christ as man and of his Mystical Body the Church, in which under the weakest and most common symbols the greatest mysteries are operated. Happy those who do not take any subject of scandal in Jesus Christ. They are not only convinced of the truth of religion, but also they see in its mysteries an incomprehensibility worthy of God spread throughout all his works. They see in the humility of Jesus Christ the power and the wisdom of God [1 Corinthians 1.17-29], in the weakness of the Church an admirable providence and the never-failing assistance of the Holy Ghost.

O my divine Saviour, so far from being scandalized in you, grant I may adore, love, and obey you and put all my trust in you. Enlighten my mind, make me walk in the practice of your holy law, purify my soul from its sins, open my heart to your sacred word that I may taste and practice its divine maxims which will procure my happiness in time and eternity.

L068 – First Sunday after Epiphany, Holy Family Sunday, 13 January 1850, Covington, Kentucky; about 1220 words on Luke 2.42-52; from AASF 1850 loose document # 46.

Sixteen times during this sermon, Father Lamy calls his listeners to imitate Jesus, Mary, and Joseph, the three members of the Holy Family. Lamy attributes a maximum human intelligence to Christ (see pages 29-32).

First Sunday after Epiphany [Luke 2.42-52; Holy Family]

The Son of God became man not only to be our Redeemer but

also to be our model. As the gospel relates, our divine Saviour went to the Temple with his parents when he was twelve years old to teach us what ought to be our zeal for the worship of God. He assisted himself to the exercises of religion that we who are his disciples should neglect nothing of that in which the service of God is concerned. It is not enough to adore and worship God, but [we] are also by our examples to bring others to glorify him. No doubt our Saviour assisted to the divine worship with the most profound attention, respect, and fervor. We have to imitate his virtues in our prayers whether in public or in private. We can do nothing better than to honor God and worship him. With what cheerfulness then should we assist to the exercises of our religion? We should not dispense ourselves from it except in cases of extreme necessity, when we see our blessed Redeemer going with his parents to the Temple though he lived at a considerable distance from it. At least we ought to employ to the service of God at the time which he requires of us. Jesus Christ then has left us an example that as he has done we also might do, that we should not neglect the duties of our holy religion, that we should not suffer every trifle or any temporal or worldly concern to exempt us from coming to church, to the temple of God, when our Christian duty requires us.

The gospel tells us that Jesus Christ went down with Joseph and Mary to Nazareth and was subject to / them [Luke 2.51]. Take model from the peace, union, and good understanding that reigned in the Holy Family, and endeavor to practice the same virtues wherever you are. Jesus Christ could have performed miracles, he could have preached and made himself admired by everyone, but for our instruction he shuns this brilliant career and chooses a private and retired life. In that retreat or private life, he strictly obeys his parents, he puts himself under their control. He serves then in the meanest offices, he works with his reputed father at his mechanic trade.

A pious curiosity would wish to have a long and exact detail of the words and actions of our Saviour to the time where he commenced to preach publicly his Gospel, but the God-man who was to teach the universe his doctrine and to save the world with the price of his blood, when the time should have come for him to

speak and to suffer, has only been pleased at first to edify mankind by his private life and by the examples of his domestic virtues. All the gospel says of Jesus Christ of his private life is that he was submitted to his parents, that "he increased in wisdom and age and grace with God and with men" [Luke 2.52]. Could the Son of God give us a more striking lesson of humility? He is willing to pass for the son of a tradesman, he does not deny it, he calls him his father and Saint Joseph calls him his son. His house was that of a mechanic, consequently poor, composed only of the most indispensable furniture. So was his clothing and his diet. His employment and occupation were the same with those of his reputed father. His divine hands were employed at an humble trade. We have to learn from this great example to be ever humble, meek, and obedient, to sanctify our ordinary employments and even our common activities by recollection and mental prayer. /

How far we are from our divine Model. We indulge pride and vanity, we wish to appear and to shine, whilst our Saviour spent almost [all] his life but only three last years privately and in retirement to teach us that the highest perfection may be found in the exercise of the lowest and meanest offices, if in those we only take care to keep close to our God and to refer to him all our actions. "Learn of me," said our Saviour, "that I am meek and humble of heart" [Matthew 11.29], and this we have to learn specially from his private life.

Obedience alone gives merit to our actions; also the inspired writer had said, "Better is obedience than sacrifice."[2] Though being the Lord of heaven and earth, Jesus Christ obeys his creatures to repair the glory of his Father offended by the disobedience of our first parents, to give us the example, to put us in the way of the submission we owe to God, in obeying men for the sake of God. Christians should then obey their parents [and] their superiors as Jesus obeyed Joseph and Mary, and the superiors and parents should command their inferiors as Joseph and Mary commanded Jesus.

It is written of our Lord with relation to this private part of his life that "he increased in wisdom and age and grace with God and men" [Luke 2.52]. Our God from the first moment of his conception was

full of all heavenly wisdom and divine grace, but as the sun though equally luminous in itself yet shines with more splendor according as he rises and advances, so Jesus Christ the true Sun of Justice who enlightens every man coming into the world [John 1.9] was pleased in proportion to his advancing in age to show forth every glory more than other in his words and actions – the admirable treasures of wisdom and grace that were hidden in his / soul, to teach us to make a continual progress in the way of God and to advance every day by large steps from virtue to virtue till we come "unto a perfect man, unto the measure of the age of the fullness of Christ" (Ephesians 4.13).

"He increased in grace before God," that is to say, the virtues which appeared in him were sincere and true in the sight of God. For what will it profit to us to regulate our exterior, to compose ourselves before men, if before God our sins increase and multiply? We would have then only apparent and reputed virtues, but in reality it would be nothing else but hypocrisy.

Would to God, beloved friends, that according to our divine Model it were true to say of us that as we increase in age we also increase in wisdom and grace before men and before God, that our virtue may be true and sincere before men, that we may edify them. How unhappy should we be if we were to increase in malice as we advance in age and thus multiply our sins in the place of multiplying our merits. All that the bountiful hand of God has bestowed upon us we have to employ to his divine service, not to outrage him and offend him. Our body, our soul, our heart, fortunes, health, talents – we must not make of these instruments of iniquity, we must make them serve to be instruments of justice and merit "that we may," as the great apostle says, "present ourselves a living sacrifice, holy [and] pleasing unto God, our reasonable service" [Romans 12.1].

L087 – Third Sunday after Epiphany, 26 January 1851, in or near San Antonio, Texas, to an English-speaking congregation; about 1970 words which ought to have treated Romans 12.16-21 and Matthew 8.1-13, the curing of a leper and of the believing centurion's servant, but perhaps because he had lost most of his

possessions a couple of weeks earlier in the shipwreck at Port Lavaca and did not have a Bible to consult, the young Bishop got Matthew's one leper confused with the ten lepers of Luke 17.11-19. The sermon is focuses on how the Sacrament of Penance (confession) heals us of our sins and maintains us in good health; AASF 1851 loose document # 21.

Third Sunday after Epiphany (also 13th aft. Pentecost)

"Go and show yourselves to the priests." Saint Luke 17.14.[3]

Such was the order that the Saviour of the world gave to those lepers who came to him to be delivered from the dreadful contagion with which they were afflicted. The same remedy is offered to us by the Church in the name of Christ to be purified of a spiritual leprosy of sin. She hands us to the priest as to the physician of our souls, and she commands us to acquaint them thoroughly of the state of our spiritual maladies. "Go and show yourselves to the priests." My intention is not to establish by lengthy arguments the precept of confession. If we are children of the Church, we should submit ourselves to her decisions. "For if he will not hear the Church," says Jesus Christ, "let him be to you as a publican and a heathen" [Matthew 18.17].

Now one of the most essential precepts of the Church is confession. This command is founded upon the words of the Son of God which he spoke to his apostles when according to Saint John (20.28) he appeared to them after his resurrection and, breathing upon them, said, "Receive ye the Holy Ghost. Whose sins you shall forgive they are forgiven, whose sins you shall retain, they are retained." These words need no commentary. This precept is authorized by tradition confirmed by the councils of the Church, received in all ages, observed by all the faithful. It is only of late that some Christians, despising the authority of the Church, have looked upon confession as an observance that was no more binding. They have rejected it, saying as those of whom we read in the gospel that when our Saviour proposed to them a mystery which seemed to them an absurdity, they went away saying, "This is a hard saying, and who can bear it?" [John 6.61].

But without entering into a great controversy on this subject, I

maintain and I hope I will prove that confession is one of the most useful, salutary practices in the Christian religion. To be convinced of this, we can consider ourselves in two different states: in the state of sin, or in the state of grace. In the state of sin, we need a remedy to cure our souls, in the state of grace we need strength to maintain us.

1. Nothing better than confession to heal us from the leprosy of our sins. We must all acknowledge that in order to obtain pardon for our sins, we have to use the means or the remedy / which the almighty God has appointed. Any other means would have no efficacy because God would not accept of it. Now it has pleased the divine Mercy to make the remission of sin depend upon the confession, the acknowledgement of it, and though at the first appearance this seems to be a law of justice, yet we may easily discover in it an effect of his goodness, for is it not a prodigy of goodness that to be absolved of a crime which exposed [me] to eternal damnation, it be sufficient to accuse myself, that God be satisfied with such a declaration? Human justice proceeds in a very different manner; they punish only what is declared and make known; but in divine justice there is severity and punishment only for what is kept hidden. This confession which the Catholic Church requires of her children in the tribunal of penance must be a free and voluntary confession in which we accuse ourselves of our own accord with repentance and love because we have learned from the apostle that if we judge ourselves now we shall not be judged [1 Corinthians 11.31]. If then we declare our sins, God will conceal them. This is the reason why we confess even the most secret sins. The prophet David had understood the efficacy of this confession and declaration of our sins when asking mercy of God in these words, "Wash me more and more from my iniquity, and cleanse me from my sins" [Psalm 50.4]. He would give God no other motives to obtain pardon but that he acknowledged and confessed his iniquity: *quoniam iniquitatem meam ego cognosco* – for I know my iniquity" [Psalm 50.5].

But someone will say, You would require of me to acknowledge my sin not only before God but also before man, but this is going too far, and I cannot believe that the almighty God would request of me such an act of humiliation. Had some Christians of our times

been in the place of those whom our Saviour was pleased to sent to the priests as a condition upon which they were to be healed, no doubt they would have protested against such a precept, and they would have told Christ, We come to you, not to men, to be cured of our leprosy, and you send us off to the priests – "Go and show yourselves to the priests." What, are you not more than the priests? Are you not God?[4] Does not all power come / from you? What does that mean that we have to apply to men? We do not see any reason in that request. Had the poor lepers spoken of in the gospel made the same objection, none of them would have been healed. But when the Son of God told them, "Go and show yourselves to the priests," they readily and cheerfully obeyed because they knew God commanded them.

It does not become man to dictate to God the conditions of his reconciliation. He should rather be in the disposition of Samuel when he said to God, "Speak, o Lord, for thy servant heareth" [1 Samuel 3.1-10], that is to say, he is ready to do what thou command. Even if it is before a man that we have to acknowledge our sins, we should remember that it is only to a man authorized by the almighty God, holding the place of God, the minister of the mercies of God, as Saint Paul expressed it: "God has given to us the ministry of reconciliation; for Christ we are ambassadors" (2 Corinthians 5.5). We know that God alone can forgive sins; but if he makes the forgiveness of sins depend upon the confession of those sins made to a man authorized by him, should not we prove ourselves guilty of the crime of arrogance and rebellion against God if we refused to comply with this easy condition? The first Christians did not fear to make a public confession before all the congregation. Should we not show the same submission for private confession that they did for public confession? Let us follow the advice of the apostle who admonished us to "go with confidence to the throne of mercy that we may obtain mercy and find grace in seasonable aid" (Hebrews 4.16).

By Baptism, original sin [is forgiven] and any sins we may have committed before Baptism, if we receive it when we are adults, but the same thing takes place in Baptism as in the Sacrament of Penance. It is only a man who administers Baptism as it is only a man

[who] exercises [Penance]; God invests of his authority to forgive sins committed after Baptism. We should not find one more surprising than the other. Confession has the greatest efficacy to destroy sin because it humbles the sinner, excites in him sorrow and contrition for his sins, and is in itself a most salutary penance. The root of sin is pride; to destroy sin in its very root there is nothing better than the humility of confession, not of that confession by which we acknowledge in general that we are sinners but of that established by Jesus Christ [and] practiced in the Church by which we specify everything. Any other confession is no confession, for God knows very well what sins we are guilty of, and we cannot hide them from his knowledge. Also the wise man has said, "He that confesses his sins and forsakes them shall obtain mercy, but he that hides them shall not be directed" [Proverbs 28.13]. The more this confession is humiliating, the more it is repugnant to human pride, so much the more / it is pleasing to God and salutary to our souls. Christian brethren, if we took as much trouble to please God as we do to please men, to procure the welfare of our souls as we do for the welfare of our body, we would not find fault with this practice of religion. We would approach with good dispositions to this salutary bath to cleanse our conscience. Confession as we have seen is then the most powerful means to obtain pardon for our sins.

2. It is also the best preservative and remedy against relapses into sin. To be justified by the grace of repentance and the Sacrament of Penance would be only a small advantage for us poor sinners had we not some means to guard us against relapses. Now the virtue of Confession is not only to reconcile us with God but also if we are well disposed to keep us as much as human weakness will permit in that state of reconciliation, for it is the best remedy religion furnishes us against sin. The Sacrament of Penance has peculiar graces – virtue which consists in enabling us to maintain and defend ourselves against temptations. But the will of God [is] that we should go and gather those graces in this salutary institution; hence it follows that the longer a Christian keeps himself from this sacrament, the more he deprives himself of those graces so essential to salvation. The enemy of our souls knows well the efficacy of it; also, he loses

no time but employs all his cunning and malice to poison or to dry up this source of all graces, to poison it by the evil use we make of it, to dry it up by persuading us that it is not necessary. In this respect he imitates the conduct of Holophernes, who in order to reduce the inhabitants of Bethulia cut off all the aqueducts [Judith 7.6]. Thus the seducer endeavors to cut off all the means or canals by which the blood of Christ flows into our souls. He represents to us Confession as too difficult [and] impracticable.

Besides, what influence, what power has not a priest in his capacity of minister of Christ to direct our souls and to maintain them in the path of Christian justice? He is a true friend who is bound before God to maintain our spiritual interest, to open our eyes to the dangers to which we are daily exposed, who will correct us with charity and mildness. Experience teaches us that the tribunal of penance has a great virtue, a secret power to make us refrain from criminal activities. The thought that we shall have to confess that sin will often be able to make us avoid it. We have a striking instance of this in what happened in the beginning of the Reformation in Germany. When the people had thrown off the salutary yoke of Confession, they lost all sense of virtue, gave a free scope to their passions, became so wicked that it was thought necessary to reestablish the ancient discipline of Confession as the best remedy against licentiousness.

There [are] abuses in Confession. Unhappily, man abuses of everything, but the abuse comes only from our malice. Still, this does not take off the advantage of Confession, which is, as we have proved, a means of conversion and of perseverance and opens to us a sure and easy way to heaven.

L070 – First Sunday of Lent, 17 February 1850, Covington, Kentucky; about 1400 words on Matthew 4.1-11. The liturgical season of Lent is meant to be purgative, and what Lamy here calls "a sense of the guilt of our sins" might better be called "sin-consciousness," which is a very great gift of God and poles apart from the psychologically paralyzing guilt feelings that Calvin and Jansenius bequeathed to the world. Lamy allegorizes the gospel episode, especially at very end of his

sermon. Thoroughly reworked in 1855 and translated into Spanish, this became sermon L120; in English it is AASF 1850 loose document # 48.

First Sunday of Lent[5] [Matthew 4.1-11]

Fasting is recommended to us in the word of God by the great example of Christ, by the example of his saints as well of the Old as of the New Testament. Christ says that his children will fast during his absence from them (Saint Matthew 9.15) [and] that the devil is not to be cast out but by prayer and fasting (Saint Mark 9.28). What caused man originally to fall from God? Intemperance. He returns to him by fasting.

Exterior fasting must be joined with a penitential spirit which implies a deep sense of the guilt of our sins, a hearty sorrow and grief for them, a sincere desire to return to God and to renounce our sinful ways for the future. Fasting performed in this manner cannot fail of moving God to mercy.

Let also prayer and almsdeeds be joined with fasting. It is not without reason that the Church has appointed the precise number of forty days fast in Lent since this same number of forty days fast has been recommended by the Law and the prophets and sanctified by the example of Christ himself. Moses fasted forty days (Exodus 24.18) whilst he conversed with God on Mount Sinai when he received the divine law. Elias fasted for forty days in the wilderness before he came to the mountain of God (3 Kings 19.8). Our divine Saviour before he commenced to preach his Gospel retired into the wilderness and employed forty days in prayer and fasting.

Fasting will not fail of moving God to mercy if we join it with fervent prayer, but above all if we endeavor to abstain from sin, for this is the great and general fast of Christians. It ["fasting" from sin] obliges all sorts of persons young and old, sick and healthy, at all times and in all places. God rejected the fast of the Jews (Isaias 58) / because on the days of their fasting they ceased not to provoke him by their customary sins. Our exterior penance will be nothing but hypocrisy if we do not renounce pride, covetousness, malice, and all our bad habits. "Let the wicked man," says the prophet (Isaias 55.7), "forsake his ways and the unjust man his thoughts, and let him

return to the Lord, and then he will have mercy on him."

From the gospel of this day we have to learn that Jesus Christ humbled himself to be tempted for our sake, to teach us also what should be our conduct in temptation. We should never expose ourselves rashly to temptation, but in regard to the temptations which God has deemed necessary in our present state and condition, when we resist them generously, we prove our fidelity to God, we glorify him, increase our merits, and strengthen our virtue.

There are temptations of the heart, of the mind, and of the senses. We learn from the example of our Saviour how to oppose all these temptations.

1° Temptations of the heart flatter our inclinations and bring us from light offenses to the greatest disorders. Our Saviour at the close of forty days' fast was willing to feel hungry. The devil, seeing that our divine Master was exhausted, proposed to him some ready means to supply his wants. "You suffer," did he say to him, "and there is nothing in this wilderness to relieve you, but you know the power of God and what you are yourself. If you are the Son of God, command that those stones be made bread." Thus the devil, taking advantage of our situation, weakness, and wants, examining our weak side, suggests to us to satisfy ourselves. At first he seems only to propose something permitted, but if we listen to him only he will soon / make [us] fall in sin. Jesus Christ answers him, "Not by bread alone doth man live but by every word that proceedeth out of the mouth of God." That is to say, what makes a man live is not so much the food which he takes as the will of God which he must follow. At the example of Jesus Christ we must answer the tempter by the maxims of faith. Does [Should] he wish us to give way to sensuality and voluptuousness, let us answer him that there is more pleasure and comfort in the word of God and his love, in the obedience to his law, in prayer and practice of virtue than in the satisfaction of brutal passions and a soft and sensual life.

2° Temptations of the mind flatter our pride. The devil, defeated by the wise answer of our Saviour, did not lose courage but using the power that God granted him on that occasion took him in the Holy City and set him upon a pinnacle of the Temple. Our Saviour

had answered him by the holy scripture; this father of lies dared to use this word of truth and of sanctity to teach error and crime. "If thou be the Son of God," did he say, "cast thyself down, for it is written, 'He hath given his angels charge over thee and in their hands they shall bear thee up, lest perhaps thou dash thy foot against a stone.'" Satan has the power to bring us to the edge of the abyss, he can suggest to us extraordinary ways which flatter our pride, motions thereof [whereby] we abandon the common and ordinary way of humility and the obedience we owe to our superiors and to the Church. Our safety depends from our humility and obedience to the authority appointed by the almighty God. Jesus Christ, without stopping to observe to the wicked spirit that he falsified the passage of the scripture, answered him by this firm maxim so well known, "It is written also, 'Thou shalt not tempt the Lord thy God.'" We should oppose to the seductions of the tempter the most known, most common principles of religion.

3° Temptations of the senses flatter with the prospect of the most brilliant hopes to endure unto the most shameful actions. Furious of the resistance he met with, the wicked spirit took our Saviour up into a very high / mountain and showed him all the kingdoms of the world and the glory of them. That is, he put before his eyes a lively representation of all the kingdoms in the world with their riches and splendor. "All this is mine," did he say; "I can dispose of it, and I will give it to you at one condition, if thou wilt fall down and adore me." What an imposture, what a horrible blasphemy, what a proposition! Thus it is that Satan moves our imagination [and] troubles our mind by vain hopes and false illusions. He makes us every fair promise if we will only give ourselves to him [and] shake off the yoke of God. But if we are so unhappy as to believe him, we will soon experience how hard is his yoke and how false his promises. Our Saviour teaches us that violent temptations must be rejected with indignation. "Begone, Satan," said he to him, "for it is written, 'The Lord thy God shalt thou adore, and him only shalt thou serve,'" words truly worthy to be written in our hearts in indelible characters. It is in the service and love of God that we find grandeur, honor, glory, and perfect happiness. Now, beloved friends, is it God

alone we adore, it is God alone we serve? We must know that to serve the world, to follow its maxims, to seek after the goods, the pleasures of this world is to fall down at the feet of Satan and to adore him at the expense of the adoration and love we owe to God alone.

Observe what the gospel says when our Saviour had suffered all these temptations: "Then the devil left him, and behold, angels came and ministered to him," that is, gave him to eat. There is no food so delicious as the consolation that a soul feels after having resisted the temptation. Our eternal welfare depends on the manner with which we shall have sustained temptations. If we yield to temptation, the punishment of our cowardice will be to burn with Satan, but if we resist it, strong in faith, our recompense will be to reign in heaven with Christ and his angels. Grant us, God, that we may shun the one and obtain the other.

L044 – Second Sunday of Lent, 4 March 1849, Covington, Kentucky; about 1640 words on Matthew 17.1-9, from AASF loose document 1849 # 18. The unique, spectacular, and mysterious Transfiguration gives rise to a strong, fast-moving sermon with a great deal of variety.

Second Sunday in Lent

"And he was transfigured before them, and his face did shine as the sun, and his garments became white as snow." Matthew 17.2.

Jesus Christ made choice of only three of his disciples to be the witnesses of his transfiguration, of his glory. We are to learn from this that visions and revelations are not the portion of all the saints but only of some souls favored in a particular manner according [to] the choice and the good pleasure of the Saviour. How happy were these apostles to whom our Lord manifested his glory. We are not, certainly, worthy of the same favor, but on this occasion we should ask by their intercession the grace to profit of the wonders they have seen and to be penetrated as they were of the truth of the divinity of Christ.

This transfiguration took place on Mount Thabor. It is on moun-

tains that Jesus Christ has operated most of his great mysteries to show us how much our minds and hearts should be raised above earthly things to be able to meditate upon his divine mysteries, to relish them, and to profit by them. Jesus Christ was in prayer when his heavenly Father conferred on him the honor of his transfiguration. It is in silence and in prayer that God will manifest himself to us. If we were more faithful to prayer and more recollected in this exercise, how many lights would we not receive upon the glorious attributes of our Saviour and upon the necessity of obeying him. "His face was shining as the sun, and garments white as snow." This glorious light of the transfiguration of our Lord, which charmed the eyes without dazzling them, surpassed whatever makes the admiration of men, yet it was only a ray of the glory of his [human] soul which enjoyed the vision of God from the first moment of its creation and of its union with the Second Person of the Trinity.[6] Not so with the shining appearance of men. It often conceals shameful and black defects. How often the soul is most horrible and ugly in a body possessed of all exterior quality and decorated of shining and rich clothes. Unwise are those who fix their eyes on this vain splendor, and more unhappy those whose hearts are taken up with such vanity.

Blessed is he who has heart, affection, and / desires upon thee; your splendor and glory, o my Saviour, is not a borrowed one, it is your own by nature. You have concealed it during your mortal life on earth, for the sake of instructing us and dying of [sic] us. You have manifested it once, to maintain our courage and raise our hope. He also conceals his glory and divinity in the Sacrament of the Eucharist to be the food and nourishment of our souls, but he will openly manifest himself in all his splendor in his kingdom to be our beatitude. What powerful motives to love you, o my Saviour! Let my heart withdraw from the love of earthly things to love only Jesus Christ and trust in him alone.

Moses and Elias were seen with our Saviour. One the great leader of the people of God, the other the father of the prophets, they both came to render homage and testimony to Christ who is the end of the law and of the prophets, who makes truth succeed to figures and

events to promises and predictions. After having contemplated at leisure the glory and majesty of their divine master and heard his conversation with Moses and Elias, the apostles understood that these two great personages were going to disappear. Then Peter, always zealous for the glory of Jesus Christ, said to him, "Lord, it is good for us to be here. If thou wilt, let us make here three tabernacles, one for thee, one [for] Moses, and one for Elias," expressing by these words how happy he would be to be permitted to stay there with Christ. But earth is not the place for rest and comfort. If God sometimes makes us feel the sweetness of his presence, it is a passing favor which is granted us to encourage us to labor and suffer with him. "Peter was yet speaking; behold, a bright cloud overshadowed them, and lo a voice of the cloud saying, 'This is my beloved Son in whom I am well pleased. Hear ye him.'"

In this oracle there is a precept by which we are commanded to hear Jesus Christ with submission and docility, to believe his doctrine, to practice his laws, to imitate his example, to take his spirit, to follow his maxims; in these words we learn that before God there is nothing great, worthy of approbation and esteem but Jesus Christ, but only what is united to Jesus Christ, what is done for him by his Spirit and by his grace; and anything else, though it may have the name of grandeur and glory, is nothing before God and shall be of no account in eternity. Now beloved friends, do we truly listen to Jesus Christ? Do we not rather listen to the world / and to our own will and humor?[7] Do we hear Jesus Christ when he tells us to renounce sin, to break off from that evil habit, to check those motions of our hearts, to repress our senses, to watch upon our sight, to hold our tongue, to shun pride, vanity, dissipation, to give up ourselves to prayer and recollection in the divine presence. Have we not on the contrary the misfortune to choke up his voice and to shut our ears lest we should hear him? The apostles were frightened, they fell on the ground, the cloud that overshadowed them [and] the voice they heard caused their fear, but Jesus came and touched them, saying, "Arise and be not afraid." Reassured by the word of our Saviour, they rose up and looking about they saw nothing but Jesus Christ alone in his human ordinary state. Blessed are those to whom our Saviour

says as to the apostles, "Arise, be not afraid." Blessed are they who are
with Jesus Christ, who in everything and everywhere see only Jesus
Christ and act only for him! They can say with the apostles, it is
good for us to be with him, to be in his company.

We are in his company, we enjoy his society when we are living
members of the true Church and participate to his sacraments. Then
such practical members of the Church can say, it is good for me to be
here, to be a child of the true Church, to be admitted in the company
of the saints. Beloved friends, is it not a most special blessing to have
Jesus Christ for our only master, to be one of his disciples, to have
been made a child of heaven, an heir of God by baptism, to be a
partaker of the sacraments of the Church, to have our souls fed not
only with the grace of God but also with the body and blood of
Christ, to be in communion with the saints and all the true servants
of God from the beginning of the world, to have a share to all the
prayers and good works that are performed by all the members of
the true Church throughout the universe?

Yes, beloved friends, we ought to say with the apostles, it is good
for us to be here, to be within the pale of the Catholic Church. Let us
build here a tabernacle; that is to say, let us raise up the spiritual
building of virtue, let it be grounded on the foundation of humility
and perfected by charity, on the love of God and our neighbor. Christians, if we look upon it with the light of God, is it not the choicest of
all blessings to have been called to the knowledge and true faith of
Christ? What would all other favors or advantages either of nature
or grace have availed you if this had been wanting? How miserable,
how wretched must you have been for time and / eternity if like so
many others you had been left to sit in darkness and in the shadow
of death" [Luke 1.79]? Indeed you may well exclaim with the prophet,
God has not dealt so mercifully with every nation, and he has not
manifest[ed] his judgments to them" [Psalm 147.20]. Having received
such favor from God, let us be grateful for it and pray him that we
may profit of the benefits we have already received. "Ask and you
shall receive; seek and you shall find; knock and it shall be opened
unto you" [Matthew 7.8]. Ask then upon this occasion that he may
grant you the grace to hear and receive with docility his command-

ments and those of his Church which he has appointed to teach you and to speak to you in his name, that you may never hear a voice opposed to truth. Firmly believe all he has revealed and the Church teaches you that you may practice all he has commanded and live in the constant expectation of that day when, according to Saint Paul, he will reform your body and from a weak and corruptible body he may make it spiritual and incorruptible and make you partaker of the splendor and glory of which he has given you a sketch in his glorious resurrection.

Here we move from the Sunday cycle to a single example from the Saints' cycle, which is composed of feasts on the given date of a given month.

Lamy delivered sermon LOO3A on the Feast of the Conversion of Saint Paul, 25 January c1849, in Danville, Ohio; about 1420 words on Acts 9.1-22 and Matthew 19.27-29; from AASF 1876 loose document # 14d. In 1849, 25 January fell on a Sunday, and so the feast displaced the Sunday Mass. A priest today would find it difficult to declaim 1400 words about Paul's apostolic practice without ever mentioning his theology of salvation.

Saint Paul

The conversion of Saint Paul gives us an admirable instance of the power of divine grace and of the incomprehensible wisdom of the ways of God. An ignorant fisherman as Saint Peter was seems indeed no ways qualified to be a preacher, an apostle, and the prince of the apostles; but then he was humble, and such God usually chooses for the greatest things. But as for Saint Paul, he was not only not qualified to be a preacher of the Gospel but positively disqualified by dispositions directly contrary to the humility and simplicity of the Gospel. He was a proud Pharisee, a fiery zealot, a persecutor, a ravenous wolf, scattering and destroying the sheep of Christ; and yet in a moment by a miracle of grace he is made a vessel of election to carry the name of Christ before nations. From a wolf he becomes a lamb. Here is a change of the right hand of the Most High. Saint Paul was favored with the most extraordinary ecstasy in which he

was taken up to the third heaven, in which he heard and saw sublime mysteries [2 Corinthians 12.2]. For his humiliations under these favors, he suffered with a temptation of the flesh.[8] This apostle, not satisfied with his incredible labors, chastised his body with severe fasting, watchings, and other great mortifications "lest whilst he preached to others he might himself become a reprobate" [1 Corinthians 9.27]. Notwithstanding his immense fatigues and wonderful actions, he did not think he had attained anything, but forgetting all that was behind he had his eyes open only to the duties and obligations that were before him and upon what remained yet for him to do that he might finish his career. As a man who is running a race by looking behind could only be tempted to stop by imagining that he has already gone a great distance, whereas by looking forward he sees how far he has yet to go to carry the prize and spurs himself forward lest he lose the advantage he may seem to have already gained. So did this apostle in the path of virtue, stretching himself forward always with fresh vigor and daily redoubling his fervor to do what still remained for him to accomplish [1 Corinthians 9.24-27]. He despised himself as an unprofitable servant [Luke 17.10] and condemned himself as falling short of what he owed to God, whom he always served in holy fear. He gloried and pleased himself in persecutions and humiliations, in his own weakness and insufficiency, that God alone might be considered and glorified in all things. He feared no dangers, was deterred by no difficulty, but rejoiced in the greatest sufferings, fatigues, and labors that he might make God everywhere known and served by all his creatures. To defend the dignity of his apostleship upon which the success of his preaching depended, he mentioned once his revelations and privileges, but he was compelled by necessity for the salvation of many souls and conversion of nations, and he speaks of them in such a manner as to show he gave all the glory to God alone and made no account of them himself but trembled and humbled himself more under such favors. Speaking of his sufferings, the apostle passes over the innumerable conversions, miracles, and wonders which he wrought and only mentions his sufferings, for the cross was his glory. He tells us that he had undergone more labors and suffered

more frequent imprisonments and more stripes than any other. He was often near death by rivers, thieves, and dangers from the Jews and from false brethren, in towns and in deserts. He endured all manners of fatigues, frequent watchings, fasting, hunger, thirst, and nakedness. He had been five times publicly whipped by the Jews, receiving each time thirty-nine stripes, and had been thrice beaten with rods, had thrice suffered shipwreck, had been a day and a night in the depth of the sea [2 Corinthians 11.23-27].

We have in the Acts of the Apostles a summary account of the missions of Saint Paul. After his conversion and baptism, he changed his name Saul into that of Paul. He preached first to the Jews, then to the gentiles; he visited many places and preached Christ everywhere. At Lystra, upon the cure of a lame man which the apostle performed, the heathens there took him for a god. In this persuasion / the people prepared to offer sacrifice to Saint Paul and his fellow apostle Saint Barnabas. For that purpose the priests of Jupiter brought oxen dressed up with garlands after the gentile manner to the place where they were. Paul and Barnabas rent their garments to testify their abhorrence of such an attempt and prevented their abominable sacrifice [Acts 14.6-14]. Soon after, Saint Paul was stoned by the same giddy mob and was dragged out of the city for dead, but by the care of the disciples he recovered and returned into the city with them [Acts 14.18-19]. After that he went again to Jerusalem and assisted at the first general council held by the apostles at Jerusalem. The great apostle stayed some time in that city to confirm in the faith the new converted flock and then set out to visit the churches he had founded in the east [Acts 15]. At Lystra he took Saint Timothy for his disciple. He went to the Galatians who as Saint Paul himself testifies received him as an angel. Having known by a revelation that he was called into Macedonia, he proceeded to Philippi where he delivered a young girl of an evil spirit, was put into prison, but delivered by a miracle. He converted and baptized the jailer himself with his whole house [Acts 16]. At that time Saint Luke the evangelist, who had been converted at Antioch, became a disciple of Saint Paul and his inseparable companion. They traveled through Macedonia, established a church in the capital of that province; at Athens the

apostle preached to the Jews in their synagogue and to the gentiles in all public places, even in the Supreme Court of the Magistrates, most venerable over all Greece for their wisdom and learning. Dionysius, one of these judges, embraced the faith and several others [Acts 17]. From the last place he was conducted by a call of the Holy Ghost to Corinth; having stayed there eighteen months he brought many, both Jews and Greeks, over to the faith. He visited again the new converts through Asia, everywhere encouraging the faithful and watering his young plants [Acts 18]. At Ephesus God confirmed his preaching by such miracles that even there were brought from his body to the sick handkerchiefs and aprons, and the diseases departed from them.[9] By the labors and miracles of the apostle the word of God spread exceedingly, but he had many adversaries. He suffered much from the persecutions of the Jews, was every hour exposed to divers dangers, and protests himself that he was continually exposed to lose his very life. Being prisoner at Caesarea he was permitted to defend himself against the accusations of the Jews [Acts 24]. The king, Agrippa, who heard him, could not but confess that he had almost persuaded him to become a Christian; it was only because this king, Agrippa, being a worldly man, shut his heart against the motion of grace, the Christian faith not being the fashionable religion in the world [Acts 25-26]. They who neglect to listen to the call of heaven and to improve the favorable visit of the Holy Ghost, in punishment of their abuse of grace usually perish in their sin.

But at length the happy term of our apostle's labors approached, and he beheld with joy the moment in which Christ called him to his glory. He was beheaded at Rome in the year of our Lord 65. His dignity of a Roman citizen did not allow him to be crucified. The body of Saint Paul is kept at Rome with the body of Saint Peter. The day of the death of the renowned conqueror has been forgotten, whilst that of these two apostles is everywhere honored. Men have a greater respect for the tombs of these apostles than for any prince of the world. To the place where the bones of these apostles lie people come from all parts of the world with wonderful piety and zeal to implore the intercession of these two great saints. The greatest glory

then, the greatest honor is to serve God; this is truly to reign here
and a sure pledge to reign hereafter with God.

*The English-original talks conclude with two instructions — subjects presented for
meditation or contemplation, especially to sisters, brothers, or priests.*

*L039 – Instruction on Marriage, dated 1848, read in Covington, Kentucky;
about 475 words. The talk is addressed to the couple about to be wed, and Lamy
might have used it over and over as part of the Nuptial Mass; from AASF 1849
loose document # 4. Lamy uses several scriptural sources — Genesis 2, Job 6,
Mark 10 and Matthew 19, John 3, and Ephesians 5 — but surprisingly ignoring
Mary and Joseph.*[10]

[Marriage]

Marriage is a contract by which two persons become one in
affection, in interest, and [in] every temporal consideration.

Marriage was first established in the earthly paradise, when God
gave to man the woman and blessed this union. Jesus Christ has
raised the contract of matrimony to the dignity of a sacrament, a
spiritual and holy thing among Christians.

There is no state, no condition of life but what needs the blessing
of God, nor any state happy without it.

Your respective duties to each other are very important. The peace,
union, and love which is going to exist between you is for life. Nothing can dissolve it but death, for the Word of Truth says, "What God
joins, let no man separate" [Mark 10.2-12; Matthew 19.3-12]. You
must be kind and indulgent to each other, bear with each other's
humor, weakness, and imperfections. Concur together all the concerns of life. Your mutual fidelity must remove every suspicion from
each other's mind.

The union of the married couple should be such as to represent
the blessed union of Christ with his Church. Saint Paul calls Marriage a great Sacrament, but he says in Christ and in the Church;
and he recommends to them the same union, fidelity, [and] submission as there is between Christ and his Church (Ephesians 5. 22-33).

If the married couple is blessed with children, both their temporal and spiritual good must be procured, for the end of marriage is not only to fill the world with inhabitants but also to give to the Church true Christians who under God ... intent to matrimony ... and fill the Church with good Christians and heaven with saints.[11] /

Do not neglect to recommend your undertaking to God and to invite our Saviour to your marriage like that happy couple of Cana in Galilee, which our Redeemer was pleased to honor with his divine presence and with his first miracle. Having instituted marriage he gave it a sanction and a blessing by assisting to it. The Son of God came to marry as it were by his incarnation our human nature with his divine person; he came to marry himself to his Church and to raise Christian matrimony to a higher dignity which should be a sacred sign of his perpetual union with his Church. He came to espouse our souls to himself, and for this reason he was pleased to favor this marriage with his first miracle. Happy are those who invite our Saviour, his mother, and his disciples to their wedding, who far from shutting our God from themselves and from their mind enter this state with motives worthy of a Christian. Such ones will not fail to have their marriage sanctioned and blessed by the Almighty (Job 6.17).

.

L200 – Instruction on Perseverance, delivered about 1875 in Santa Fe; about 715 words on the topic, mainly from Matthew 10.22; from AASF 1876 loose document # 14g.

Perseverance

"He who shall persevere to the end shall be saved." Matthew 10.22.

To reconcile ourselves with God and resolve to lead a virtuous life is good, but it is not all. We must besides persevere in our fidelity to God, for our divine Saviour has said, "He who shall persevere to the end shall be saved."

Many reasons of perseverance. I will speak only of one *motive*. We have to persevere [in being true to] *the promises* we made to Al-

mighty God, in our Baptism, which we renewed afterwards in the receiving of the sacraments of Penance and of Holy Eucharist, to serve him, to keep his commandments.

The sacraments are not only exterior and sensible signs, established by our Lord to sanctify our souls, but they are also signs of the engagement and solemn treaty by which God on his part pledges himself to give his graces and guarantees eternal life to us; and man on the other part binds himself to serve God, to obey and love him. In the twenty-ninth chapter of Deuteronomy, we read that Moses assembled Israel at the foot / of Mount Sinai and proposed to them the eminent necessity to make a treaty with God, which was the keeping of the law they had received. The prophet asked them if after all the wonders they had seen since their leaving Egypt they were willing to choose the Lord for their God. They accepted in the most solemn manner. Then the prophet declared to them that as they had chosen God for their master, God also chose them for his people.

We have made the same solemn treaty [or] engagement with our divine Saviour, and we are in duty bound to keep our engagement. Reason, faith, our own interest should induce us to be faithful to our promises not only for a short time, [a] few days, [a] few months, but until death. "He who shall persevere to the end shall be saved," says our Saviour.

Without perseverance we cannot succeed even in worldly affairs. Much less can we expect to succeed in the most important affair of our salvation. Without energy, constancy, perseverance, we cannot expect to save our souls and to secure the greatest of all rewards, the glory of heaven. /

Beloved brethren, among the different means of perseverance I will propose only three for your consideration: prayer, frequentation of the sacraments, devotion to the Blessed Virgin Mary.

Prayer. "Watch and pray," says our Saviour, "that you may not fall into temptation (Matthew 26.41), for though the spirit is quick, the flesh is frail." By prayer we keep in remembrance of God. Were we to stop praying, we would be separated from the Author of all good, we would be lost in the midst of creation; our spiritual life would be

stopped. Prayer is so necessary that Jesus Christ himself taught us
how to pray. *"In meditatione mea exardescet ignis"* – [In my meditation a
fire shall flame out" Psalm 38.4]. What oil is to keep a lamp burning,
this prayer is to entertain the keep[ing] of divine love in our souls.

Frequenting the sacraments. To maintain material life, food is necessary, so it is in the spiritual order. The Holy Eucharist is the food of
our souls. "He who / eats this bread," says our Saviour, "shall have
life everlasting, and the bread I will give you is my flesh" (John 6.52).
We receive this bread in the holy Communion; the oftener we receive it, the stronger we will be.

Devotion to the Blessed Virgin Mary. When our Saviour was dying on
the cross, he gave us his mother in the person of Saint John. "Behold
thy mother," said he to his beloved disciple, and Saint John from that
time considered her as his mother. So every good Catholic takes her
for his mother, invokes her, prays to her; as long as we have a true
and filial devotion to her, she will protect us as a mother protects her
child; and it has never been heard that anyone had invoked her in
vain.[12]

Endnotes

[1]   This concluding paragraph is very effective in beginning with two apostro-
phes before the speaker addresses his congregation. Lamy composed it two years
before he could have heard of Nuestro *Padre* Jesús Nazareno – Our *Father* Jesus the
Nazarene (Christ in his passion), the focal Person of the penitential Brotherhoods
of New Mexico.

[2]   "Obedience is better than sacrifices" occurs in 1 Kings 15.22 (now called 1
Samuel), with a slight variant in Ecclesiastes 4.17. "Mercy is better than sacrifice"
occurs in Osee (Hosea) 6.6, and Christ quotes it in Matthew 9.13 and 12.7.

[3]   The requirement that the leper or lepers show themselves to priests in order
to be readmitted to society is found in Leviticus 14.

[4]   Few if any scripture scholars today would say that during his public life
anyone recognized Jesus as God.

[5]   Lamy reused this sermon in 1855 – L120. He dropped the triple-temptation
schema of L070 and went to a division by concupiscence, pride, and avarice.

[6]   On the problems of the human intellect of Jesus Christ and its knowledge,
see pp. 29-32.

7   Lamy uses the word "humor" to refer to the particular mixture of the four humors in given persons: our characteristic psychological tilt, our mood of the moment, our idiosyncratic hobby-horse. The humors explain the quality of sensory-emotional awareness that we have in common with brute animals, and they impact the intellectual-voluntary level of consciousness, rational mind and will, only indirectly.

8   Lamy here seems to blend 2 Corinthians 12.7, "a sting [or thorn] of my flesh" and Galatians 4.13, "your temptation in my flesh [or my bodily ailment]."

9   More readably, "that handkerchiefs and aprons from his body were even brought to the sick, and the diseases departed from them" [Acts 19.12].

10   See Enrique R. Lamadrid, *"Las Entriegas," New Mexico Historical Review* 65 (1990), 5, 8.

11   This passage started out saying "… to fill the Church with good Christians and heaven with saints," but then Lamy tried to improve it and reduced it to complete unintelligibility.

12   Lamy concludes with an echo of the "Memorare," a fifteenth-century prayer to Mary that includes the passage "Never was it known that anyone who fled to thy protection or implored thy help was left unaided." In 1849 the Vatican had attached an indulgence to the recitation of the prayer

Sermons in Spanish

Domingo Tercero de Cuaresma

"El último estado de aquel hombre viene a ser peor que el primero."
San Lucas 11.26 [todo = 11-32]

Las condiciones fáciles que nuestro Señor Jesucristo nos ha impuesto para procurar nuestra conversión y salvación sirven muchas veces por razón de nuestra malicia, a endurecer nuestros corazones en la mala costumbre de pecado. Pero si queremos considerar delante de Dios y con los ojos de la fe el peligro de abusar de la gracia de Dios y de provocar su bondad, seguramente nos pondremos en el estado del saludable temor de Dios que es el principio de la sabiduría Cristiana y tomaremos los medios necesarias para ser fieles a nuestros deberes.

El pecado produce tres grandes males en el alma del hombre. El primer perjuicio, que es el origen de todos, es de separar nuestra alma de Dios, como lo dice el profeta Isaías (59.2), "Vuestras maldades pusieron división entre vosotros y vuestro Dios"; el pecado nos hace perder la inocencia y causa a nuestra alma una enfermedad porque el estado de pecado es una enfermedad, una lepra espiritual. Por eso el profeta David rogaba a Dios y le decía, "Señor, sana mi alma, porque he pecado contra ti" [Salmo 40.5]. Nuestro divino Salvador ha instituido el Sacramento de Penitencia para reconciliarnos con Dios, volver a nuestras almas su inocencia y salud. Entonces los que abusan de este sacramento de reconciliación y vuelven otra vez a cometer los mismos pecados son reos de la ingratitud la mas negra.

Sermons Translated from Spanish

L089 – Third Sunday of Lent, 14 March 1852, Santa Fe, New Mexico; about 2,375 words on Luke 11.11-32; from the Loretto Archives, Nerinx, Kentucky. This is Lamy's earliest surviving sermon in Spanish, delivered after his arrival in Santa Fe on 9 August 1851, his epic trip to Durango, Mexico, and his return to Santa Fe in early 1852; he delivered it just before he left for the First Plenary Council in Baltimore in mid-May. He planned to make side trips to New York on business, to New Orleans to visit his niece Marie in the Ursuline convent school, and to Nerinx, Kentucky, to recruit sisters for a school in Santa Fe; he returned to Santa Fe 26 September 1852.[1]

Third Sunday of Lent

"The last state of that man becomes worse than the first." Saint Luke 11.26.

The easy conditions that our Lord Jesus Christ has imposed on us to bring about our conversion and salvation often serve as a reason for our malice, for hardening our hearts in the evil habit of sin. But if we wish to consider before God and with the eyes of faith the danger of abusing God's grace and provoking his goodness, we will surely put ourselves in a state of that saving fear of God which is the beginning of Christian wisdom and we will take the necessary means to be faithful to our duties.

Sin produces three great evils in the human soul. The first bad result, which is the root of the others, is to separate our soul from God, as the prophet Isaias says (59.2), "Your iniquities have divided between you and your God"; sin makes us lose our innocence and causes in our soul a sickness, for the state of sin is a sickness, a spiritual leprosy. Therefore the prophet David would pray to God and say, "O Lord, heal my soul, for I have sinned against thee" [Psalm 40.5]. Our divine Saviour has instituted the Sacrament of Penance to reconcile us to God and return innocence and health to our souls. Then those who misuse this sacrament of reconciliation and turn again to committing the same sins are guilty of the blackest ingratitude. Therefore our Lord says in the gospel, "The last state of / that man becomes worse than the first."

Por eso nuestro Señor dijo en el evangelio, "El último estado de /
aquel hombre viene a ser peor que el primero." Por el Sacramento
de Penitencia habíamos renovado nuestra amistad con Dios,
habíamos confesado nuestras iniquidades y prometido de guardar
la ley de Dios. Como seguridad del contrato que hicimos con nuestro
Salvador, subimos el altar para recibir la sagrada Comunión, el cuerpo
y la sangre de Jesucristo, pero a cayendo en las mismas faltas nos
arrepentimos de nuestro arrepentimiento, faltamos a nuestras
promesas. Por eso nuestro último estado es peor que el primero.
Mas veces recaemos, mas difícil se hace nuestra conversión. Mas
inveterada la costumbre, mas dificultoso de corregirse de ella. Aunque
Cristo nos hubiera dejado en los sacramentos tanta facilidad para
procurar nuestra salvación, es un error muy fatal de creer que
podemos pasar nuestra vida en una inconstancia perpetua. Hoy
limpiando nuestras almas de sus pecados en el baño saludable de
penitencia, y mañana volviendo a mancharlas por los mismos
pecados. Un día sentándonos al divino banquete con Cristo, otro día
con el demonio: no se puede ofrecer a nuestra santa religión un
ultraje mas insultante. Si quieren ustedes excitar en su alma un
horror por el pecado de recaída, escuchad la palabras de San Pablo
sobre este asunto: "No contristéis," dice el apóstol (Efesios 4.30), "el
Espíritu Santo de Dios"; es obligarlo contra su voluntad a salir del
templo de nuestras almas que él había tomado para su morada y
crucificar otra vez a nuestro Señor Jesucristo y poner bajo de nuestros
pies su preciosa sangre. /

El apóstol San Pedro usa las expresiones las mas fuertes contra el
pecado de recaída. Deploramos la suerte infeliz de las pobres naciones
bárbaras que no han recibido el Evangelio, que no saben los misterios
del reino de Dios, y que perecen en su ignorancia. Pero San Pedro
nos dice que "Mejor nos era no haber conocido el camino de la
justicia que después del conocimiento volver las espaldas a aquel
mandamiento santo que les fue dado. Pues les ha acontecido lo que
dice aquel proverbio verdadero, Tornase el perro a lo que vomitó, y
la puerca lavada a revolcarse en el cieno" (2 Pedro 2.21-22).

Lo que dice nuestro Señor del demonio cuando él toma posesión
otra vez de nuestras almas es para enseñarnos que el enemigo de

By the Sacrament of Penance we renewed our friendship with God, confessed our iniquities, and promised to keep God's law. As surety for the contract we have made with our Saviour, we go up to the altar to receive holy Communion, the body and Blood of Jesus Christ, but by falling into the same faults we repent of our repentance and fail in our promises. Therefore our last state is worse than the first. The more times we fall, the more difficult our conversion becomes. The more inveterate the vice, the more difficult it is to correct. Although by the sacraments Christ has let it be so easy for us to achieve our salvation, it is a very deadly mistake to believe that we can spend our life in perpetual fluctuation, today cleansing our souls of their sins in the saving bath of penance and tomorrow returning to dirty them with the same sins, one day seated at the divine banquet with Christ, the next day with the devil: we cannot offer our holy religion any outrage more insulting. If you wish to arouse in your soul a horror of the sin of relapse, listen to the words of Saint Paul on this point: "Grieve not," says the apostle (Ephesians 4.30), "the Holy Spirit of God"; it obliges him against his will to leave the temple of our souls which he had taken for his dwelling place, and it crucifies our Lord Jesus Christ again and puts his precious blood under our feet. /

The apostle Saint Peter uses the strongest expressions against the sin of recidivism. We deplore the misfortune of the poor barbarous nations who have not received the Gospel, who do not know the mysteries of the kingdom of God, and who perish in their ignorance. But Saint Peter tells us that "It had been better for us not to have known the way of justice than after knowing it to turn their backs on that holy commandment which was given them. For what the true proverb says has happened to them: The dog is returned to his vomit, and the sow that was washed to her wallowing in the mire'" (2 Peter 2.21-22).

What our Lord says about the demon when he again takes possession of our souls should instruct us that the enemy of our salvation is stronger in power, stronger in number (seven for one), stronger in malice ("seven others worse"), and stronger in firm possession ("they fix their dwelling in the soul"). Then the last state of that Christian soul is worse than the first.

nuestra salvación es mas fuerte en poder, mas fuerte en numero (siete por uno), mas fuerte en malicia ("siete otros peores"), mas fuerte en estabilidad ("fijan su morada en el alma"). Entonces el último estado de aquella alma Cristiana es peor que el primero.

Para guardarnos de tantas recaídas en el pecado, sería necesario de ver cual es la causa de estas recaídas y conociendo eso tomar medidas y poner remedio a esta desgracia. Hallamos estas causas en la conducta del demonio, y en la nuestra, después de haberlo expulsado de nuestro corazón el demonio es inquieto y por nuestra parte nos quedamos quietos. "Cuando un espíritu inmundo," dice nuestro Señor Jesucristo, "ha salido de un hombre, se va por sitios áridos, buscando lugar donde repose, y no hallándole dice, 'Me volveré a mi casa de donde salí.'" Él siente la pérdida que ha sufrido y no tiene descanso ni paz. Por el contrario, después de su reconciliación con Dios, muchos Cristianos se quedan quietos e indiferentes, después de pocos momentos dados a la piedad, olvidan sus obligaciones / por el perdón y los favores que han recibido. Se olvidan que la vigilancia es necesaria para perseverar en el santo servicio de Dios, porque dice San Pedro (1 Pedro 5.8-9), "El diablo vuestro adversario anda como león rugiendo alrededor de vosotros buscando a quien tragar. Resistidle fuertes en la fe." Las resoluciones que tomamos son muy débiles, pero el adversario de nuestra salvación es determinado de tomar posesión de nuestras almas. Nos considera como suyos, y dice, "Me volveré a mi casa de donde salí." Las resoluciones que tomamos deberían ser renovadas todos los días con el mismo fervor, la misma determinación, como cuando nos hemos convertido a Dios. Si queremos permanecer fieles a Dios, se necesita de observar lo que manda nuestro Señor (Mateo 26.41), "Velad y orad para que no entréis en tentación. El espíritu en verdad pronto está, mas la carne enferma." La vigilancia es muy necesaria porque hay mucho peligro de perder la gracia de Dios; "La hemos en vasos frágiles," como dice San Pablo [2 Corintios 4.7], muchas tentaciones a penas hemos vencido, una que sobreviene otra: velad y orad. La vigilancia sola sin el auxilio divino no puede ser suficiente. Una oración humilde, fervoroso es necesario para obtener la gracia de Dios, que nos hace capaces para cumplir con nuestros deberes,

To guard ourselves from falling again into sin, it would be necessary to see what causes these relapses, and once this is known to take measures and remedies for this misfortune. We discern these causes in the behavior of the demon and in our own: after having been expelled from our heart, the demon is disturbed and we on our part remain quiet. "When an unclean spirit," says our Lord Jesus Christ, "is gone out of a man, he goeth through places without water seeking rest, and not finding it, he saith, I will return into my house whence I came out.'" He feels the loss he has suffered and finds neither rest nor peace. On the other hand, after their reconciliation with God, many Christians remain quiet and unconcerned, and after a few minutes devoted to piety, they forget their obligations / for the pardon and the favors they have received. They forget that watchfulness is necessary for perseverance in God's holy service, for Saint Peter says (1 Peter 5.8-9), "Your adversary the devil goes about like a roaring lion seeking whom he may devour. Resist ye him, strong in the faith." The resolutions we make are very weak, while the adversary of our salvation is determined to take possession of our souls. He thinks he owns us and says, 'I will return into my house whence I came out." The resolutions we make should be renewed every day with the same fervor, the same determination, as when we were converted to God. If we wish to remain faithful to God, we must observe what our Lord commands (Matthew 26.14), "Watch ye and pray that ye enter not into temptation. The spirit indeed is willing, but the flesh weak." Watchfulness is very necessary for there is great danger of losing God's grace; "We have it in fragile vessels," as Saint Paul says [2 Corinthians 4.7], we have barely survived many temptations, one after another: Watch and pray. Vigilance alone without divine help cannot be sufficient. A humble, fervent prayer is needed for receiving God's grace, which makes us able to comply with our duties, practice virtue, and avoid sin. Watch and pray, maintaining yourselves in complete humility; place your confidence in God, and assure your salvation by your good works. Live in the healthy fear of God so as to merit the grace of living in his holy love, which is the grace I ask of God for all.

practicar la virtud y evitar el pecado. Velad y orad, resguardados en toda humildad, poned vuestra confianza en Dios, asegurad vuestra salvación por vuestras obras buenas. Viváis en el saludable temor de Dios, para merecer la gracia de vivir en su santo amor, que es la gracia que pido a Dios por todos.

[Notes at the bottom of 4th page, left margin of 1st]
En mi ausencia, el mayor gozo que podré tener será de oír que mis feligreses, mi hijos, andan en la verdad, andan en el camino de la virtud.

La escuela [de las] Hermanas − Concilio, como asamblea de la iglesia.

Viernes de Dolores[2]

"Hijo mío, Hijo mío, quien me diera que yo muriese por ti!" Lo que decía el rey David a la ocasión de la muerte de Absalón su hijo (2 Reyes 18.33, 19.4) con mas razón puede decirlo María santísima, al pie de la cruz, mirando a su Hijo divino en su última agonía.

Al considerar los dolores de María santísima en el misterio de hoy, hemos de admirar su fe. No era por un mero sentimiento de compasión que nuestra señora se había avanzado hasta el pie de la cruz, al tiempo que crucificaban a su Hijo; esta madre afligida se había acercado a este lugar triste del suplicio de nuestro Salvador en un espíritu de fe, y para cooperar a la redención del mundo.[3] Ella sola conocía el secreto de este misterio de la cruz; ella se acordaba lo que le había dicho el ángel el día / de su anunciación, que su Hijo salvaría a su pueblo y que su reino sería eterno [Lucas 1.31-33]. Tampoco María santísima se había olvidado de la profecía de Simeón que le dijo que este querido Hijo sería un objeto de contradicción, que ella misma tendría su alma traspasada por una espada de dolor [Lucas 2.29-35]. Esta madre virgen había oído muchas veces a nuestro Señor hablar de su pasión y muerte ignominiosa, como también de su gloriosa resurrección. Ella meditaba estas palabras en su corazón, las comparaba, y quedaba testigo de su cumplimiento. El escándalo

[Notes at the bottom of 4th page, left margin of 1st]
In my absence, the greatest joy I could have would be to hear that my parishioners, my children, are walking in truth, walking in the way of virtue.

The Sisters' school – Council, like an assembly of the church.

L202 – Friday of Our Lady of Sorrows, 3 April 1868, Santa Fe; about 2000 words on the occasion of the lunar feast of Mary's sorrows under the cross, a week before Good Friday; from AASF 1868 loose document # 19.

Friday of Our Lady of Sorrows[2]

"My son, my son, would that I might have died rather than you!"

That is what King David said on the occasion of the death of Absalom his son (2 Kings 18.33, 19.4). With more cause Mary most holy could have said these words at the foot of the cross, looking at her divine Son in his final agony.

In considering the sorrows of Mary most holy as part of today's feast, we must wonder at Mary's faith. It was not out of a mere feeling of compassion that Our Lady had gone forward all the way to the foot of the cross at the time they crucified her Son; this afflicted Mother had drawn near to this sad place of our Savior's suffering in a spirit of faith and so that she might cooperate in the redemption of the world.[3] She alone knew the secret of this mystery of the cross; she often recalled what the angel had said to her on the day / of the Annunciation, that her Son would save his people and that his kingdom would be eternal [Luke 1.31-33]. Mary most holy had also not forgotten the prophecy of Simeon, when he told her that her beloved Son would be an object of contradiction, that she herself held out her soul to be transfixed by the sword of sorrow [Luke 2.29-35]. This virgin mother had often heard our Lord speak of his ignominious passion and death, and also of his glorious resurrection.

del Calvario podía mover y debilitar la fe de los demás, hasta de los apóstoles, pero este mismo ese. No servía mas que para asegurar la suya.

Con respeto al dolor que María santísima sintió a la vista de los suplicios de su Hijo divino, es cosa imposible de hacerse una idea de este grado de dolor, es para honrar estos dolores de la virgen madre / y el ánimo tan sublime de María que la Yglesia guarda este Viernes y que lo llama Viernes de Dolores en honor de los sentimientos dolorosos de nuestra Señora.

Nunca, jamás, ninguna madre padeció un martirio tan cruel. ¿Quién pudiera contener el llanto, como lo dice la Yglesia en el *Stabat Mater,* al ver la madre de Dios en una desolación tan grande, en una tristeza tan profunda?[4] Qué espada de dolor le atravesó el corazón cuando esta tierna madre vio a su querido Hijo en las manos de los verdugos, oyó los golpes de los martillos para meter los clavos en sus pies y en sus manos para atar a la cruz su cuerpo sagrado, y lo mas horrible y amargo eran los insultos, ultrajes y derisiones que le hacían. "¿Oh quién me dará de morir por ti, oh Hijo mío, para librarte," decía esta santísima Madre. Solamente un milagro de la gracia de Dios pudo mantenerla y darle la fortaleza necesaria para no ser oprimida por el dolor y no caer muerta al pie de la cruz.

Nuestro Señor Jesucristo da San Juan por hijo a María santísima. "Mujer," le dijo nuestro Señor, "aquí tienes a tu hijo," y luego al discípulo: "Ahí tienes a tu madre" [Juan 19.25-27]. Este era el testamento del Salvador divino. Para procurarle a su santísima madre algún alivio, consuelo, Jesucristo la encomendó a su discípulo él mas amado, y en la persona de San Juan, él nos ha dado como hijos a su santísima madre. Y desde aquel día encargose de ella el discípulo y la tuvo consigo. Oh que don tan grande nos hace Jesús dándonos a su santísima madre. Cada uno de nosotros puede entonces decirle con verdad, Oh María, yo soy tu hijo, y tu eres mi madre. Pero es por la pureza y la humildad que la honraremos, le agradecemos esta santísima virgen se quedará con nosotros, si nuestra vida es pura, si somos hijos dóciles y respetuosos, también ella nos protegerá en los peligros, en las tentaciones, para que después de haberla honrado, imitado, logramos de tener la dicha de su compañía en el cielo.

She would meditate on these words in her heart and examine them, and she stood there to witness their fulfillment. The scandal of Calvary could shake and weaken the faith of the others, even that of the apostles, but this same event could only strengthen Mary's.

In regard to the sorrow Mary most holy felt at the sight of her divine Son's sufferings, it is impossible to form any idea of this depth of sadness. It is to honor these sorrows of the virgin mother / and the sublime soul of Mary that the Church keeps this Friday feast and calls it the Friday of Sorrows in honor of the sorrowful emotions of our Lady.

Never, never has any mother suffered a martyrdom so cruel. "Who could refrain from weeping," as the Church says in the Stabat Mater, "at seeing the mother of God in so great a state of desolation, in a sadness so profound."[4] What sword of sorrow pierced her heart when this tender mother saw her beloved Son in the hands of the executioners, when she heard the blows of the hammers driving the nails into his feet and into his hands to fix to the cross his sacred body; and even more awful and more bitter were the insults, the outrages, and the taunts they voiced. "Oh who will grant me to die instead of you, oh my Son, to deliver you?" said this most holy mother. Only a miracle of God's grace could sustain her and give her the courage needed not to be overwhelmed by the sorrow, not to fall down dead at the foot of the cross.

Our Lord Jesus Christ gave Saint John as a son to Mary most holy: "Woman," our Lord said to her, "here you have your son," and then to the disciple, "there you have your mother" [John 19.25-27]. This was the last will and testament of the divine Savior. To leave his most holy mother some relief, some consolation, Jesus Christ gave his most beloved disciple to her, and in the person of Saint John, he has given us as sons to his most holy Mother. And from that day, the disciple took her into his care and kept her with him. O what a great gift Jesus has given us, the gift of his most holy mother. Each one of us can then say with truth, "O Mary, I am your son, you are my mother." But it is for her purity and humility that we will honor her; we are grateful that this most holy virgin will stay with us if our life is pure, if we are obedient and reverent children. She

Jueves Santo
Consagración de los Santos Óleos
   Se distinguen tres clases de santos óleos:
         1° el aceite de olivas mezclado con el bálsamo, que se llama
              crisma;
         2° el aceite de los catecúmenos, que es de olivas, llamado
              los santos óleos;
         3° el aceite de los enfermos que se llama también
              vulgarmente santo óleo.
   El crisma se emplea en la unción de los bautizados, confirmados
y obispos, en la unción de las Yglesias, altares, cálices. El aceite de los
catecúmenos sirve para ungir a los bautizados, Yglesias, altares, y
sacerdotes. El aceite de los enfermos sirve para aplicar a los que
reciben la extrema unción.
   La unción exterior significa la unción interior de la gracia sobre
nuestra alma. Por el aceite hemos de entender la pureza de la
conciencia, por el bálsamo la fragancia de una buena reputación –
"*Sicut ... balsamum ... aromatizans dedi suavitatem odoris*" (Eclesiástico 24.20).
   El bautizado recibe una unción sobre el pecho para poder desechar el
error y la ignorancia / por el don del Espíritu Santo y recibir la verdadera
fe. El recibe otra unción entre los hombros para que por la gracia del
Espíritu Santo pueda evitar la pereza espiritual, y ejercerse en buenas
obras. Se le hace al bautizado otra unción en la cabeza que es el sitio de
la inteligencia, para que pueda dar razón de su fe cuando es necesario;
todavía otra unción sobre la frente, para que profese su fe con toda libertad,
y que nunca tenga vergüenza de su religión.

will also protect us in all danger, in all temptations, for when we have honored and imitated her, we come to possess the happiness of her company in heaven.

L160 – Holy Thursday (Thursday of Holy Week), 21 April 1859, Santa Fe; about 1950 words on the blessing of the three holy oils, used as part of many of the church ceremonies, on the Mandatum or Maundy (Christ's washing of the disciples' feet), and on the institution of the Eucharist.

Holy Thursday
Consecration of the Holy Oils
There are three different sorts of holy oils.

1. olive oil mixed with balsam, called chrism;
2. the oil of catechumens, from olives, called the holy oils;
3. oil of the sick which is also called holy oil.

Chrism is used for anointing those baptized, those confirmed, and bishops, and in the anointing of churches, altars, and chalices. The oil of catechumens serves to anoint the baptized, churches, altars, and priests. The oil of the sick is applied to those who receive Extreme Unction.

The outward anointing signifies the interior anointing of grace upon our soul. By the oil we mean purity of conscience, by the balsam the fragrance of a good reputation – *"Sicut ... balsamum ... aromatizans dedi suavitatem odoris"* (Ecclesiasticus 24.20).

The baptized receives an anointing on the breast that can remove error and ignorance / by the gift of the Holy Spirit and makes him receive the true faith. He is anointed again between the shoulders so that by the grace of the Holy Spirit he can escape spiritual sloth and can perform good works. The baptized person receives another anointing on the head, the seat of intelligence, so he can give reasons for his faith when necessary, and he always gets another anointing on the forehead so he will confess his faith with complete liberty and never be ashamed of his religion.

Tal es la significación de los santos óleos. Tan grande es el respeto que debemos llevar a los santos óleos que solamente los sacerdotes pueden tocarlos y solos los obispos consagrarlos. /

La Última Cena

En la última cena del nuestro Señor Jesucristo, consideramos solamente su humildad y su inmensa caridad.

1° Su humildad tan profunda que lo hace bajar hasta lavar los pies de sus apóstoles, pues ¿qué, se había olvidado Jesucristo que es el Hijo de Dios e igual a Dios, que su humanidad sagrada va ser glorificada y sentada a la derecha de Dios en el cielo. No, seguramente él lo sabe bien, sin embargo él quiere hacer este acto tan grande de humildad para dar un remedio a nuestra soberbia. La delicadeza y vanidad del mundo con su deseo de guardar cada uno su rango hubiera dicho que no podía nuestro Señor mandar a sus apóstoles para que le lavasen ellos los pies a su divino Maestro, y no él a ellos, y los hubiesen hecho con gusto. Pero la humildad de Jesucristo nos da un ejemplo muy contrario, para que cumplir con su preceptos cuando él decía "Aprended de mi que soy humilde y manso de corazón" [Mateo 11.29], "No he venido para ser servido antes bien para servir" [Mateo 20.28].

El jefe de los apóstoles se escandalizaba del servicio tan humilde del Hijo de Dios, diciendo, "Señor, tu lavarme a mi los pies? Jamás, jamás," y él no se rindió hasta que nuestro Señor le amenazó que si no le dejaba lavar los pies, entonces no tendría parte con el. Después de tanta humildad practicada por el Hijo de Dios, como / podremos quejarnos nosotros que tenemos que pasar muchas humillaciones y servir a los demás? "Os he dado el ejemplo," dice el Señor, "para que como yo he hecho, así también lo hagas" [Juan 13.15].

2° Su inmensa caridad en la institución del santísimo Sacramento del altar. "Y cenando ellos, tomó Jesús el pan y lo bendijo y lo partió, y lo dio a sus discípulos diciendo, 'Tomad y comed, este es mi cuerpo." Y tomando el cáliz, dio gracias y se les dio, diciendo, 'Bebed de este todos, porque esta es mi sangre del nuevo testamento, que será derramada por muchos para remisión de pecados'" (Mateo 26.26).

Such is the meaning of the holy oils. So great is the reverence we ought to have toward the holy oils that only priests can touch them and only bishops can consecrate them. /

The Last Supper

Concerning the Last Supper of our Lord Jesus Christ, we consider only his humility and his immense charity.

1. His humility was so profound that it makes him stoop to wash the feet of his apostles. Had Jesus Christ forgotten that he is the Son of God and equal to God [the Father], that his sacred humanity was going to be glorified and seated at the right hand of God in heaven? No, surely he knew it well, but nevertheless he wished to perform this great act of humility to offer a remedy for our pride. The trickery and vanity of the world, along with everybody's desire to protect his status, might cause one to say, Couldn't our Lord have commanded his apostles to wash his feet and not himself to wash theirs, and they would have done so with delight. But Jesus Christ's humility gives us an example quite the opposite so that it would fit with his commands when he said, "Learn of me because I am meek and humble of heart" [Matthew 11.29] and "I have not come to be ministered to but to minister" [Matthew 20.28].

The chief of the apostles was scandalized by the humble servitude of the Son of God, saying, "Lord, dost thou wash my feet? Never, never!" and he did not cooperate until our Lord threatened him that if he did not let him wash his feet he would have no part with him. After the Son of God practiced such great humility, how / can we ourselves complain about having to undergo many humiliations and serve others? "I have given you an example that as I have done to you, so you do also" [John 13.6-15].

2. His immense charity in the institution of the most holy Sacrament of the altar. "And while they were at supper, Jesus took bread, blessed it, broke it, and gave it to his disciples saying, 'Take ye and eat. This is my body.' And taking the chalice, he gave thanks and gave it to them saying, 'Drink all ye of this, for this is my blood of the new testament, which shall be shed for the many unto remission of

Nuestro Señor por un milagro de su caridad inmensa nos deja su sagrado cuerpo y su sangre preciosa en el santísimo Sacramento. En la noche misma en que fue entregado a sus enemigos para morir sobre la cruz, mientras que ellos están buscando la ocasión de perderle, nuestro Señor halla medio de quedarse siempre con nosotros. No quiere dejarnos huérfanos [Juan 14.18]. ¿Cómo podemos apreciar la caridad inmensa de un padre tan tierno "Tomad y comed, este es mi cuerpo"? Jesucristo quiere ser nuestra herencia, nuestro tesoro, nuestro patrimonio, y por eso en su último testamento él nos deja su cuerpo y su sangre.

¿Qué tesoro puede el corazón del hombre poseer comparable a este del cuerpo de Jesucristo, cuando lo recibe en un espíritu de humildad y de devoción. Prepárense pues / a recibirlo con el mas grande respeto. Miren como la mayor de las desgracias, el ser privado de este pan celestial, guárdenlo con la vigilancia del amor, para que el enemigo no les quita este precioso tesoro. Y por eso roguemos a Dios para que el mismo nos guarde nuestro corazón y que no permita entrada en el a ninguna cosa contraria a santa voluntad.

"Haced esto en memoria de mi" (Lucas 22.19). La última voluntad de nuestro Padre es que habiéndose muerto por nosotros, guardemos la memoria de un beneficio tan inefable, particularmente cuando subimos al altar recibiendo su cuerpo y su sangre con la debida disposición para la santificación de nuestras almas, y el acuerdo de su pasión y muerte por nosotros.

Mi corazón, Señor, no puede prepararse a recibiros dignamente sino por la meditación de vuestra sagrada pasión y como os habéis entregado todo por mi salvación, así deseo yo entregarme todo a vos. Oh mi Dios, os doy mi corazón para amaros, os doy mi voluntad para seguir vuestra santa ley. Os doy mi entendimiento para considerar vuestros inefables misterios, os doy mi memoria para acordarme de vuestra muerte, os doy mi alma y mi cuerpo para emplearlos y consumirlos en vuestra servicio. Amen.

sins'" (Matthew 26.26-28). By a miracle of his immense charity, our Lord leaves us his holy body and his precious blood in the most holy Sacrament. On the very night when he was betrayed to his enemies so he would die on the cross, while they are seeking an occasion to destroy him, our Lord finds a means of remaining always with us. He does not wish to leave us orphans [John 14.18]. How can we appreciate the immense charity of a father so tender: "Take and eat, this is my body"? Jesus Christ wishes to be our inheritance, our treasure, our patrimony, and so in his last testament he leaves us his body and blood.

What treasure can the heart of man hold that is comparable to this of the body of Jesus Christ, when we receive him in a spirit of humility and devotion? Prepare yourselves, then, / to receive him with the greatest respect. Consider that the greatest misfortune is being deprived of this heavenly bread; protect it with all the watchfulness of love so that no enemy robs them of this precious treasure. And for this we ask God himself to guard our heart and not allow entrance to anything contrary to his holy will.

"Do this for a commemoration of me" (Luke 22.19). The last will of our Father is that having died for us, we should preserve the memory of a benefit so ineffable, particularly when we come up to the altar to receive his body and his blood with a suitable attitude for the sanctification of our souls and the remembrance of this passion and death for our sakes.

My heart, Lord, cannot prepare itself to receive you worthily without meditating on your sacred passion and recalling how you handed over the whole of yourself for my salvation; so I wish to hand myself entirely over to you. O my God, I give you my heart to love you, I give you my will to follow your holy law. I give you my understanding to contemplate your ineffable mysteries, I give you my memory to recollect your death, I give you my soul and my body to be used and consumed in your service. Amen.

Para la Pascua

"Poder tengo para poner mi vida, y poder tengo para volverla a tomar — *Potestatem habeo ponendi animam meam, et potestatem habeo iterum sumendi eam.*" San Juan 10.18.

Ningún otro sino solo Dios hubiera podido decir estas palabras y tener tal poder. Después de la muerte de nuestro Salvador, sus enemigos cierran su sepulcro, y ponen una guardia fuerte de soldados para que sus discípulos no viniesen a llevar su cuerpo, pero todo en vano; su malicia y su diligencia sirven solamente para poner la resurrección de Jesucristo fuera de toda controversia. Porque verdadero es lo que ha dicho el sabio en Los Proverbios 21.30, "No hay sabiduría, no hay prudencia, no hay consejo contra el Señor." En el día de su resurrección, se cumplieron estas palabras que nuestro Señor había dicho, "Tengo poder para poner mi alma, y poder tengo para volverla a tomar — *Potestatem habeo ponendi animam meam, et potestatem habeo iterum sumendi eam.*" El había dado su resurrección como la prueba la mas grande de su misión divina. "Ciertos escribas y Fariseos querrían ver un milagro de Cristo; él les respondió diciendo, 'La generación mala y adulterina señal pide, mas no le será dada señal sino la señal de Jonás el profeta. Porque así como Jonás estuvo tres días y tres noches en el vientre de la ballena, así estará el Hijo del Hombre tres días y tres noches en el corazón de la tierra'" (Mateo 12.38-40), significando su resurrección el tercero día.

Este misterio siendo el mas grande de los milagros de nuestro Señor Jesucristo y el fundamento de nuestra fe, Dios quiso hacerla el mas incontestable no solamente en obligando sus enemigos a admitirla pero también con las / dificultades que tuvieron algunos de sus apóstoles para creerlo.[5] Tomás, uno de los doce, no estaba con ellos cuando les apareció Jesús, y no solamente él se rehusaba a creer la resurrección de su divino Maestro sobre la autoridad de los otros discípulos, pero también no quería creer el testimonio de sus ojos, y "les decía, 'Si no veré en sus manos la hendidura de los clavos

L092 – *Easter, 27 March 1853, Santa Fe; about 1450 words on John 10.11-16 (actually the gospel for the Second Sunday after Easter). This sermon begins a run of seven straight 1853 sermons, L092 to L098.*

For the Pasch [Easter]

"I have power to lay down my life, and I have power to take it up again – *Potestatem habeo ponendi animam meam, et potestatem habeo iterum sumendi eam.*" Saint John 10.18.

Nobody but God alone could have said these words and possess such power. After our Saviour's death, his enemies sealed his tomb, and they set a strong guard of soldiers so that his disciples should not come to carry his body off, but all in vain; their malice and their carefulness served solely to place the resurrection of Jesus Christ beyond all question. For it is true what the wise man has said in Proverbs 21.30, "There is no wisdom, there is no prudence, there is no counsel against the Lord." On the day of the resurrection, these words which our Lord had spoken were fulfilled, "I have power to lay down my life, and I have power to take it up again – *Potestatem habeo ponendi animam meam, et potestatem habeo iterum sumendi eam.*" He had given us his resurrection as the greatest proof of his divine mission. "Some of the scribes and Pharisees wished to see one of Christ's miracles; he answering said to them, 'An evil and adulterous generation seeketh a sign, and a sign shall not be given it but the sign of Jonas the prophet. For as Jonas was in the whale's belly three days and three nights, so shall the Son of Man be in the heart of the earth three days and three nights'" (Matthew 12.38-40), signifying his resurrection on the third day.

Since this miracle is the greatest of the miracles of our Lord Jesus Christ and is the foundation of our faith, God wanted to make it the most unimpeachable miracle not only in forcing his enemies to admit to it but also with the / difficulties that some of his apostles found in believing it.[5] Thomas, one of the twelve, was not with them when Jesus appeared, and he not only refused to believe in his divine Master's resurrection on the authority of the other disciples, but he also did not wish to believe the testimony of his own eyes, and "he said to them, 'Except I shall see in his hands the print of the

y meteré mi dedo en el lugar de los clavos, y meteré mi mano en su costado, no lo creeré.'" Su divino Maestro le concedió la evidencia que él había pedido, entonces "Tomás exclamó, 'Señor mió y Dios mió.' Jesús le dijo, 'Porque me has visto, Tomás, has creído; bienaventurados los que no vieron y creyeron'" [Juan 20.25-29].

La resurrección de nuestro Salvador mantiene nuestra fe en la resurrección futura de nuestros cuerpos. Quedando ciertos que resucitaremos un día a una vida inmortal para ser eternamente felices o infelices, deberíamos considerar la virtud como la cosa la mas grande, la mas sublime, y el pecado como la cosa la mas fea, la mas horrorosa, como la desgracia la mas grande que pueda sucedernos.

Este articulo de nuestra fe [de] una vida futura nos debe animar para practicar la virtud y proveer de antemano para una resurrección gloriosa. Escuchad las palabras del apóstol San Pablo a los Gálatas (6.8): "Aquello que sembraré el hombre, eso también segura. Y así el que siembra en su carne, de la carne cosechara corrupción; mas el que siembra en el espíritu, de espíritu segura vida eterna."

Si queremos participar con la intención de la Iglesia en esta grande solemnidad y hacer de una manera cristiana la conmemoración del misterio de la resurrección de nuestro Salvador, el / mismo apóstol San Pablo nos dirá cuales deberían ser nuestras disposiciones: "Si resucitasteis con Cristo, buscad las cosas que son de arriba, en donde está Cristo sentado a la diestra de Dios; pensad en las cosas de arriba, no en los de la tierra" (Colosenses 3.1-2).

Excitemos en nosotros sentimientos de fe, de esperanza y de amor de Dios; si hemos tenido la desgracia de perder la vida de la gracia, resucitemos de nuevo a la gracia de Dios y vivamos una vida del todo angélica, del todo divinizada. Gustemos las cosas del cielo; este es la manera la mas propia y mas útil de celebrar la pascua de la resurrección y de asegurarnos una resurrección gloriosa.

nails and put my finger into the place of the nails and put my hand into his side, I will not believe.'" His divine Master granted him the evidence he had requested, and then "Thomas exclaimed, 'My Lord and my God.' Jesus saith to him, 'Because thou hast seen me, Thomas, thou hast believed; blessed are they that have not seen and have believed'" [John 20.25-29].

The resurrection of our Saviour supports our faith in the future resurrection of our own bodies. Being sure that we will rise again some day to an immortal life to be eternally happy or unhappy, we ought to consider virtue as our most important and most sublime fact and hold sin as the ugliest and most horrible fact, as the greatest disaster that can happen to us.

This article of our faith about a future life should animate us to practice virtue and provide beforehand for a glorious resurrection. Listen to the words of the apostle Saint Paul to the Galatians (6.8): "What things a man shall sow, those shall he reap. For he that soweth in his flesh, of the flesh shall also reap corruption, but he that soweth in the spirit, of the spirit shall reap life everlasting."

If we desire to take part in the Church's intention during this great solemnity and to commemorate the mystery of our Lord's resurrection in a Christian manner, the / same apostle Saint Paul will tell us what our disposition should be: "If you be risen with Christ, seek the things that are above, where Christ is sitting at the right hand of God; mind the things that are above, not the things that are upon the earth" (Colossians 3.1-2).

Let us excite in ourselves sentiments of faith, hope, and love of God; if we have had the misfortune of losing the life of grace, let us rise up anew to the grace of God and live a life altogether angelic, altogether divinized. Let us savor the things of heaven; this is the most appropriate and most effective way to celebrate the passover of the resurrection and to assure ourselves of a glorious resurrection.

Segundo Domingo después de Pascua

"Y soy el Buen Pastor; conozco mis ovejas, y las que son mías me conocen a mí." Juan 10.14 [todo = 11-16].

En el evangelio de este día, el Hijo de Dios desea que le consideremos bajo la amable calidad de Buen Pastor de nuestras almas. En verdad nuestro Señor es el Buen Pastor que bajo del cielo para buscar la oveja infeliz que se había estragado y perdido, y cuando le hallo, la carga sobre sus hombros para llevarla con gozo al rebaño. Él ha dado su vida para sus ovejas. El mercenario que no toma interés alguno por las ovejas, las desampara en el peligro porque él no cumple con su deber, por la gloria de Dios, ni por el celo de la salvación de las almas inmortales, pero solamente por su interés. El mercenario no quiere otra cosa que su comodidad, conseguir riquezas. No dejará de lisonjear sus ovejas para agradar a ellas, cerrará los ojos a sus faltas, no les hablará de sus deberes, no les enseño las virtudes, las dejará en la ignorancia la mas crasa, y cuando están en el camino de la perdición, no las avisara del peligro, y porque se necesita algún trabajo, algún sacrificio, para que procure el interés eterno de sus ovejas, él las desampara las dejará antes bien que de molestarse.

Que diferente es el verdadero pastor, cuyo nuestro Salvador es el perfecto modelo. Conoce muy bien sus ovejas, y ellas la conocen a el. Conoce lo que les hace provecho y lo que las puede dañar. Este Buen Pastor está proveyendo todos los días por sus ovejas, y lo hace con el mayor gusto. En el Salmo 22 el profeta real nos hace la mas elocuente descripción de todos los oficios que el celestial Pastor ha rendido a nuestras almas: "El Señor me gobierna, y nada me faltará. En un lugar de pastos allá me ha colocado; me ha colocado junto a una agua de refección. Llevo me por senderos de justicia. / Preparaste una mesa delante de mi, contra aquellos que me atribulan. Ungiste con óleo pingüe mi cabeza, y mi cáliz que embriaga, que excelente

L093 – Second Sunday after Easter, 10 April 1853, Santa Fe; about 1100 words on John 10.11-16; from the Loretto Archives. Lamy translated much of this from the English of his 1850 sermon L075. It is interesting to reflect that "Lamb" was Lamy's nickname in the seminary, probably the Franglish pun "Lamby."

Second Sunday after Easter

"I am the Good Shepherd; I know my sheep, and mine know me." John 10.14.

In today's gospel, the Son of God wishes us to consider him under the loveable image of the Good Shepherd of our souls. Our Lord is truly the Good Shepherd who came down from heaven to seek the unfortunate sheep that had strayed and gotten lost, and when he found her, he put her on his shoulders to carry her joyfully back to the flock. He has given his life for the sheep.

The mercenary, who has no real concern for the sheep, abandons them in time of danger because he does not do his duty either for the glory of God or out of zeal for the salvation of those immortal souls but acts only for his own benefit. This hireling is interested only his own comfort and getting rich. He will not fail to flatter his sheep so as to please them, he will shut his eyes to their faults, he will never speak about their duties, never instruct them about virtues, and leave them in crass ignorance. When they are on the road to perdition, he will not warn them of the danger, and since it takes some effort and sacrifice to safeguard the eternal interests of his sheep, he will abandon them, he will quit them rather than be bothered.

How different the true shepherd for whom our Saviour is the perfect exemplar. He knows his sheep thoroughly, and they know him. He knows what will do them good and what will harm them. This Good Shepherd provides for his sheep day by day, and he does so with great pleasure. In Psalm 22 the royal prophet [David] offers us the most eloquent description of all the benefits the heavenly Shepherd has granted to our souls: "The Lord ruleth me, and I shall want nothing. In a place of pasture he hath set me, he hath set me at the water of refreshment, ... he hath led me on the paths of justice. / ... Thou hast prepared a table before me against them that afflict me, thou has anointed my head with oil, and my chalice which

es ella, y tu misericordia va en pos de mi, todos los días de mi vida, afín de que yo more en la casa del Señor en longitud de días." Tales son los beneficios que hemos recibido del divino Pastor de nuestras almas. él nos ha preparado una mesa sobre la cual ha puesto el pan de los ángeles, su cuerpo, su sangre, su alma, su divinidad que recibimos en la comunión, y por razón de tantos favores podemos decir con el profeta que su misericordia nunca nos desamparé y que nos quedaremos fieles a su santa ley todos los días de nuestra vida.[6]

Tendremos perfecta seguridad si queremos obedecer a la voz de este Buen Pastor. Como discípulos de Cristo, sus ovejas, hemos de vivir una vida inocente y sin mancha. De todos los animales, la oveja es la mas sencilla y la mas inocente. Tal debería ser el carácter de los buenos Cristianos: deberán ser inocentes, ni llevar odio, aversión, malicia a nadie, acordándose de la que dice San Pablo (Romanos 12.14, 17-20): "Bendecid a vuestros perseguidores; bendecidles, y no los maldigáis … no pagando a nadie mal por mal, procurando bienes, no solo delante de Dios sino también delante de todos los hombres. Si se puede, cuanto esté de nuestra parte, teniendo paz con todos los hombres, no defiendoos a vosotros mismos mas dad lugar a la ira, porque escrito está, "'a mi me pertenece la venganza, yo pagaré," dice el Señor.' Por tantos, si tu enemigo tuviera hambre, dale de comer; si tiene sed, dale de beber; porque si esto hicieses, carbones encendidos / amontonarás sobre su cabeza. No te dejes vencer de la malo, mas vence el mal con el bien."

A mas de la inocencia, de la simplicidad, otra virtud del verdadero Cristiano es la mansedumbre. Por eso nuestro Señor llama a sus hijos y a todos los que creen en él sus ovejas. El proverbio es bien conocido que dice: tan manso como un cordero. Así ha de ser un Cristiano pues si no representa en si mismo esta calidad de mansedumbre que nuestro Señor nos manda que practicaríamos de una manera tan particular, cuando dijo (Mateo 11.29): "Aprended de mi que manso soy y humilde de corazón" – si uno no se aplica con todo su corazón a practicar esta virtud de mansedumbre, nuestro Señor Jesucristo no lo reconocerá por su discípulo. Esta virtud de mansedumbre viene de la mortificación de sus pasiones y deseos, del desprecio del mundo, y de la caridad verdadera; tal es el origen

inebriateth me, how goodly it is. And thy mercy will follow me all the days of my life, that I may dwell in the house of the Lord unto length of days." Such are the benefits we have received from the divine Shepherd of our souls. He has set us a table whereon he has put the bread of angels, his body, blood, soul, and divinity that we receive in Communion, and because of his generosity we can say with the prophet that his mercy will never desert us and that we will remain faithful to his holy law all the days of our life.[6]

We will possess perfect security if we choose to obey this Good Shepherd's voice. As disciples of Christ, his sheep, we must live a life innocent and without stain. Of all beasts, the sheep is the simplest and most innocent. Such should be the character of good Christians, who should be innocent and bear no hatred, dislike, or malice toward anyone, recalling what Saint Paul says (Romans 12.14, 17-20): "Bless them that persecute you, bless and curse not. ... To no one render evil for evil, providing good things not only in the sight of God but also in the sight of all men, if it be possible, as much as is in you, having peace with all men. Revenge not yourselves but give place unto wrath, for it is written, "Revenge is mine, I will repay," saith the Lord.' But if thy enemy be hungry, give him to eat, if he thirst, give him to drink, for doing this thou shalt heap / coals of fire upon his head. Be not overcome by evil, but overcome evil by good."

In addition to innocence and simplicity, another virtue of the authentic Christian is meekness. For this reason our Lord calls his children and all those who believe in him his sheep. As the well-known saying puts it, "gentle as a lamb." Such it is to be a Christian, and if this trait of gentleness is not visible in us as our Lord commanded us to practice it in a special manner when he said (Matthew 11.29) "Learn of me because I am meek and humble of heart" – if anyone fails to apply himself with all his heart to the practice of this virtue of gentleness, our Lord Jesus Christ will fail to acknowledge him as his disciple. This virtue of meekness stems from the mortification of our passions and desires, from contempt for the world, and from true charity; such is the source of that tranquil serenity that we so much admire in the saints and that we must imitate very carefully. If we mortify and repress our passions, then it would be a

de esta tranquilidad y calma que tanto admiramos en los santos, para que hemos de imitar con mas cuidado. Si tuviéramos nuestras pasiones mortificadas y reprimidas, entonces seria una cosa muy fácil de practicar la virtud de mansedumbre.

Una calidad notable de la oveja es la obediencia. Se deja llevar a donde uno quiere, siempre se queda cerca de su pastor, es fiel a su voz, lo sigue, y si algunas veces se extravía un poco, vuelve luego al rebaño cuando el pastor le llama. Esta obediencia hace conocer a los que verdaderamente pertenecen a Dios, de los que no le pertenecen. / "Las mías me conocen a mi," dice nuestro Señor, "y oirán mi voz." Tengan cuidado, pues de no seguir su propia voluntad, y de oponerse a la voz del divino Pastor cuando nos llama y desea llevarnos al pasto pingüe de su Iglesia en donde nuestras almas tendrán el mas abundante mantenimiento.

El Hijo de Dios no os reconocerá como su ovejas, como miembros de rebaño, si no quisierais oír su voz, cumplir con su voluntad, que nos es bien conocida por la Iglesia, pues "No todo él que me dice, 'Señor, Señor,'" dice nuestro Redentor, "entrará en el reino de los cielos, sino él que hace la voluntad de mi Padre, que está en los cielos, ese entrará en el reino de los cielos" (Mateo 7.21).

Nuestro Salvador ha cumplido con todos los deberes de un Buen Pastor, ahora que nada falte de parte de ustedes para corresponder a su gracia, mas bien después de haber sido admitidos sobre la tierra en la Iglesia que es el rebaño del Señor, por nuestra obediencia, mansedumbre, caridad, y todas las demás virtudes, merezcamos de ser agregados en el rebaño de los escogidos en el cielo. Es el favor que pido a Dios por todos.

Cuarto Domingo después de la Pascua

"Me voy a aquel que me envió." Juan 16.5.

Nuestro Señor estaba cumpliendo con las ordenes de su Padre eterno. No quería ir fuera del camino que le había enseñado. Como discípulos de Cristo, hemos de seguir el mismo camino. "Me voy a

very simple thing to practice the virtue of meekness.

A notable characteristic of the sheep is obedience. She will be led wherever the shepherd wishes; remaining always close to the shepherd, faithful to his voice, she follows him; and if at times she strays a little ways away, she comes right back to the flock when the shepherd calls her. This obedience distinguishes those who really belong to God from those who don't. / "Mine know me," says our Lord, "and they will hear my voice." They are careful not to follow their own will or reject the voice of the divine Shepherd when he calls us and wishes to lead us to the rich pastures of his Church, where our souls find abundant food.

The Son of God does not know us for his sheep, for members of his flock, if we do not wish to hear his voice and do his will, as the Church has plainly told us: "'Not everyone that saith to me 'Lord, Lord,'" says our Redeemer, "'shall enter into the kingdom of heaven, but he that doth the will of my Father who is in heaven, he shall enter into the kingdom of heaven'" (Matthew 7.21).

Our Saviour has fulfilled all his duties as a Good Shepherd; now may nothing be lacking on your part, especially after having been admitted into his Church on earth which is the flock of the Lord, in corresponding to his grace by our obedience, gentleness, love, and all the other virtues. May we merit entrance into the flock of those chosen ones in heaven. This is the favor I ask of God for all of you.

L095 – Fourth Sunday after Easter, 24 April 1853, Santa Fe; about 800 words on John 16.5-14; from the Loretto Archives. The preacher draws a set of stark contrasts between hell and heaven in an attempt to lead his listeners to shun the one and seek the other.

Fourth Sunday after Easter

"I go to him that sent me." John 16.5.

Our Lord always complied with the orders of his eternal Father. He never wanted to walk other than in the path he had been shown. As disciples of Christ, we must follow the same path. "I go to him

aquel que me envió." En esta vida se nos presentan dos caminos, uno que lleva al cielo y el otro que lleva al infierno. Largo como de todo la vida, y penoso como muy empinado es el camino del cielo. Es preciso de andar con fatiga, en este camino del cielo, pues es muy cuesta arriba, y para hacer la voluntad de Dios es preciso de renunciar a nuestra propia voluntad. "'Si uno,' dice nuestro Redentor, 'quiere venir en pos de mi, que renuncie a si mismo, lleve su cruz, y sígame'" [Mateo 16.24]. Se necesita de pasar por muchos trabajos y dificultades para poder entrar en el reino de Dios.

En el otro camino que lleva al infierno uno anda a placer, a gusto, pues hace solamente lo que le da gana, y si quiere, no se sujeta a ninguna ley, a ningún trabajo, a ninguna mortificación. Por este camino de cuesta abajo, va guiando el demonio, atiza con su espíritu, propone la carga al parecer ligera, pero a la verdad muy pesada. Pues / todo es asco, inmundicias, lodo, cieno, y por fin el infierno sin fin.

En el camino de la virtud, Jesucristo va adelante de nosotros como un guía seguro, y para que lo sigamos nos da su gracia, su espíritu. Nos manda tomar la cruz, el yugo de su divina ley. En este camino hay trabajo, dificultad, pero con las fuerzas que se reciben de parte de la gracia de Dios, todo es bondad, santidad, limpieza, y al fin eterna gloria. Se experimenta lo que dice el profeta real de la ley de Dios, que "es sin mancilla, convierte las almas, da sabiduría a los pequeñuelos; las justicias del Señor, … sus juicios verdaderos, justos en si mismos. Son mas de codiciar que el oro, … y mas dulces que la miel" (Salmo 18.8-11).

"Vuestro corazón se llena de tristeza porque os digo estas cosas," dijo Jesús a sus discípulos, "mas yo os hablo la verdad: os conviene que yo me vaya, porque si no me voy, el Espíritu Consolado no vendrá a vosotros; pero si me voy os le enviaré. El Espíritu Consolado él vendrá a consolaros y vuestra tristeza se convertirá en gozo.

"Cuando vendrá este Espíritu, convencerá al mundo en orden al pecado, en orden a la justicia, y en orden al juicio. En orden al pecado, por cuanto no han / creído en mi" [Juan 16.6-7, 20, 8-9]. El día mismo de Pentecostés el Espíritu de Dios descendió sobre los apóstoles. San Pedro, el primero de ellos, convenció a los Judíos de

that sent me." This life offers us two paths, one of which leads to heaven and the other to hell. The road to heaven is as long as the whole of life, and it is difficult because it is very steep. The going is truly wearisome on this heavenly road, for it is uphill all the way, and to do God's will is precisely to renounce our own will. "If any man," says our Redeemer, 'will come after me, let him deny himself and take up his cross and follow me'" [Matthew 16.24]. It is necessary to pass through many labors and difficulties so as to enter into the kingdom of God.

On the other road, which leads to hell, one goes at his pleasure, comfortably, for he does only what he feels like doing, and if he wishes he is subject to no law, no labor, no mortification. He goes along this downhill pathway led by a devil, keeps company with his spirit, and carries a burden that seems light but in actuality is quite heavy. And / all is loathsomeness, filth, muck, slime – and endless hell at the end.

On the path of virtue, Jesus Christ goes before us as our trustworthy guide, and that we might follow him he grants us his grace, his Spirit. He bids us take up the cross, the yoke of his divine law. On this road are work and difficulty, but with the strength we get from God's grace, everything is goodness, holiness, cleanliness – and with heaven eternal at the end. One experiences what the royal prophet speaks of in connection with God's law, which "is unspotted, converting souls, … giving wisdom to little ones. The justices of the Lord, … his true judgments, just in themselves. They are more to be desired than gold, … and sweeter than honey" (Psalm 18.8-11).

"Because I have spoken these things to you, sorrow hath filled your heart," said Jesus to his disciples, "but I tell you the truth: it is expedient to you that I go, for if I go not, the Consoler Spirit will not come to you; but if I go I will send him to you. The Consoling Spirit will come to comfort you and turn your sorrow into joy.

"When this Spirit comes, he will convince the world of sin, and of justice, and of judgment; of sin, because they / believed not in me" [John 16.6-7, 20, 8-9]. The very day of Pentecost, the Spirit of God came down upon the apostles. Saint Peter, the foremost of them, convinced the Jews of their sin in a manner so powerful that three

su pecado de un modo tan fuerte que se convirtieron tres mil y recibieron el bautismo y el Espíritu Santo [Hechos 2.41]. En otra predicación convirtió cinco mil [Hechos 4.4]; en fin desde aquel tiempo hasta ahora el crimen de los Judíos y de todos los que recusan de creer en Jesucristo y en su doctrina ha sido probado con tanta evidencia que nunca han podido ni nunca podrán justificarse.

Este Espíritu divino convencerá al mundo en orden de la justicia, que quiere decir que le convencerá de la inocencia de Jesucristo, de la justicia de su causa. ¿Si nuestro Señor no hubiera sido el Hijo de Dios, si él no hubiera fortalecido a sus apóstoles con los dones de su divino Espíritu, como les hubiera sido posible ellos de hacer tantos milagros, y de convertir al mundo?

Este mismo Espíritu convencerá al mundo en orden del juicio porque el príncipe de este mundo ha sido juzgado ya. Nuestro Señor destruyo el reino de Satanás, lanza los demonios en la Judía, y sus discípulos de su Espíritu divino los lanzaron en todas las partes de la tierra. Tales son las profecías consonantes que hizo nuestro Señor a sus discípulos poco tiempo antes / de su muerte, ya nosotros hemos visto el cumplimiento de estas profecías.

¿Ahora a quién creeremos? a quién daremos nuestro corazón? al demonio, que nos ha engañado tantas veces? al mundo, que nos ha seducido también tantas veces, y nos seduce todos los días? ¡A Dios! No los permita nuestro Señor; el vencedor del mundo y del demonio tiene derecho a nuestro servicio, tiene derecho a nuestro corazón; a el solo lo daremos, a el solo seguiremos, a el solo amaremos, a el solo obedeceremos en este tiempo, en esta vida, para merecer de poseerle después de la muerte y por toda la eternidad.

thousand of them converted and received baptism and the Holy Spirit [Acts 2.41]. In another oration, he converted five thousand [Acts 4.4]; in sum, between that time and today the crime of the Jews and of all who refuse to believe in Jesus Christ and in his doctrine has been proven with such evidence that they never have been able to justify themselves and they never will.

This divine Spirit will convince the world of justice, which means that he will convince it of the innocence of Jesus Christ and of the justice of his cause. Had our Lord not been the Son of God, had he not strengthened his apostles with the gifts of his divine Spirit, how would their doing such miracles and converting the world have been possible?

This same Spirit will convince the world of judgment because the prince of this world has already been judged. Our Lord destroyed the kingdom of Satan; he has expelled the demons in Judea, and his disciples, through the divine Spirit, have scattered them to all parts of the world. Such are the consoling prophecies our Lord voiced to his disciples a short time before / his death; we have already seen the fulfillment of these prophecies.

Now, in whom will we believe? To whom will we give our heart? To the devil, who has tricked us so many times? To the world, which has seduced us so often as well and continues to do so daily? To God! Our Lord will not allow them [to seduce us]; the conqueror of the world and of the devil holds title to our service, holds title to our heart. To him only will we give them, him only follow, him only love, him only obey in time, in this life, so as to deserve to possess him after death and for all eternity.

Pentecostés.

"El Consolado, el Espíritu Santo que mi Padre enviará en mi nombre, os lo enseñará todo, y os recordará cuantas cosas os tengo dichas." San Juan 14.26. [todo = 23-31]

El pueblo de Israel observaba la solemnidad de Pentecostés como una de sus principales fiestas, y la razón era que la ley antigua había sido proclamada en este día;[7] así los Cristianos guardan con solemnidad la fiesta de hoy porque en este mismo día fue promulgada la ley de gracia por la venida del Espíritu Santo bajo la forma de lenguas de fuego.

Ahora el Espíritu de Dios bajó sobre los apóstoles en forma de lenguas para significar que venía a hacerlos dignos ministros de su palabra y enriquecerlos de una sabiduría divina, los misterios de Dios y todas las verdades del Evangelio para poder enseñarlas y publicarlas en todo el mundo conocido. El Espíritu Santo no solamente apareció en forma de lenguas pero lenguas de fuego para que entendiésemos que este divino Espíritu enciende las almas en las cuales viene a morar. Así como el fuego transforma en fuego / todas las materias de la cuales se ampara, del mismo modo el Espíritu de Dios enciende las almas de los apóstoles con un amor, un celo que consuma todas sus aficiones terrestres y les muda en otros hombres. "Yo rogaré al Padre, y os dará otro Consolado para que more siempre con vosotros, el Espíritu de la verdad ... " (San Juan 14.16-17). Este Espíritu de verdad fue prometido a los pastores de la Yglesia para estar siempre con ellos, guiarlos en toda verdad para enseñar los hijos de la Yglesia, para estar siempre con los verdaderos discípulos de Cristo, y así guiarlos en toda verdad en su fe y en sus acciones.

Pero para que el Espíritu Santo venga en nuestras almas y que las purifique de todas sus manchas, de todos sus defectos, y que las transforme como hizo de los primeros discípulos, hemos de ponernos

*L164 – Pentecost, 12 June 1859, Santa Fe; about 870 words on John 14.23-31
and the descent of the Holy Spirit on the apostles fifty days after the resurrection;
from the Loretto Archives. Lamy quotes several passages from the church hymn
"Veni, Sancte Spiritus – Come, Holy Spirit."*

Pentecost.

"The Consoler, the Holy Ghost whom my Father will send in my name, will teach you all things and will bring all things to your mind, whatsoever I have said to you." Saint John 14.26.

The people of Israel observed the solemnity of Pentecost as one of their main feasts, and the reason was that the Old Law was proclaimed on this day;[7] and so Christians keep the feast with solemnity today because on this very day was promulgated the law of grace through the coming of the Holy Ghost in the form of tongues of fire.

Today the Spirit of God came down on the apostles in the form of tongues to signify that he came to make them worthy ministers of his word and to enrich them with a divine wisdom, the mysteries of God and all the truths of the Gospel so that they could teach and publicize them throughout the whole known world. The Holy Spirit appeared not only in the form of tongues but of tongues of fire so we might understand that this divine Spirit kindles the souls in whom he comes to dwell. Just as fire transforms / all the material it catches, in the same way the Spirit of God burns the souls of the apostles with love, with a zeal that may consume all the earthly affections and make changed men of them. "I will ask the Father, and he shall give you another Consoler that he may abide forever with you, the Spirit of truth" (Saint John 14.16-17). This Spirit of truth was promised to the shepherds of the Church to be with them always, to guide them unto all truth so as to teach the children of the Church, to be always with the true disciples of Christ and so to guide them unto all truth in their faith and in their actions.

But so that the Holy Ghost will come into our souls and purify them of all their stains, of all their defects, and transform them as he did with the first disciples, we must get ourselves into the same attitudes and ask humbly along with the Church, "*Veni Sancte Spiritus*

en la misma disposición y de rogarle humildemente con la Yglesia, *"Veni Sancte Spiritus* – Ven, oh Santo Espíritu – *Mentes tuorum visita* – dignase visitar las potencias de tus siervos para llenar con los dones de tu gracia las almas que has criado."[8]   Este debería ser el fruto de esta grande solemnidad. No podemos tener una dicha / mas grande que de poseer el Espíritu Santo en nuestras almas, como también por otro lado, no hay estado mas infeliz sin este divino Paracleto. Pues en donde no hay el Espíritu de Dios, allí es Satanás. Pues dice San Pablo (Romanos 8.9), "Pero él que no tiene el Espíritu de Cristo este tal no es de el." Pero si no pertenece a Jesucristo a qué entonces pertenecerá? Qué parte tendrá en Cristo y en su reino? Oh como deberíamos considerar lo que nos enseña la Yglesia en el oficio de hoy: *Sine tuo numine, Nihil est in homine, Nihil est innoxium* – Sin vuestra divinidad, oh Espíritu Santo, el hombre es nada, en él no hay nada santo, nada recto." Pero si deseamos con todo nuestro corazón participar a los dones del Espíritu Santo, no dejaremos pasar esta solemnidad sin rogar a nuestro Señor Jesucristo que nos dé el Paracleto, el Consolado que nos tiene prometido para que "venga a visitar nuestras almas, a lavarlo que en ellas está inmundo, a regarlo que está seco, a sanarlo que está débil, enfermo, a ablandarlo que está inflexible."[9]   Este divino Espíritu, "que ha renovado la faz de la tierra" [Salmo 103.30] por / su gracia, por sus milagros, vendrá también a mundificar nuestros corazones, a transformarnos como hizo con los primeros Cristianos, si no le ponemos ningún obstáculo. Para ser verdaderos Cristianos, no basta la fe, no basta la profesión de nuestra religión, se necesita a mas de esto tener el Espíritu de Jesucristo, pues él que no tiene este Espíritu no es del Señor, no es de sus discípulos. Si el Espíritu de Dios mora en nosotros, nuestro cuerpo," dice San Pablo, "verdaderamente está muerto por el pecado, mas el espíritu vive por la justicia. Somos deudores no a la carne para que vivamos según la carne, porque si vivierais según la carne, moriréis; mas si por el Espíritu hicierais morir los hechos de la carne, viviréis, porque todos los que son movidos por el Espíritu de Dios, los tales son hijos de Dios" (Romanos 8.9-14).

La vida del verdadero Cristiano se reduce a estas tres cosas: 1° a la mortificación de los deseos de la carne, 2° a ser animado del Espíritu

– Come Holy Ghost – *Mentes tuorum visita* – deign to visit the mental powers of your servants" to fill with the gifts of your grace the souls you have created.[8] Such ought to be the result of this great solemnity. We cannot gain a greater / benefit than to possess the Holy Spirit in our souls, as on the other hand we cannot achieve a worse disaster than to be without this divine Paraclete. Where the Spirit of God is absent, there Satan exists. For Saint Paul says (Romans 8.9), "But if any man hath not the Spirit of Christ, he is none of Christ's." Then if he does not pertain to Jesus Christ, to whom does he pertain? What portion does he have with Christ and his kingdom? O how we need to consider what the Church teaches us in today's divine office, "*Sine tuo numine, Nihil est in homine, Nihil est innoxium* – Without your divinity, o Holy Ghost, man is nothing, he possesses nothing holy, nothing righteous." But if we wish with all our heart to partake of the gifts of the Holy Spirit, let us not end this solemnity without asking our Lord Jesus Christ to give us the Paraclete, the Consoler who promised us that he would "come and visit our souls, to wash what is unclean in them, to water what is dry, to heal what is weak and sick, to mollify what is rigid."[9] This divine Spirit, "who has renewed the face of the earth" (Psalm 103.30) by / his grace, through his miracles, will come also to cleanse our hearts, to transform us as he did the first Christians, if we raise no obstacle. In order to be real Christians, faith is not enough and professing our religion is not enough, for we need in addition to possess the Spirit of Jesus Christ, for whoever has him not is not of the Lord, is not one of his disciples. "If the Spirit of God dwells in us," says Saint Paul, "our body indeed is dead because of sin, but the spirit liveth because of justification. ... We are debtors not to the flesh to live according to the flesh, because if you should live according to the flesh, you will die, but if by the Spirit you mortify the deeds of the flesh, you will live, for whoever are moved by the Spirit of God are the children of God" (Romans 8.9-14).

The life of a real Christian comes down to these three things: the mortification of fleshly desires, being animated by the Spirit of God, and suffering in union with the Spirit of Christ.

Our soul is in darkness, so we must ask God to give us the Spirit

de Dios, 3º a padecer en el Espíritu de Cristo.

Nuestra alma está en las tinieblas, hemos de rogar a Dios que nos dé el Espíritu de verdad; nuestra alma es tibia y lánguida, el Consolado vendrá a animarla; nuestra alma es pobre, destituida de virtud, el Espíritu de santidad vendrá a enriquecerla, adornarla, santificarla, y así que mora en nuestra alma en esta vida y en la otra.

Día de la Santísima Trinidad

Jueves es día de fiesta de obligación: Corpus Christi.

La procesión de Corpus Christi se hará el Domingo en la tarde después de las vísperas.

Los miembros de la cofradía del Santísimo considerarán como su deber de asistir a la procesión, con toda el respeto, silencio y devoción que uno que tiene fe debe llevar en estas ocasiones.

Para ganar la indulgencia los miembros de la Cofradía han de prepararse a recibir las sacramentos de penitencia y de Eucaristía. La limosna corta y voluntaria que prometen los de la cofradía ha de entregarse cada año sin faltar si ellos quieren recibir una participación [en] las oraciones y misas que se dicen.

El primer Domingo de cada mes habrá misa en la capilla de Nuestra Señora de Guadalupe a las siete de la mañana para facilitar a los vecinos de dicha capilla oportunidad de oír misa, y el segundo Domingo de cada mes en la capilla de San Miguel a la misma hora. Estos dos Domingos se dirán la primera Misa en la capilla de Nuestra Señora de la Luz a la seis, y misa cantada como de costumbre.[10]

El último Domingo de Mayo de hoy en ocho días es la fiesta de Nuestra Señora de la Luz. /

"Tres son los que dan testimonio en el cielo: el Padre, el Verbo, y el Espíritu Santo; y estos tres son una misma cosa." San Juan 1, 5.7.

Es una verdad que nos enseña la sagrada escritura en muchos lugares y reconocido también por muchos filósofos paganos que no

of truth; our soul is tepid and listless, so the Consoler will come to enliven it; our soul is poor and empty of virtue, so the Spirit of holiness will come to enrich, adorn, and sanctify it, and in this way the Spirit abides in our soul in this life and in the other.

L097 – Trinity Sunday, 22 May 1853, Santa Fe; about 475 words on 1 John 5.7 (which is not a reading from the Mass); the sermon comes from the Loretto Archives. There is a lengthy preface first about Corpus Christi and the major procession around Santa Fe which continues even a century and a half later, then about the schedule of Sunday Masses.

Day of the Most Holy Trinity

Thursday is a holy day of obligation, Corpus Christi. The procession of Corpus Christi will take place Sunday in the afternoon after Vespers. The members of the Confraternity of the Most Holy Eucharist should consider how [they should fulfil] their duty of assisting at the procession with all the respect, silence, and devotion that a believer should bring to these occasions.

To gain the indulgence, the members of the Confraternity must prepare themselves to receive the sacraments of Penance and the Eucharist. The small and voluntary alms which the members of the Confraternity have promised must be given annually without fail if they wish a share in the prayers and Masses which are said.

On the first Sunday of each month at seven in the morning, there will be Mass at the Chapel of Our Lady of Guadalupe to make it easy for the people who live near that chapel to attend, and on the second Sunday of each month, at the Chapel of San Miguel at the same hour. On those two Sundays, the first Mass will be said in the Chapel of Our Lady of Light at six, and the high Mass as usual.[10]

The last Sunday of May, a week from today, is the feast of Our Lady of Light. /

"There are three who give testimony in heaven, the Father, the Word, and the Holy Ghost; and these three are one and the same Being." 1 John 5.7.

It is a truth which the holy scripture teaches us in many pas-

hay mas que un Dios existente por si mismo, eterno y poseyendo todas las perfecciones. Sin embargo, aunque uno en substancia, naturaleza y esencia, Dios tiene una compañía digna de si, pues la fe nos enseña que hay tres personas distintas en Dios, el Padre, el Hijo y el Espíritu Santo. Dios en contemplando y conviniendo a sí mismo desde toda la eternidad produce un pensamiento, un Verbo, en fin su Hijo eterno. El Padre y el Hijo por su mutual amor desde toda la eternidad producen la tercera persona, el Espíritu Santo.

Este misterio, como todos las demás de la fe, es incomprensible, pero creyendo en él damos a Dios el mas grande homenaje. Si pudiéramos comprender las perfecciones de Dios, entonces él dejaría de ser Dios; por eso nuestra fe tiene mérito porque creemos sobre la palabra de Dios.

En el cielo la santísima Trinidad no será un misterio, pues dice San Pablo, "En el cielo veremos, veremos a Dios faz a faz" [1 Corintios 13.12].[11] Lo que hemos de hacer ahora para merecer un día de comprender y de gozar a Dios es de adorar la santísima Trinidad en verdad y en espíritu, de servirle con fidelidad, y de honrarlo por mucha obediencia a los santos mandamientos.

Domingo infra Octava de Corpus [Christi]

"Cierto hombre dispuso una gran cena, y convido a mucha gente." San Lucas 14.16 [todo = 16-24].

Aunque esta cena se pueda entender de la gloria del cielo, aquí la aplicaremos a la sagrada Eucaristía. Cena de verás grande, el rey del cielo la preparó grande, porque se nos da una comida divina. "Envió un criado"; el Señor envió no solamente un criado pero muchos, y todavía envió y enviará; se dice uno solo por la unidad de la fe y de la Iglesia a decir a los convidados que viniesen. Todos son llamados a este celestial convite. Dios hace excepción de ninguno. Todos somos sus hijos, sus herederos, a nadie se cierran las puertas

sages and recognized as well by many pagan philosophers that there is no more than one God, existing of himself, eternal, and possessed of all perfections. Nevertheless, though one in substance, nature, and essence, God has a community worthy of himself, for faith teaches us that there are three Persons, the Father, the Son, and the Holy Ghost. God [the Father], contemplating and considering himself for all eternity, generates a Thought, a Word, indeed a Son. The Father and the Son, through their mutual love from all eternity, produce a third Person, the Holy Ghost.

This mystery, like all the rest of the faith, is incomprehensible, but by believing in it we give God the greatest homage. If we could comprehend the perfections of God, then he would cease to be God; therefore our faith possesses merit because we believe on the word of God.

In heaven, the most holy Trinity will not be a mystery because as Saint Paul says, "In heaven we will see [as we are seen]; we will see God face to face" [1 Corinthians 13.12].[11] What we must do today to merit one day the comprehension and enjoyment of God is to adore the most holy Trinity in spirit and truth, to serve God with fidelity, and to honor him with our obedience to his holy commandments.

L098 – Sunday in the Octave of Corpus Christi, 29 May 1853, Santa Fe; about 980 words on Luke 14.16-24; from the Loretto Archives.

Sunday within the Octave of Corpus Christi

"A certain man made a great supper and invited many." Luke 14.16.

Although we can understand this supper as the glory of heaven, here we apply it to the sacred Eucharist. A supper great indeed, the king of heaven has prepared it in a grand manner, for he gives himself to us as a divine dinner. "He sent a servant": the Lord sent not only one servant but many, and he sent and will send them; it mentions only one to suggest the unity of the faith and of the Church telling those who are invited to come. All are called to this heavenly feast. God excludes no one. We are all of us his children, his heirs, he

de la Iglesia, pues nuestro Señor manda a sus apóstoles, "Predicad el evangelio a todas criaturas" – que quiere decir, instruid a todas las naciones en el camino de la salud – "enseñándoles a observar todas las cosas que os tengo mandado" [Marcos 16.15, Mateo 28.20]. Veremos ahora como los convidados correspondieron a esta invitación. A un banquete tan grande, tan honorable, tan provechoso, todos hubieron debido venir, pero lo contrario sucedió, y empezaron todos como de concierto a excusarse. Aquí entran las excusas, de las que David pedía a Dios, "No le dejase caer en ellos, Señor," decía el profeta en su Salmo 140.4, "no permitas se deslice mi corazón en palabras de malicia, para alegar excusas sobre excusas en los pecados." Nadie las escucha, ellos las alegaron por seguir sus antojos y no responder al llamamiento de Dios. /

1ª excusa, la adquisición de bienes. *"Villam emi* – Compré una villa, y voy a verla. Ruégote me des por excusado." El conseguir bienes, posesiones temporales de una manera justa no es contra la ley de Dios. Pero tomar motivo de la posesión, adquisición de ranchos o de otros bienes para excusarse de servir a Dios, y de corresponder a su invitación, es un desprecio de Dios que viene de una soberbia la mas inaguantable. Este es el principio de todo pecado, tan formidable para condenar, que al primer descargo derribó del cielo a la profundo del infierno innumerables ángeles, y a la segunda perdió a todos los hombres. Pero supo abatir a los soberbios él que siendo Dios de majestad inmensa, supo humillarse a si mismo hasta la muerte de la cruz. A que vino si no a quebrar estas cervices soberbias? quien si no los pobres de espíritu, los humildes, son sus escogidos y amados? Uno es el Dios de todos, una la fe, una la Iglesia, todos somos hermanos, e igualmente decimos, "Padre nuestro."

2ª excusa. "Compré cinco quintas de bueyes, los voy a probar," dijo el segundo. Estos son los avarientos y codiciosos. "La avaricia es la raíz de todos los males," dice San Pablo, "la cual codiciando algunos se descaminaron de la fe, y se enredaron en muchas dolores" (1 Timoteo 6.10).

La inquietud por sus bienes, sus posesiones, / no les deja descansa ninguno. Al avariento todo su tiempo esta ocupado en eso, y por el miedo que tiene de perder su fortuna no la puede gozar. Es verdad

shuts to nobody the doors of the Church, for our Lord commands his apostles, "Preach the gospel to every creature" – that is to say, instruct all the nations in the paths of salvation, "teaching them to observe all things whatsoever I have commanded you" [Mark 16.15, Matthew 28.20]. We will see today how those invited respond to this invitation. To a banquet so great, so honorable, so beneficial they all should have come, but the opposite happened, and they all began in concert to excuse themselves. Here begin their excuses, concerning which David begged God, "Lord," says the prophet in his Psalm 140.4, "do not permit my heart to let itself loose in malicious words, alleging excuses upon excuses in sins." Nobody excuses them, they alleged them in order to follow their whims and not to respond to God's invitation. /

The first excuse, the acquisition of goods: "Villam emi – I have bought a farm, and I must needs go out and see it. I pray thee, hold me excused." The pursuit of goods, temporal property, in a just manner is not contrary to the law of God. But to make a life program of acquiring ranches or other goods so as to excuse ourselves from serving God, from answering his invitation, is a contempt of God which stems from a pride quite unbearable. This is the root of all sin, powerful in bringing condemnation, for in the first instance it overthrew from heaven to the depths of Hell innumerable angels, and at the second it ruined the whole human race. But being the God of immense majesty, Christ knew how to humiliate the proud, for he humbled himself even to the death of the cross. Why did he come if not to bow down the proud neck? Who if not the poor in spirit, the humble, are his chosen ones and his beloved? One is the God of all, one the faith, one the Church, all are brethren, and we say equally "Our Father."

The second excuse, "I have bought five yoke of oxen; I go to try them," says the next man. These are the avaricious and the greedy. "For the desire of money is the root of all evils," says Saint Paul, "which some coveting have wandered from the faith and have entangled themselves in many sorrows" (1 Timothy 6.10).

The restlessness for his goods, his possessions, / leave him no rest, for the greedy man is continually taken up with these things,

que el cuidado por nuestros bienes no es incompatible con nuestra salvación; tenemos derecho a cuidar lo que Dios nos ha dado, el conducirse de otro modo seria una negligencia culpable delante de Dios; pero tampoco es permitido de ser avariento, pues el codicioso ¿como había de mirar al cielo, cuando con todos sus cinco sentidos el esta engolfado, atascado en la tierra?

3ª excusa. "Acabo de casarme," dice un tercero, "y así no puedo ir allá." Por estos se entienden los lascivos, y deshonestos, lujuriosos; estos tres fuegos, dice San Juan, abrazan al mundo. "Todo cuanto hay," dice el mismo apóstol, "en el mundo es codicia de la carne, codicia de los ojos, y soberbia de la vida" (1 Juan 2.16). Esta soberbia de la vida es la primera excusa que se alega para no corresponder a la invitación de Dios, esta codicia de los ojos es el deseo inmoderado de los bienes de este mundo, o la avaricia, y esta es la segunda excusa que dan para no venir a la invitación. Este último dio una razón muy falsa, porque el matrimonio fue santificado por nuestro Salvador; y solamente los que se quedan y quieren quedarse viciados y / abandonarse como brutos a su lujuria, abusando del matrimonio, pueden dar tal excusa. Todos los que se abandonan a esta codicia de la carne como han de aceptar la invitación del rey celestial que aprecia la pureza del alma y cuerpo sobre todas las virtudes,[12] y que se deleita entre las vírgenes [Judit 15.15]. Así todos se excusaron. "Habiendo vuelto el criado, refirió todo a su amo. Irritado entonces el padre de familia dijo a su criado, 'Sal luego a las plazas y barrios de la ciudad, y tráeme acá cuantos pobres y lisiados y ciegos y cojos; hallarás, pues os protesta en verdad que ninguno de los que antes fueron convidados ha de gustar la cena.'" Así recibieran ellos el castigo que habían merecido. El reino de Dios fue cerrado por ellos; perdieron el derecho a su gloria. Hermanos míos Cristianos, Dios nos guarde de una desgracia tan grande de perder eternamente a nuestra alma, a nuestro Dios. No nos excusemos en nuestros pecados, antes bien correspondamos de buena voluntad. Al llamamiento de Dios apreciemos su invitación; como Cristianos estamos convidados a esta cena grande que se dará en el reino de los cielos, a donde los convidados que se habrán presentado con las cualidades requisitas gozaran a Dios mismo por toda la eternidad.

and for fear that he might lose his fortune he cannot even enjoy it. It is true that concern for our goods is not incompatible with our salvation. We have the right to care for what God has given us, and to do anything else would be culpable negligence before God. But neither is it permitted to be greedy, for how can the greedy man look up to heaven when all his five senses are swallowed and shackled by the earth?

The third excuse: "I have married a wife," says the third man, "and therefore I cannot come." These men stand for the lascivious, the dishonorable, and the luxurious. These three fires, Saint John says, encompass the whole world. "For all that is in the world," says that apostle, "is the concupiscence of the flesh, and the concupiscence of the eyes, and the pride of life" (1 John 2.16). This pride of life is the first excuse someone claims so as not to accept God's invitation, this desire of the eyes is the immoderate wish for the things of this world, also called avarice, and it is the second excuse given for not coming as invited. This last gave a reason that is totally false, because our Saviour made matrimony holy, and only those who remain and wish to remain vicious and / to give themselves over like brute animals to their luxury, abusing matrimony, can offer such an excuse. All those who abandon themselves to this concupiscence of the flesh though they ought to accept the invitation of the king of heaven who values purity of soul and body above all other virtues[12] and who is delighted to be among virgins [Judith 15.15]. And so everyone was excused. "The servant returned and told his master everything. Then the master of the house, being angry, said to his servant, 'Go out quickly into the plazas and neighborhoods of the city and bring here to me the poor and the disabled, the blind and the lame; go get them; but I tell you, surely none of those men that were invited shall taste of my supper.'" Thus they will get the punishment they deserve. The kingdom of God was closed to them; they lost the right to glory.

My Christian brethren, God save us from so great a misfortune as losing our soul, losing our God, forever. Let us not make excuses for our sins but rather cooperate with good will. At God's call let us value his invitation. As Christians we are invited to this great meal

Fiesta del Sagrado Corazón de Jesús

"Yo he venido a poner fuego en la tierra, ¿y qué he de querer sino que arda?" Lucas 12.49.

La devoción al Sagrado Corazón de Jesús ha sido instituida para encender en los corazones de los Cristianos aquel fuego del amor divino que por desgracia se estaba apagando, dejando vacío el corazón humano, o mas bien haciéndole olvidar de los beneficios de su Redentor, del amor inmenso de este Dios para nuestras almas. Para obviar a un abuso tan grande hemos de considerar el Sagrado Corazón de nuestro Señor Jesucristo como el modelo por el cual debemos formar y arreglar el nuestro. Aprenderemos de este divino Maestro de buscar en todas cosas la gloria de Dios, nuestra / propia santificación y perfección en la practica de todas las virtudes y el bien del prójimo. Aprenderemos a hacer el ejercicio de la oración en un espíritu de sacrificio, ofreciéndonos a Dios en unión con nuestro Señor Jesucristo y no para conseguir consuelos que no merecemos de ningún modo, a perseverar en este santo ejercicio a pesar de todos los obstáculos de repugnancia y de distracciones. Ténganse en una unión tan estrecha con Jesucristo para no tener sino un corazón con el, para amar lo que es conforme a los sentimientos de este Sagrado Corazón, y evitar lo que pudiera renovar el dolor que sintió cuando él dijo, por razón de nuestras culpas, "Mi alma está triste hasta morir" [Mateo 26.38].

Si tomamos este Sagrado Corazón de Jesús por nuestro modelo, no faltaremos de comprender que hay dos virtudes sobre todos las

which will be given in the kingdom of heaven, where the invited guests who will be present with the required qualities will enjoy God himself for all eternity.

L 197 – Sacred Heart of Jesus, 23 June 1865, Santa Fe; about 350 words on the seventeenth-century devotion; from the Loretto Archives. Lamy invites the congregation to reject any consolation that is not earned, evidently on the grounds that God owes us something from time to time. His phrasing "humble and meek of heart" is a reversal of Matthew's order at 11.29

Feast of the Sacred Heart of Jesus

"I am come to cast fire on the earth, and what will I but that it be kindled?" Luke 12.49.

The devotion to the Sacred Heart of Jesus has been instituted to light in the hearts of Christians that fire of divine love which unfortunately was being extinguished, leaving the human heart empty or at least making it forget the benefits of its Redeemer and the immense love of God for our souls. To avoid such a great abuse, let us consider the Sacred Heart of our Lord Jesus Christ as a model on which we should form and regulate our own. We will learn from this divine Master how to seek in all things the glory of God, our / own sanctification and perfection in the practice of all the virtues, and the good of our neighbors. We will learn to make the exercise of prayer in a spirit of sacrifice, offering ourselves to God in union with our Lord Jesus Christ, never in any way receiving consolations that we have not earned, and persevering in this holy exercise despite all the obstacles of repugnance and of distractions. Let there be a bonding with Jesus Christ so close that there is only one heart with him, to love whatever conforms to the attitudes of this Sacred Heart and to avoid whatever could renew the sorrow he felt when, because of our faults, he said, "My soul is sorrowful even unto death" [Matthew 26.38].

If we take this Sacred Heart for our model, we will not fail to comprehend that there are two virtues more than all the rest which / we must practice since they are like the wellspring and the foun-

otras que / hemos de practicar porque ellas son como la fuente y el fundamento de las demás virtudes. "Aprended de mi que soy humilde y manso de corazón" (Mateo 11.29). Esforzándonos de adquirir estas dos virtudes, podremos ofrecerle de este modo un digno tributo de reconocimiento y gratitud, y habiendo así tenido en nuestra vida sentimientos conformes a su Sagrado Corazón, mereceremos de quedar unidos con él por un amor y gozo eterno.

Cuarto Domingo después de Pentecostés

"Replícale Simón, 'Maestro, toda la noche hemos estado fatigándonos, y nada hemos cogido. No obstante, sobre tu palabra echaré la red.'" Lucas 5.5 [todo = 1-11]

El vivir una vida perezosa y inútil es un mal grande, pero un desorden mas deplorable y mas común es el consumir a sí mismo en trabajo y en ansia que finalmente terminan en nada solido, donde uno no puede recoger frutos; pues después de muchos trabajos hemos de decir con los apóstoles, "Nos hemos fatigado mucho tiempo, y nada hemos cogido." La razón es porque hemos trabajado en la ausencia de nuestro Salvador y en las tinieblas. Hemos trabajado por el mundo, según las máximas del mundo, para conseguir solamente los bienes del mundo. Es un trabajar en las tinieblas, fatigarse toda la noche y perder su tiempo. Si queremos lograr nuestro trabajo, tenemos que trabajar en la luz grande de la fe, conducirnos según las máximas de la fe.

Haremos dos reflexiones. Primera, la fe se pierde por la negligencia y la relajación de las buenas obras. La posibilidad de perder la fe viene de nuestra inconstancia, para el perder en realidad es la consumación de la impiedad y de la malicia. La fe se pierde por la negligencia de las buenas obras que son el fruto de esta virtud teologal.[13] Por eso Jesucristo dijo a los Judíos: "Quitado os será el reino de Dios, y será dado a un pueblo que haga los frutos de el" [Mateo 21.43]. Nuestra fe debe ser viva y animada; ahora el alma, la

dation of the rest of the virtues. "Learn of me, for I am humble and meek of heart" (Matthew 11.29). By making ourselves acquire these two virtues, we can offer in this manner a worthy tribute of recognition and gratitude, and having thus achieved in our life attitudes conformed to the Sacred Heart, we will deserve to be united with him by an eternal love and joy.

L099 – Fourth Sunday after Pentecost, 12 June 1853, Santa Fe; about 1000 words on Luke 5.1-11 and Acts 10.2-4; from the Loretto Archives.

Fourth Sunday after Pentecost

"Simon answered, 'Master, we have been wearying ourselves all the night and have taken nothing. Nevertheless, at thy word I will let down the net." Luke 5.5.

Living a dangerous and useless life is a great evil, but a more deplorable and more common disorder is to drain oneself in labor and anxiety that finally issues into nothing solid, where one cannot gather any fruit, when after considerable effort we must say with the apostles, "We have exhausted ourselves for a long time and have gotten nothing." The reason is that we have worked apart from our Saviour and in the dark. We have worked for the world, according to the principles of the world, in order to attain only the world's goods. That is working in the dark to wear ourselves out and waste our time. If we wish our work to succeed, we must work by the shining light of faith and act according to the principles of faith.

Let us consider two things. First, we lose our faith if we neglect and ignore good works. The risk of losing our faith stems from inconstancy, since the loss is really the final result of impiety and malice. Faith disappears through neglect of good works which are the fruit of this theological virtue.[13] For this reason Jesus Christ said to the Jews, 'The kingdom of God shall be taken from you and shall be given to a nation yielding the fruits thereof' [Matthew 21.43]. Our faith ought to be living and vibrant, and the very soul and life of believing is good works. They sustain it, they give it motion and

vida de la fe, son las buenas obras. Ellas la mantienen, le dan movimiento y aumento. Como sucede cuando un cuerpo deja de ejercer las funciones de la vida, se / corrompe, y se cae en disolución; así también la fe, por la interrupción de las buenas obras, se hace mas débil de día en día, y finalmente se muere, pues, dice Santiago, como el cuerpo sin el espíritu es muerto, así también la fe sin las obras es muerta" (Santiago 2.26). Así lo prueba la experiencia. ¿Puede haber alguna cosa mas muerta que la fe de un hombre que hace nada por Dios, nada por su salvación? Es verdad que la fe puede subsistir con el pecado; no se necesita nada menos de la infidelidad para destruir la fe; pero por grados uno anda a la infidelidad, cuando la fe deja de obrar, una multitud de enemigos se levanta contra nuestra alma, la soberbia, el mundo, la carne, ¿y como podremos resistir contra enemigos tan poderosos? El conservar el don de la fe en medio de una vida desordenada no seria menos de un milagro. Habiendo recibido la fe por un puro favor de Dios, si queremos perseverar en esta virtud es menester de producir frutos dignos de fe; de otro modo mereceremos de ser castigados por la justicia de Dios, que nos quitará este don, y lo dará a otros que producirán fruto. La fe es semejante a un árbol que debe producir frutos, pero si este árbol es cubierto solamente con hojas, cuando debería llevar fruto, Dios le dirá, como el dueño que tenía una higuera plantada en su huerta. Se fue a buscar fruto en ella, y no le halló; y dijo al que labraba la viña, / "Mira, tres años vengo a buscar fruto en esta higuera, y no lo hallo; córtala pues, para que ha de ocupar aun la tierra?" (Lucas 13.7).

En el centurión Cornelio tenemos un modelo que nos enseña lo que hemos de hacer para conservar nuestra fe, para perfeccionarla. Este hombre era de los gentiles, no había recibido la una fe distinta de Dios y de sus misterios, pero siendo religioso y temeroso de Dios con toda su casa, haciendo muchas limosnas al pueblo y orando a Dios incesantemente, mereció que un ángel de Dios le fuese mandado, diciéndole: "Tus oraciones y tus limosnas han subido en memoria delante de Dios" [Hechos 10.2-4], mereció por sus bienes obras, sus buenos hechos, de recibir la visita del príncipe de los apóstoles que vino en persona para instruirle antes de ser Cristiano.

growth. As happens when a body leaves off exercising the opera-
tions of life, it / corrupts and dissolves, so faith as well, by the failure
of good works, grows daily more weak and finally dies, for as Saint
James says, "Even as the body without the spirit is dead, so also faith
without works is dead" (James 2.26). So experience shows. Can anything be more dead than the faith of a man who does nothing for
God, nothing for his own salvation? It is true that faith can coexist
with sin, for it takes nothing less than infidelity to destroy faith; but
by stages one arrives at infidelity, and when faith stops working a
host of enemies arises against our soul – pride, the world, the flesh –
and how can we resist enemies so powerful? Preserving the gift of
faith in the midst of a disordered life would be nothing less than a
miracle. Having received the faith by a pure gift of God, if we wish
to persevere in this virtue we must produce fruit worthy of faith;
otherwise we earn punishment by God's justice, who will take this
gift away and give it to others who will provide fruit. Faith is like a
tree that ought to produce fruit, but if this tree is covered only with
leaves when it ought to bear fruit, God will speak to him as the
owner who had a fig tree planted in his garden spoke. He went to
gather fruit from it and found none, so he said to the caretaker of the
vineyard, / "Behold, these three years I come seeking fruit on this
fig tree and find none, so cut it down; why doth it cumber the earth?"
(Luke 13.7).

   In the centurion Cornelius we find a model who teaches us what
we must do to preserve our faith and bring it to perfection. This man
was a gentile, he had not received the one true faith about God and
his mysteries, but being religious and God-fearing along with his
whole household, giving generous alms to people and praying un-
ceasingly. He merited to have an angel of God sent to him to say,
"Thy prayers and thy alms are ascended for a memorial in the sight
of God" [Acts 10.2-4], so he earned by his good works, his good
deeds, the visit of the prince of the apostles who came in person to
instruct him before he became a Christian. He was respectful of
God's justice, who rewards virtue and punishes vice. This fact alone
taught him that being rich he ought to give alms, that being the
head and father of a family he saw it was his duty to bring up his

Era temeroso de la justicia de Dios, que recompensa la virtud y castiza el vicio. Esto solo le enseñaba que siendo rico tenía que dar limosnas, siendo la cabeza y el padre de una familia, el sabio que era su obligación de criar a sus hijos en el temor y amor de Dios y de mantener en sus corazones el espíritu de religión, que siendo pecador tenía que orar a Dios, hacer penitencia y pedir perdón.

El evangelio nos dice que nuestro Señor Jesucristo subió en la barca de San Pedro para predicar al numeroso concurso. Esto nos enseña que nuestro divino Redentor puso su cátedra en San Pedro y que en el estableció la unidad de su Iglesia y que solo y sus sucesores son la cabeza visible de ella, a pesar de todo lo pueden decir / los que se quedan separados de la Iglesia Católica. "El cielo y la tierra pasarán," dijo Jesucristo, "pero mis palabras no pasarán" [Marcos 13.31]; he aquí sus palabras a Simón (Mateo 16.18-19): "Yo te digo que tu eres Pedro y que sobre este piedra edificaré mi Iglesia, y las puertas del infierno no prevalecerán contra ella; y a ti te daré las llaves del reino de los cielos, y todo lo que atares sobre la tierra, era también atado en los cielos, y todo los que desatares sobre la tierra será también desatado en los cielos." Creyendo estas palabras con toda la Iglesia Católica por mas de diez y ocho siglos, habiendo tenido la dicha de recibir la verdadera doctrina de la fuente misma de la verdad, de la flote de San Pedro, si nos conformamos a las reglas de esta misma fe, de esta misma doctrina, no nos fatigaremos en vano sin coger nada, pero recibiremos el fruto de nuestro trabajo, que es la gracia de Dios en esta vida y la bienaventurada eternidad en la otra.

children in the fear and the love of God and to maintain in their hearts the spirit of religion, and that being a sinner he was bound to pray to God, do penance, and ask pardon.

The gospel tells us that our Lord Jesus Christ went into the bark of Saint Peter to preach to a large crowd. Thus we learn that our divine Redeemer set his cathedral upon Saint Peter, that on him he established the unity of his Church, and that he alone and his successors are its visible head, despite everything that those / who remain apart from the Catholic Church can say. "Heaven and earth shall pass away," said Jesus Christ, "but my words shall not pass away" [Mark 13.31]; behold his words to Simon (Matthew 16.18-19): "I say to thee that thou art Peter and upon this rock I will build my church, and the gates of hell shall not prevail against it; and I will give thee the keys of the kingdom of heaven, and whatsoever thou shalt bind upon earth shall be bound also in heaven, and whatsoever thou shalt loose on earth shall be loosed also in heaven." Believing in these words together with the whole Catholic Church for more than eighteen centuries and having had the happiness of receiving the true doctrine from the very wellspring of truth, from Saint Peter's boat, if we conform to the rules of this very faith, of this very doctrine, we will not wear ourselves out in vain and obtain nothing, but we will instead receive the fruit of our work, which is the grace of God in this life and a blest eternity in the other.

Noveno Domingo después de Pentecostés

"Al llegar Jesús cerca de Jerusalén, poniéndose a mirar esta ciudad, derramó lágrimas sobre ella, diciendo, 'Jerusalén, si conocieses también tu por lo menos en este día que te se ha dado, lo que todavía podría atraerte la paz! Mas todo eso está oculto a tus ojos.'" [Lucas 19.41-42; todo = 41-47]

Por el espacio de tres años nuestro Señor era la admiración de toda la Palestina por sus milagros. El había obrado muchos en Jerusalén, pero esta ciudad resistía con la mayor obstinación a todas sus gracias, pues la causa de las lágrimas era la infidelidad de los habitantes de Jerusalén. Muchas ciudades de Judea y de Samaria eran convencidas de que Jesús era el Mesías y no resguardaban mas que el ejemplo de la capital para reconocerle públicamente, pero los principales de Jerusalén le unían la oposición la mas ciega. Se habían caído en el mas deplorable estado; la paz que les ofrecía su Salvador no la podían, no la querrían entender. Su bien, su interés verdadero, todo eso era oculto a sus ojos. Su mala disposición, su malicia, no les permitía de ver las venganzas que estaban pendiendo ni las calamidades que se preparaban.

La falta de corresponder a los favores que habían recibido, a las visitas de su / Dios, les mereció la ruina de su pueblo, de su nación; la predicción que nuestro Señor les hizo sucedió y se cumplió literalmente cuarenta años después, cuando los Romanos, ministros de la venganza del cielo, tomaron Jerusalem y la destruyeron de tal modo que no se queda en ella una piedra sobre piedra;[14] por cuanto habían desconocido el tiempo en que Dios les había visitado.

La ruina de Jerusalén y de toda la nación de las Israelitas se quedará por ejemplo a las ciudades y naciones culpables. Este ejemplo las debería hacer temblar. Pues la justicia de Dios tendrá su tiempo, y sabrá castigar cuando una nación o una ciudad habrá llevado la mitad de sus ofensas, de sus pecados.

L101 – Ninth Sunday after Pentecost, 17 July 1853, Santa Fe; about 760 words on Luke 19.41-47; from the Loretto Archives. In an announcement at the end, Lamy pleads for respectability – a persistent goal of the clergy during the middle of the nineteenth century.

Ninth Sunday after Pentecost

"And when he drew near to Jerusalem, placing himself to see the city, he wept over it, saying, 'If thou also hadst known, and that in this thy day, the things that are to thy peace! But all that is hidden from thy eyes." [Luke 19.41-42]

For the space of three years our Lord was the wonder of all Palestine because of his miracles. He had worked many in Jerusalem, but this city resisted his graces with great stubbornness, and so the cause of his tears was the unbelief of the inhabitants of Jerusalem. Many cities of Judaea and Samaria were convinced that Jesus was the Messiah and would have needed no more than the capital's example to recognize him openly, but the leading men of Jerusalem formed a completely blind opposition. They had fallen into a most deplorable state; the peace the Saviour offered they could not, they would not understand. Their good, their true interest, all this was hidden from their eyes. Their bad attitude, their malice, kept them from seeing the impending vengeance and the disasters prepared for them.

The failure to cooperate with the favors they had received, with the visits of their / God, merited them the ruin of their people and their nation; the Lord's prediction occurred, fulfilled itself literally, forty years later when the Romans, ministers of heaven's vengeance, captured Jerusalem and destroyed it in such a manner that not one stone remained on another,[14] and all because they had failed to recognize the time when God had visited them.

The ruin of Jerusalem and of the whole nation of the Israelites stands as an example for guilty cities and nations. This instance ought to make them tremble, for God's justice will bide its time, will know how to punish, when a nation or a city will have accumulated half as many offenses and sins [as Jerusalem].

Consideramos nosotros en esta ocasión si hemos conocido el día del Señor o si no hemos tenido la desgracia de caer en el funesto estado de ceguedad en que se hallaba la ciudad de Jerusalem. ¿Como hemos conocido el precio del tiempo presente? Los santos lo supieron apreciar, y no perdieron ni un instante. Si nosotros también lo supiéramos apreciar, si conociésemos cuanto nos importa de aprovecharnos del día del Señor, de su visita, que bienes infinitos nos están / prometidos, si correspondamos con la gracia de Dios; como también que desgracias, que calamidades nos preparamos si abusamos de los beneficios de Dios, de sus gracias. Dios no permita que todo esto sea oculto a nuestros ojos.

En las calamidades publicas, los infieles y los impíos no ven mas de la apariencia de las cosas; hacen reflexiones según les parece a su razón débil tocante a los males, a las desgracias que afligen su patria. Pero un Cristiano debe considerar estas calamidades publicas con los ojos de la fe y ver en estos eventos un castigo justo de Dios que les aflige para que hagan penitencia y se conviertan.

Nuestro Señor lloró sobre los pecados de los hombres, sobre su mala disposición; el estaba proveyendo que su pueblo se quedaría en su infidelidad, que todos las milagros que había obrado en su favor no servirían que hacer su condenación mas rigurosa, que su sangre sería derramada en vana pro ellos.

Pero si viniese nuestro Señor en la tierra, que lágrimas de sangre lloraría / a la vista de tantos pecados, de tantos escándalos y excesos que ciertamente pasan los de los Judíos. Tantas gracias y beneficios de los cuales abusan los hombres, tantos sacramentos de que abusamos, fueron instituidos por nuestra salvación, pero que cambiamos por nuestra condenación.

Es en nuestro poder de consolar a nuestro Salvador, de parar las lágrimas que esta derramando. Y eso lo haremos llorando nosotros mismos por nuestros pecados, haciendo penitencia, nunca volviendo a cometer pecado, pero aprovechándonos de todos los medios de salvación que tenemos.

We consider on this occasion whether we have known the day of the Lord, whether we have not suffered the disgrace of falling into the deadly state of blindness in which Jerusalem found itself. How well have we understood the value of the present moment? The saints knew how to appreciate it and never wasted an instant. If we knew also how to appreciate it, if we understood how important it was to benefit from the Lord's day, from his visitation, what incalculable blessings are / promised us, if we cooperated with God's grace – and also what misfortunes, what calamities we prepare for ourselves if we misuse God's benefits and graces. May God not allow all this to be hidden from our eyes.

In public calamities, the faithful and the ungodly do not see more than the outward appearance of things; they reflect on what seems to their feeble minds to concern the evils, the misfortunes that afflict their homeland. But a Christian ought to consider these national disasters with the eyes of faith and see in these occurrences God's just punishment that afflicts them so that they will do penance and be converted.

Our Lord wept over the sins of men, over their bad attitude; he was disposing matters so that his people would remain in their unbelief, so that all the miracles he had worked in their favor would serve only to make their condemnation more rigid, and so that he would shed his blood in vain for them.

But if our Lord came on the earth, what tears of blood would he weep / at the sight of so many sins, so many scandals and excesses that certainly surpass those of the Jews. Such graces and blessings that men abuse, such sacraments that we misuse, all instituted for our salvation, but we transform them into our condemnation.

It is in our power to console our Saviour, to stop the tears he sheds. And we ourselves can do this by weeping for our sins, doing penance, and never again committing sin but instead availing ourselves of all the means of salvation that we possess.

Una palabra sobre el respeto en los templos – "Mi casa es casa de oración, mas vosotros la tenéis hecho una cueva de ladrones" [Lucas 19.46]. Aquí se ve cuan criminal es las falta de respeto en la casa de Dios. Es un ultraje que se hace a Dios.

El templo es un lugar a donde venimos para humillarnos, conseguir perdón y misericordia, y si faltamos de respeto, salimos del templo mas culpables, y hallamos nuestra condenación a donde habíamos debido hallar gracia. Su respeto rendirá nuestros templos respetables a todos.[15]

Décimo Domingo después de Pentecostés

"Todo hombre que se ensalza será humillado y él que se humilla será ensalzado." Lucas 18.14 [todo = 9-14]

Antes de considerar la oración del Fariseo y del publicano, oración, tan diferente una de otra, veremos primero a quien nuestro Señor dirigió esta parábola. La dijo, según refiere el evangelio, a cierta clase de gente que se tenían como justos viviendo muy satisfechos de sí mismos, y al mismo tiempo despreciaban a los demás.

1° Esta confianza, seguridad en nosotros mismos es opuesta a la confianza que hemos de tener en Dios, a su temor y al respeto que le debemos. Esta confianza tiene su origen de la soberbia y es incompatible con la humildad. Los que están en tal disposición no pueden hacer una oración agradable a Dios, porque se presentan delante de Dios con esta propia confianza, con esta buena opinión de sí mismos, y piden la gracia de Dios no como una gracia pero mas bien como una deuda.[16]

2° Se tenían como justos. Muchos se caen en este defecto. Como unos pretendidos justos que delante de Dios tienen demasiado motivos para aludir de su justicia, como algunos pecadores cuyos desordenes y ofensas no son conocidos de los hombres. Cuantos vienen delante de Dios en su templo con una familiaridad, una confianza, una soberbia, que escandalizan a los hombres y provocan

A word about respect for our churches – "My house is a house of prayer, but you have turned it into a den of thieves" [Luke 19.46]. Here we see how criminal is the lack of respect for God's house. It is an outrage against God.

The church is a place where we come to humble ourselves, to seek pardon and mercy; and if we lack respect, we emerge from church more guilty, and achieve our condemnation where we should have found grace. Your respectful behavior would render our churches respectable to all.[15]

L102 – Tenth Sunday after Pentecost, 24 July 1853, Santa Fe; about 1050 words on Luke 18.9-14; from the Loretto Archives.

Tenth Sunday after Pentecost

"Everyone that exalteth himself shall be humbled, and he that humbleth himself shall be exalted." Luke 18.14.

Before considering the prayer of the Pharisee and that of the publican, a prayer so different one from the other, let us look first at those to whom our Lord directed this parable. He spoke it, as the gospel tells us, to persons of a certain sort who held themselves just, living very satisfied with themselves and at the same time disdaining others.

1. This confidence and security in ourselves is contrary to the confidence we ought to have in God, the fear of him and the respect we owe him. This [false] confidence arises from pride and is incompatible with humility. No persons with this attitude can make a prayer acceptable by God, for they present themselves before God with this self-confidence, this good opinion of themselves, and they ask for God's grace not as a grace but rather as something he owes them.[16]

2. They think themselves just. Many fall into this defect like many self-styled just men who have plenty of reason to refer to their justice in God's presence, like some sinners whose disorders and offenses are unknown to others. How many of them come before God in his temple with a familiarity, a confidence, a pride that scandal-

a Dios. Cualesquiera que seamos, la fe nos enseña que delante de
Dios somos todos pecadores, y si queremos que Dios oiga nuestras
oraciones, hemos de ser convencidos de nuestra indignidad. /
3° Despreciaban a los demás como siendo bajo de ellos, indignos
de ser comparados a ellos mismos. Puede ser que el amor propio no
nos permitirá de ver este vicio, pero a la menos hemos de conocerlo
en sus efectos que son el despreciar al prójimo. No hubiera lugar en
nuestras almas para tal disposición si quisiéramos practicar lo que
recomendaba San Pablo a las Filipenses 2.3, "Nada hagáis por porfía
ni por gloria, sino con humildad, teniendo cada uno por superiores
a los otros."

Tal era la clase de gente a quienes Jesucristo dijo esta parábola:
"Dos hombres subieron al templo a orar, el uno Fariseo," quiere decir
perteneciente a una clase de gente que pretenden ser mas rigurosos
observadores de la ley, que los demás, "y el otro publicano,"
perteneciente a una clase de gente generalmente conocidos por sus
desordenes y mala conducta. Estos dos hombres de una profesión
tan diferente se hallaron al mismo tiempo en el templo. Quien no se
hubiera figurado que el Fariseo, siendo tan exacto, tan escrupuloso,
iba a hacer una oración la mas sublime y aceptable a Dios, digna de
ser propuesta por modelo, mientras que el publicano, poco instruido
en la ley de Dios, haría una oración que Dios no pudiera oír; pero
sucedió todo el contrario. Eso nos debería aguardar con la humildad,
y prevenirnos para no juzgar de nadie.

La oración del Fariseo: él se prefiere a todos, se considera mejor
que todos. El Fariseo estando en pie así él oraba para significar la
confianza que tenía en sí mismo y la ostentación que él lleva en la
casa de Dios. No oraba de rodillas, eso era / bueno para los demás
de los hombres, que eran pecadores.[17] El en su opinión no tenía
pecados, por eso no era menester de tomar una postura humillante.
El agradecimiento forma seguramente una parte de la oración, pero
esta gratitud debería ser fundada sobre nuestra indignidad; también
debería ser acompañado con el sentimiento de no haber
correspondido con los beneficios recibidos. A mas de eso debería ser
dirigido a la gloria de Dios y no a la nuestra, debería terminar en el
amor de Dios y del prójimo y no al amor propio y al desprecio del

izes men and provokes God. Whoever we might be, our faith teaches us that before God we are all sinners and if we want God to listen to our prayers, we must be convinced of our unworthiness. /

3. They looked down on the rest of men as below them, unworthy of being compared with themselves. It could be that self-love does not allow us to see this vice, but we ought at least to know it in its effect, which is to belittle others. There should be no room in our souls for such an attitude if we wish to practice what Saint Paul recommends to the Philippians (2.3), "Let nothing be done through contention or for glory, but in humility, let each one hold other as his betters."

Such was the sort of person to whom Jesus Christ told this parable. "Two men went up to the temple to pray, the one a Pharisee" – that is to say, belonging to a class of persons who pretend to be more rigorous observers of the law than the rest – "and the other a publican," belonging to a class of persons widely known for their disorders and bad conduct. These two men, each of a profession vastly different from that of the other, found themselves in the temple at the same time. Who would not think that the Pharisee, being so precise, so scrupulous, would go on to pray a prayer so very sublime and acceptable to God, worthy of being offered as a model, while the publican, only slightly acquainted with God's law, would pray a prayer which God would never listen to; but it turned out the exact opposite. This fact ought to safeguard us in humility and keep us from judging anyone.

The Pharisee's prayer: he set himself ahead of all other persons, he considers himself better than all the rest. The Pharisee, standing upright, prays so as to express his confidence in himself and the showy manner he brings into God's house. He does not kneel to pray; that might have been / good enough for the rest of men, who were sinners.[17] In his opinion, he had no sins, and therefore there was no need to adopt a humble posture. Gratitude certainly formed part of his prayer, but this gratitude ought to be based on our unworthiness; further, it ought to accompany the attitude of not having cooperated with the benefits received. Further yet, it ought to be directed to the glory of God and not our own glory, it ought to issue

prójimo. "Oh Dios, gracias te doy que no soy como los otros hombres, robadores, injustos, adúlteros." Si no tomemos la obligación por nuestro oficio de corregir las faltas de los otros, debemos huir este vicio que es demasiado común de censurar la conducta del prójimo.[18] Cuando deseamos compararnos con otros, debería ser con los santos que la Iglesia de Dios honra o con los buenos y ejemplares Cristiano que viven entre nosotros. Entonces lejos de despreciar a los demás, nos veremos obligados de humillarnos siendo tan inferiores a ellos en virtud. A la vista de los escándalos del mundo hemos de pedir perdón a Dios por los infelices pecadores, que Dios les dé tiempo para arrepentirse, y también que su gracia nunca nos desamparé para que no tengamos la desgracia de caer en el mismo estado. El Fariseo da gracia a Dios porque no es como el publicano. El orgullo no perdona a nadie. Él juzga a todos, a los mismos que se humillan delante de Dios en su templo / y que muchas veces consiguen misericordia o por su arrepentimiento y su humildad. La fe nos enseña que la oración es pedir a Dios algún favor, reconocer nuestra dependencia, pero que pide el Fariseo? Qué gracia por si mismo, por sus amigos, por otros? No hace otra cosa que tomar complacencia en sus pretendidas virtudes y despreciar al prójimo.

Que diferente la oración del publicano! Que modelo para los Cristianos. El lugar que ocupa, estando lejos, cuando entramos en la Iglesia de Dios, si no nos quedamos lejos cerca de la puerta, a lo menos es necesario de llevar el mas grande respeto por la divina majestad en su templo. No osaba ni aun alzar los ojos al cielo. Que humildad, que respeto por la casa de Dios! Cuan pocos Cristianos se conducen en el templo con la misma humildad y respeto. En lugar de tener los ojos abajo están mirando todo al rededor de si, volteando la cabeza por todos lados, en fin tomando mas libertad que tomarían en presencia de una persona que respetarán. El publicano hería su pecho diciendo, "Dios mío, muéstrate propicio a mí que soy pecador." Esta disposición de humildad, de sincero arrepentimiento, le mereció de conseguir perdón y misericordia, porque la sentencia de nuestro Señor sea de quedarse verdadera, "El que se humilla será ensalzado." Si nos presentamos delante de Dios con la misma disposición del publicano, conseguiremos todavía misericordia y perdón.

into the love of God and of neighbor and not into self-love and scorning our neighbor: "Oh God, I give thee thanks that I am not as the rest of men, extortioners, unjust, adulterers." If we have not been given the duty by some office we have of correcting the faults of others, we ought to flee this vice, altogether too common, of censuring the conduct of our neighbor.[18] When we wish to compare ourselves with others, it ought to be with the saints whom God's Church honors or with the good, exemplary Christians who live among us. Then far from belittling the rest, we should humble ourselves as being inferior to them in virtue. In view of the scandals of the world we ought to ask pardon of God for the unhappy sinners, that God will give them time to repent and also that his grace will never abandon us so that we will not have the misfortune of falling into the same condition. The Pharisee gives thanks to God because he is not like the publican. Pride pardons no one. He judges all, he judges the very men who humble themselves before God in his temple / and who oftentimes obtain mercy either for their repentance or their humility. Our faith teaches us that prayer means asking some favor of God and acknowledging our dependence, but what does the Pharisee ask? What gift for himself, for his friends, for others? He does nothing but congratulate himself for his pretended virtues and demean his neighbor.

How different the prayer of the publican! What a model for Christians. He stands far off. When we enter the Church of God, if we do not stay far off near the door, at least we must possess a great respect for the divine majesty in his temple. He did not dare to raise his eyes to heaven. What humility, what reverence for God's house! How few Christians comport themselves in church with the same humility and reverence? Rather than keep their eyes down, they gawk at everything around them, turning their heads from side to side, and in short taking more liberty than they would take in the presence of a person they respect. The publican struck his breast, saying, "My God, show yourself merciful to me, a sinner." This attitude of humility, of sincere repentance, merits for him pardon and mercy, for the maxim of the Lord still remains true, "Whoever humbleth himself shall be exalted." If we present ourselves before God with the same

Domingo Veintiuno después de Pentecostés

"El rey quiso entrar en cuentas con sus siervos." Mateo 18.23 [todo = 23-35].

La parábola que nos propone nuestro Señor Jesucristo en este evangelio es para acordarnos que Dios nos pedirá cuenta a cada uno de nosotros por todos beneficios y gracias que hemos recibido de su bondad y misericordia. No seamos tan ciegos como los impíos y los infieles que piensan [que] no cuida Dios de lo que hacen. Todos toman cuentas a sus mayordomos, se las forman según los recibos, y no les abonarán los que hayan gastado contra sus ordenes y con ofensa de sus dueños. Dios nos pedirá razón de todo lo que nos ha dado. Contados tiene nuestros cabellos, y hasta de una palabra ociosa nos ha de pedir razón. Ahora es el tiempo de misericordia; la oportunidad es muy favorable para entrar en cuenta con Dios. El siervo que le debía diez mil talentos a su amo no teniendo con que pagarlo recibió el perdón de su deuda por haber rogado a su señor. Debemos mucho a Dios, todos somos pecadores, y no el pecado mas leve podemos pagar sino a costa del fiador. "Mas luego que salió aquel siervo, hallo a uno de sus consiervos, que le debía cien denarios y trabando de él le quería ahogar, diciendo, 'Paga lo que me debes.' Y arrodillandose a sus pies su compañero le rogaba diciendo, 'Ten un poco de paciencia, y todo te lo pagaré.' Mas él no quiso, que fue y le hizo poner en la cárcel hasta que pagase lo que debía."

Este primer siervo del cual se había compadecido su señor y le había dejado / libre, tenía muy buena ocasión de hacer digno del perdón que él había recibido remitiendo el mismo lo que le debía otro. ¿Y que era esta deuda en comparación de la que le habían perdonado a el? Que eran cien denarios con diez mil talentos que le había perdonado su señor? Y que son las deudas que nos debe el

disposition the publican had, we will always receive mercy and pardon.

L107 – Twenty-First Sunday after Pentecost, 9 October 1853, Santa Fe; about 1150 words about Matthew 18.23-35; from the Loretto Archives.

Twenty-First Sunday after Pentecost

"The king wished to settle accounts with his servants." Matthew 18.23.

The parable our Lord Jesus Christ proposes to us in this gospel lets us know that God will demand an account from each of us for all the blessings and graces we have received from his goodness and mercy. We should not be blind like the ungodly and the faithless who think that God keeps no account of what they do. All men settle accounts with their managers, they arrange things according to the receipts, and they do not reward those who have spent money against orders and thus harmed their masters. God will ask us to explain everything he has given us. He has counted the hairs of our head, and he will even require an explanation for some thoughtless word we have uttered. It would be best for us to settle up now in the time of mercy; the moment is very favorable to come to terms with God. The servant who owed his master ten thousand talents, not having anything to pay him with, received pardon for his debt because he asked his lord. We owe God a great deal, all of us are sinners, and we cannot even pay off the least sin except at the cost of the surety [Christ]. "But as the servant went out, he met one of his fellow slaves who owed him a hundred denarii, and laying hold of him he throttled him and said, 'Pay what thou owest.' And his companion, falling at his feet, begged him, saying, 'Have a little patience and I will pay you all.' But he would not, and he went and had him put in jail until he paid what he owed."

This first servant, whom his lord had pitied and set / free, had a perfect opportunity to be worthy of the pardon he had received by remitting what the other man owed him. And what was that debt in comparison with what had been forgiven him? What was a hun-

prójimo por las faltas que hubiera tenido hacer nosotros por las injurias o perjuicios que nos hubiera hecho, si las comparemos eso con los pecados que hemos cometido contra Dios? Le debemos a Dios mas de diez mil talentos, él nos ha perdonado, y nos perdonaré si perdonaremos de corazón al nuestro hermano, al prójimo. La crueldad con que este siervo trato a su compañero nos hace horror, nos indigna, pero examinémonos con imparcialidad y veremos que hemos tratado al prójimo, a nuestros hermanos con el mismo rigor. Despreciamos sus excusas, sus súplicas, y no nos paramos hasta que hemos tomado venganza por algunas pretendidas faltas e injurias, pero que va [a] suceder? "Viendo los otros siervos sus compañeros lo que pasaba, se entristecieron mucho y fueron a contar a su señor todo lo que había pasado." Dios no ha menester que nadie le venga a contar lo que ha sucedido. El mira todas las cosas y tiene compasión de las lágrimas que derraman los pobres oprimidos, pero la indignación de los santos y de los ángeles en el cielo, los suspiros y gemidos de los justos en la tierra solicitan la venganza del cielo, [para] que aprenda el Cristiano duro y sin misericordia que la justicia de Dios no faltará de caer sobre el, pronto o tarde, y con tanta mas severidad que se habrá dilatado mas a castigarle: / "Entonces le llamó su señor, y le dijo, 'Siervo malo, toda la deuda te perdoné porque me lo rogaste.'" Cuando Dios nos llamará y mandara sus ordenes para que nos presentemos en su presencia, no habrá quien podrá resistir. Ricos, poderosos, reyes, presidentes, maestros del mundo, Dios os llama, no de esta voz de gracia y misericordia, por la cual os llamo a su amor, a la observancia de sus leyes, y que casi siempre habéis despreciado, pero por esta voz absoluta que todos han de obedecer. Que se presenten delante de su Criador para darle cuenta de su conducta. Nos conducimos siempre como no teniendo maestro sobre nosotros que no pedirá cuenta de todas nuestras acciones? ¿Viviremos siempre como si nunca hubiéramos de morir? ¿Qué responderemos a nuestro Señor cuando él nos llamará y nos dirá, "Siervo malo, todo te he perdonado, porque me lo rogaste, pues no debías tu también tener compasión de tu compañero así como yo la tuve de ti? Yo, tu Señor y tu Dios, te he perdonado a ti, mi criatura y mi siervo, ofensas atroces y sin numero, y tu no has querido perdonar

dred denarii against the ten thousand talents his lord had written off? And what are the debts our neighbor owes us for the faults he has committed against us, for the injuries or damages he has done us, if we compare them with the sins we have committed against God? We owe God more than ten thousand talents, he has pardoned us, and he will pardon us if we pardon our brother, our neighbor, from the heart. The cruelty with which this servant treated his companion horrifies and angers us, but let us examine ourselves candidly and we will see how we have treated our neighbor, our brethren, with the same rigidity. We dismiss their excuses, their pleas, and we do not stop until we have taken vengeance for some pretended faults and injuries, but what will happen? "The other servants, their fellows, seeing what was done, were very much grieved and went and told the lord all that was done." God has no need for anyone to come tell him what goes on. He sees everything and takes compassion on the tears the poor and oppressed shed, but the indignation of the saints and the angels in heaven, the sighs and groans of the just on earth call down vengeance from heaven so that the hard and merciless Christian might think that the justice of God will not [sic] fail to fall on him sooner or later, and with more severity the longer it has delayed in punishing him? / "Then his lord summoned him and said to him, 'Wicked servant, I pardoned thee all the debt because thou besoughtest me.'" When God calls us and sends his summons that we appear in his presence, no one will be able to resist. The rich, the powerful, kings, presidents, rulers of the world – God calls you, not with the gracious and merciful voice with which he calls us to his love and to the observance of his laws, the voice we have nearly always disdained, but with the absolute voice which all men must obey, that they must present themselves before their Creator to give an account of their conduct. We continually behave as if there were no master over us who will demand an accounting of all our actions. Will we live always as if we never had to die? What will we reply to our Lord when he calls us and says to us, "Wicked servant, I have pardoned you everything because you pleaded with me, but should you not also have had pity on your companion as I had pity on you? I, your Lord and your God, have

a tu hermano una falta muy leve. Yo porque me rogaste y arremetiste te he vuelto a dar mi amistad, mis gracias, y tu has despreciado con dureza la oración y las suplicas de tu hermano y has llevado contra él un odio mortal. Yo tu Criador he tenido compasión de ti, he sobrellevado tus defectos, imperfecciones en mi servicio, he excusado tu inconstancia, tus faltas de todas clases, y tu no has querido pasar nada en otro que estaba a mi servicio como tu, mas bien te has tenido por ofendido en las mas de sus acciones / y enojado su señor le hizo entregar a los atormentadores hasta que pagase todo lo que debía." Hemos de entender que es Dios mismo que se enoja, que los ministros de su justicia son los demonios, que el suplicio es el fuego del infierno y que el plazo del pago es una eternidad que no tiene fin.

Del mismo modo concluye nuestro Señor, "Hará también con vosotros mi Padre celestial, si cada uno de vosotros no perdonaré de corazón a su hermano." Oh que consolación, que fondo de misericordia para los pecadores si supieron aprovecharlo.

¿Señor, podré tratar a mis hermanos con dureza, después de haber experimentado de parte vuestra la indulgencia la mas excesiva? Dios mío, Usted me perdona las mas grandes culpas, me las perdona enteramente sin sentimiento ninguno, y sería yo inexorable por las mas ligeras faltas que [se] cometen contra mí? ¿Pretendería dispensarme de las deberes de caridad que me habría impuesto para con el prójimo, para con mis hermanos? No, Señor, lejos de mi tal injusticia. En adelante me acordaré que bienaventurados son los misericordes porque ellos hallaron misericordia [Mateo 5.7]. En adelante arrancaré de mi corazón todo y cualquier sentimiento contra el prójimo, para que mi Juez supremo no tenga ningún sentimiento contra mi. Así tendremos derecho de poder esperar misericordia de Dios.

Escuela de la niñas … De los muchachos. Every other Sunday there will [be] instruction in English in the Sisters' chapel at 4 in the evening.

pardoned you, my creature and servant, of awful offenses beyond number, and you did not wish to pardon your brother a trivial fault. Because you pleaded and went down on your knees, I have given you again my friendship, my favors, and you have harshly disdained the prayer and pleading of your brother and bent a mortal hatred against him. I your Creator have had compassion on you, have borne your defects and imperfection in my service, have excused your wavering, your faults of all sorts, and you have not chosen to let anything pass in another man who is in my service as you are, but rather you have remained offended beyond what his actions warrant," / and enraged, his lord ordered him handed over to the torturers until he paid off everything he owed. We are meant to understand that it is God himself who is enraged, that those ministers of his justice are the demons, that the punishment is the fire of hell, and that the term of the sentence is an endless eternity.

In the same way, our Lord concludes, "My heavenly Father will do the same with you if each one of your does not pardon his brother from the heart." Oh what a consolation, what a depth of mercy, for sinners – if they knew how to profit by this.

Lord, will I be able to treat my brethren harshly after having experienced from you the greatest forgiveness? My God, pardon my greatest sins, pardon me entirely and without holding a grudge, and will I be uncompromising about the slight faults committed against me? Would I tend to excuse myself from the duties of charity imposed on me toward my neighbor, toward my brethren? No, Lord, far be such injustice from me. Henceforth I will recall how blessed the merciful are, for they found mercy [Matthew 5.7]. Henceforth I will root out from my heart each and every feeling against my neighbor so that my supreme Judge might hold no such feeling against me. Thus we will have the right to expect mercy from God.

Girls' school ... Boys'. Every other Sunday there will be instruction in English in the Sisters' chapel at 4 in the evening.

Domingo 24 [y último] después de Pentecostés

El Juicio: "Entonces verán venir al Hijo del Hombre sobre las nubes resplandecientes del cielo con gran poder y majestad." Mateo 24.30. [todo = 15.35]

1° La Venida del Juez. Pasado el tiempo que Dios tiene señalado para la duración de este mundo, y después de muchas señales y presagios horribles que harán a los hombres secarse de espanto y de temor, vendrá el Juez soberano con gran poder y majestad. El será rodeado de sus ángeles que llevarán delante de si su cruz como estandarte de gracia para los buenos y de rigor para los malos. Que diferencia de su última venida con su primera aparición, cuando se encarnó. Vino entonces con la mas grande mansedumbre y humildad, pues venia en aquel tiempo para redimirnos por su misericordia, sin ninguna señal de poder y de terror. Pero en su segunda venida, ha de llegar para vengar sus derechos, para dar a cada uno según sus méritos. Ahora en este mundo se hace la justicia muy raras veces. Los hombres se quedan sujetas a tantos errores, tantas pasiones, que es muy difícil que cada uno pueda conseguir su derecho; ni tampoco la justicia humana puede alcanzar todos los crímenes, todas las infracciones de la ley. Pero Dios en el último juicio pondrá todas las cosas en orden, y hará justicia a todos.

2° La Separación de los Buenos y los Malos. En fuerza del decreto de este soberano Juez que se ejecutará al instante, serán separados los buenos de los malos, poniendo los unos a su derecha y los otros a su izquierda. Separación eterna, después de la cual jamás podrán volverse juntas estas dos compañías. / Hecho esta separación, se abrirán los libros de las conciencias, y se verá claramente la malicia de los malos, y el desprecio que hicieron de Dios; y por otra parte la penitencia de los buenos y los efectos de la divina gracia que recibieron. Nada quedará oculto. ¡O Dios, que confusión para los unos y que consuelo para los otros! ¿En cual de estas dos compañías esperamos hallarnos en aquel último día? Tenemos ahora el poder

L112 – Twenty-Fourth and Last Sunday after Pentecost, 20 November 1853, Santa Fe; about 1020 words on the General Judgment as narrated by Matthew 24.15-35; from the Loretto Archives.

Twenty-fourth [and Last] Sunday after Pentecost

The Judgement: "And then they shall see the Son of Man coming on the shining clouds of heaven with great power and majesty." Matthew 24.30.

1. The Coming of the Judge. When the time that God has marked out for the duration of this world has passed, and after many signs and horrible omens that will make men shrivel with shock and fear, the supreme Judge will come with great power and majesty. He will be surrounded by his angels who will bear his cross before him like the banner of grace for the good and of rigor for the evil. What a difference between his final coming and his first appearance, when he became incarnate. Then he came with extreme meekness and humility, for he came at that time to redeem us by his mercy, with no least sign of power or terror. But in his second coming, he must come to vindicate his rights, to give to each according to his merits. Today in this world justice is seldom done. Men are subject to so many mistakes and so many emotions that it is very hard for each to follow the right, nor can human justice pursue all crimes, all infractions of the law. But God at the last judgment will put all things in order and do justice to all.

2. The Separation of the Good and the Evil. By means of a decree of this sovereign Judge which will take effect in an instant, the good will be separated from the evil, the former put on his right and the latter on his left – a perpetual division, after which the two groups will never rejoin again. / Once this separation happens, the books of conscience will open and the malice of evil men and the disdain they had toward God will appear clearly, as on the other hand will the penitence of the good and the effects of divine grace they received. Nothing will remain hidden. O God, what consternation to those, what consolation to these! In which of these two groups do we expect to find ourselves on that last day? We have today the power to choose between the two, living faithful to God's law, keep-

de escoger entre estas dos compañías, viviendo fieles a la ley de Dios, separándonos de los vicios, de los escándalos del mundo, nos aseguraremos la compañía de los buenos. Pero que sentimientos tendrán los réprobos en esta ocasión cuando verán a los pobres de espíritu, que ellos despreciaron tanto en esta vida, ahora honrados y exaltados? El Espíritu de Dios en el libro de la Sabiduría (5.2-6) nos dice de los malos, de los réprobos que "A vista de esto ellos se llenarán de turbación, y de un horrible terror. … Se dirán a sí mismos, arrepentidos y suspirando por la angustia de su corazón, Estos son a los que tuvimos en otro tiempo por objeto de nuestros escarnios. … Nosotros insensatos considerábamos su vida como una locura. Sin embargo he los aquí ensalzados entre los hijos de Dios, no extraviemos pues del camino de la verdad."

3° Este gran juicio será concluido por una sentencia definitiva por la cual los justos serán llamados a la posesión del reino de Dios y los réprobos condenados al fuego eterno.

Escuchad, hermanos míos, la invitación amable con que nuestro Señor llamará a todos sus siervos fieles, a sus amigos, a sus verdaderos discípulos a la posesión de su eterna felicidad. "Venid," les dirá el Juez / soberano, "benditos de mi Padre, poseed el reino que os está preparado desde la constitución del mundo."

¿Qué va suceder con los réprobos cuando habrán sido separados y puestos a la izquierda del Juez soberano? ¿No habrá alguna misericordia por ellos? Se olvidará el Criador de las obras de sus manos? No, no habrá ninguna misericordia por ellos. Ha pasado el tiempo del perdón, ahora ha llegado el lugar de la justicia. Dios recompensará a los justos de una manera digna de Dios, y castigará a los réprobos de una manera digna de Dios, con un castigo eterno. Dios no se olvidará de las obras de sus manos, el tendrá bien presente los beneficios que ha concedido a los pecadores, y el desprecio que ellos han hecho de su Criador y de su ley. El no se olvidará de la malicia, de la rebelión de los malos: "Id, malditos," les dirá "al fuego eterno que está preparado para el demonio y sus compañeros. Lejos de mí, apártense de mi para siempre, de la felicidad de mi reino: el lugar que habéis preferido antes de mi paraíso os [vais a] recibir. Les ha gustado mas de servir al demonio que a su Dios, pues seréis

ing ourselves from vice, from the world's scandals, we will assure ourselves of the companionship of the good. But how will the reprobates feel on that occasion when they see the poor in spirit, whom they so despised on earth, now honored and exalted? The Spirit of God in the Book of Wisdom (5.2-6) tells us of bad men, the reprobates who "seeing it, shall be filled with dismay, with a terrible fear. … They shall say to themselves, repenting and sighing in the anguish of their heart, 'These are they whom we held at that time as objects of our scorn. … We fools esteemed their life as madness. Nevertheless, behold them exalted among the children of God; … therefore we have erred from the way of the truth.'"

3. This great judgment will conclude with a definitive sentence by which the just will be invited to possess the kingdom of God and the damned will be condemned to everlasting fire.

O my brethren, listen to the loving invitation with which our Lord will call all his faithful servants, his friends, his true disciples to the possession of eternal happiness. "Come," the supreme Judge will / say to them, "ye blessed of my Father, possess the kingdom prepared for you from the foundation of the world."

What will become of the wicked when they have been separated and placed at the supreme Judge's left? Will he not have mercy on them? Will the Creator forget the works of his hands? No, he will have no mercy on them. The time for pardon has passed; now the time for justice has arrived. God will reward the good in a manner worthy of him, and he will chastise the wicked in a manner worthy of him, with everlasting punishment. God will never forget the works of his hands; he will be totally aware of the benefits he has given to sinners and of the disdain they have shown their Creator and his law. He will not forget the hatred, the rebellion of the evil: "Depart from me, you accursed," he will say to them, "into everlasting fire which was prepared for the devil and his angels" [Matthew 25.41]. Far from me, leave me forever and the happiness of my kingdom; the place you preferred to my paradise is going to receive you. Serving the demon pleased you more than serving your God, so you will be his companions. Go far from me; yes, you will carry God's curse forever. I would have wished to give you my blessing, my

compañeros de demonio. Iréis lejos de mí, si llevaréis para siempre
la maldición de Dios. Yo hubiera querido daros mi bendición, mis
gracias, mis favores, mi cielo, mi felicidad; se los ofrecí todos los días
de vuestra vida; hubierais podido aseguraros mi gloria, mis riquezas,
con unas condiciones muy fáciles. / No habéis querido, siempre os
rehusasteis. Una maldición habéis preferido, una maldición eterna
recibiréis, una maldición sobre vuestros ojos pues nunca verán la
luz del cielo, una maldición sobre el sentido de vuestro oído pues no
oiréis otra cosa que las blasfemias y los gritos de los réprobos, una
maldición sobre vuestro gusto que será afectado con la amargura la
mas insoportable."[19]

Ponderad bien estas palabras que denotan el abandono perpetuo
de Dios con que arroja para siempre de su vista a estos infelices. Les
echa su maldición que comprende a todos los males, maldición irrevocable que se extiende a todos los tiempos y a la eternidad.

?Como no temblaremos con la memoria de esta sentencia terrible? ?Quien podrá darnos seguridad en aquel día en que las
columnas del cielo tiemblan de espanto?[20] Lo que hemos de hacer
es de detestar nuestros pecados, pues solo ellos pueden perdernos
en este día horroroso. Hemos de juzgarnos a nosotros mismos ahora
para no ser juzgados, examinar nuestra conciencia, condenarnos,
acusarnos, enmendarnos para que el Juez soberano no nos condene
en aquel día terrible; antes bien merezcamos de oír estas palabras de
consuelo, "Venid, benditos de mi Padre, poseed el reino que os está
preparado desde la constitución del mundo."

La Natividad

"Y esta os será por señal: hallaréis al Niño envuelto en pañales
y echado en un pesebre." Lucas 2.12. [todo = 1-14]

Tal fue la señal que dio el ángel a los pastores para conocer al

graces, my favors, my heaven, my happiness. I offered it to you every day of your life; you could have attained my glory, my riches, by means of easy conditions. / You did not want it, you always refused it. You have preferred a curse, you have received a curse everlasting, a curse on your eyes never to see the light of heaven, a curse on the hearing of your ears never to hear anything but the blasphemies and shouts of the wicked, a curse on your taste which will be afflicted with the most unbearable bitterness."[19]

Ponder these words well which denote God's perpetual abandonment with which he dismisses forever the very sight of these unhappy beings. He inflicts his curse, which carries with it all evils, an irrevocable malediction which reaches through all time and unto eternity.

How could we not tremble at the recollection of this horrifying sentence? Who can offer us assurance on that day when the pillars of heaven tremble with horror?[20] What we must do is to detest our sins, for they alone can doom us on that terrible day. We must judge ourselves now so that we will not be judged then, examine our conscience, condemn ourselves, accuse ourselves, change ourselves for the better so that the supreme Judge will not condemn us on that terrible day. Instead, we will be worthy to hear these consoling words, "Come, ye blessed of my Father, possess the kingdom prepared for you from the foundation of the world."

L137 – Christmas, Friday 25 December 1857, Santa Fe; about 1000 words on Luke 2.1-14 and Titus 2.11-15, the gospel and epistle for midnight Mass; from the Loretto Archives. I find most interesting the statement "If he became man it is with the goal of making us participate in the divine nature," which richly echoes the Greek Orthodox notion of human participation in the very being of the Divine.

The Nativity

"And this shall be a sign unto you: you shall find the infant wrapped in swaddling clothes and laid in a manger." Luke 2.12.

Such was the sign the angel gave to the shepherds so they would

Hijo de Dios hecho hombre por nosotros, señal de humildad para que entendiésemos que todo es humildad en este misterio. Por falta de hallar posada, su santísima madre tiene que reclinar a su Hijo divino en un pesebre sobre un poco de paja; unos pobres paños mas corrientes es todo lo que puede hallar esta tierna madre para envolver al Hijo que ella adora y que ha de ser adorado en el cielo y en la tierra. ¿Qué clase de comodidad es esta en el invierno, en una noche tan fría?

Así hemos de ver en este misterio una naturaleza semejante a la nuestra, enfermedades como las nuestras, fuera de pecado, una pobreza mas grande que la nuestra, mas dura. Pues ¿cuál de entre los mas pobre ha nacido en un pesebre? cuál es la madre por pobre que sea que dará a sus hijos un pesebre por cuna? qué no tendrá hasta los mas infelices alguna clase de cuero, o de colchón, o cobija para el uso y la comodidad de su recién nacido. / Solo nuestro Señor se ve desamarrado con tal extremo, y es con tamaña pobreza que quiere ser reconocido.

O si él hubiese querido servirse de su poder, no le hubiera igualdad ninguna pompa del mundo. Pero siendo la gloria del mundo una gloria prestada, un brillante falso, y mas bien un obstáculo para nuestra salvación, nuestro Señor Jesucristo lo ha despreciado todo desde su nacimiento. Viene al mundo en el estado el mas débil, como un niño, pero su nombre es Admirable, El Dios Fuerte. Si él se humilla tanto es por el objeto de levantarnos, si se hace hombre es con el fin de hacernos participar a la naturaleza divina.[21] No es bastante de reconocer este misterio de la encarnación del Hijo de Dios, pero hemos de adorarlo con todo el reconocimiento debido y para conseguir las disposiciones necesarias para celebrar con fruto la memoria de una solemnidad tan grande. Entraremos en espíritu en el establo de Belén, pidiendo a María santísima que nos comunique una parte de los sentimientos de adoración, respecto, amor y devoción que le animaban su santa alma cuando dio luz a su divino Hijo, que salió de su / seno virginal como un rayo del sol por un milagro mas grande que el de su concepción por el Espíritu Santo.

know the Son of God made man for our sakes, a sign of humility so we might understand that everything in this mystery is humility. For want of a place to stay, his most holy mother has to lay her divine Son in a manger upon a little bit of straw. A few poor pieces of very ordinary cloth are all that this tender mother had to wrap the Son whom she adores and who must be adored in heaven and on earth. What sort of comfort is this in the wintertime, on so cold a night?

So we must see in this mystery a nature like our own, ailments like ours (except for sin), a poverty greater than ours, and harder. For who from among the poor has been born in a stable? What mother however poor she might be who will give her children a manger for a cradle, who even among the most unfortunate would not have some sort of sheepskin or mattress or blanket for the use and comfort of her new-born? / Only our Lord was unprovided for to such an extreme, and it is so great a poverty that it ought to be acknowledged.

O if he has wished to treat himself according to his power, no extravagance in the whole world would have equaled it. But since the world's glory is a borrowed glory, a fake gem, and more to the point a hindrance to our salvation, our Lord Jesus Christ has disdained all of it from his birth. He comes into this world in a condition of weakness, as a mere baby, though his name is "Admirable," "The Omnipotent God." If he humbles himself, it is merely to lift us up; if he becomes man it is with the goal of making us participate in the divine nature.[21] It is not enough to acknowledge this mystery of the incarnation of the Son of God, for we ought adore him with all due recognition; and so as to achieve the attitudes necessary for celebrating profitably the memory of a solemnity so great, let us enter in spirit into the stable at Bethlehem, asking Mary most holy to communicate to us part of the attitudes of adoration, reverence, love, and devotion which animated her holy soul when she had borne her divine Son, who came forth from her / virginal womb like a sunbeam by a miracle greater than the miracle of her conception by the Holy Ghost.

Poniéndonos en unión también con San José, los ángeles y los pastores que tuvieron la dicha de ofrecer sus adoraciones al recién nacido "Dios nuestro Salvador, cuya gracia," según la expresó San Pablo [Tito 2.11-12], "pareció a todos los hombres, enseñándonos aquí abandonando la impiedad y los deseos mundanos, vivamos una vida sobria, justa y piadosa." Pues tal es el provecho que hemos de sacar del misterio de la encarnación del Señor. La gracia de nuestro Salvador ha sido y es ofrecida a todos los hombres. El pecado nos había hecho caer en una ignorancia terrible de nosotros mismos y de nuestro deberes, pero nuestro Señor Jesucristo viene para enseñarnos tres cosas: la primera: que hemos de renunciar a la impiedad que es la causa de que nos pongamos en el lugar de Dios, refiriendo todo a nosotros mismos, a nuestra elevación, nuestras comodidades, y pasiones en vez de referirlo todo a Dios.[22] Ese es el origen de todos nuestros pecados y es precisamente lo que hemos de renunciar. La segunda cosa que nos enseña la Verdad eterna en el misterio de hoy es que mientras dura nuestra vida mortal, hemos de usar / de los criaturas con moderación, según las reglas de la temperancia, solamente por necesidad y no para satisfacer nuestras malas inclinaciones.[23] La tercera cosa: [lo] que nos enseña Jesucristo en su nacimiento es que habiéndose hecho hombre por amor de nosotros, habiéndonos purificado de toda iniquidad, hemos de procurar nosotros ser un pueblo digno de él por la practica de las buenas obras, por la obediencia y la fidelidad a nuestras obligaciones.

Qué beneficios tan grandes nos vienen por medio de la encarnación de nuestro Señor Jesucristo como lo enseña la fe. Pues por medio de este misterio tenemos en el Hijo de Dios un hermano, semejante a nosotros. La encarnación nos da un Salvador y un médico. El hombre se hallaba perdido con miles de trabajos, él arrastraba su vida bajo el peso del pecado, pero he aquí el Señor viene para salvarnos, él se ofrece asimismo para auxiliarnos y para curarnos. El toma sobre si nuestras enfermedades [Isaías 53.4]; en la encarnación del Señor tengo un maestro y un modelo. Todo me enseña en su nacimiento, en su vida, en su muerte. Pues que nos conceda Dios ser mas dóciles a seguir las divinas máximas del recién nacido nuestro Señor Jesucristo a fin de merecer y gozar de su gloria eterna.

Uniting ourselves also with Saint Joseph, the angels, and the shepherds who had the good fortune to offer their adoration to the new-born "God our Saviour, whose favor," as Saint Paul put it [Titus 2.11-12], "has appeared to all men, here teaching us that, doing away with impiety and worldly desires, we should live a sober, just, and devout life." For such is the benefit we should derive from the mystery of the Lord's incarnation. The grace of our Saviour has been and still is offered to all men. Sin has made us fall into a terrible ignorance of ourselves and our desires, but our Lord Jesus Christ has come to teach us three things: one, that we must renounce the godlessness which is the reason that we put ourselves in the place of God, referring all things to ourselves, our exaltation, our comfort, and our desires rather than referring all things to God.[22] Self-centeredness is the source of all our sins, and it is precisely what we must reject. The second thing eternal Truth teaches us by today's mystery is that as long as our mortal life endures we ought to use / created things with moderation, according to the rules of temperance, only out of need and not to satisfy our evil inclinations.[23] Thirdly, Jesus Christ teaches us in his nativity that having become man for love of us, having purified us from all wickedness, we must try to become a people worthy of him by the practice of good works, and by obedience and faithfulness to our duties.

What great benefits come to us by means of the incarnation of our Lord Jesus Christ, as our faith teaches! By means of this mystery we possess the Son of God as our brother, like to us. The incarnation gives us a Saviour and a Physician. Man found himself lost among thousands of labors, he dragged his life along under the burden of sin, but behold the Lord comes to save us, offering his very self to help us and cure us. He takes our infirmities upon himself [Isaias 53.4]. In the incarnation of the Lord I have a master and a model; he teaches me everything in his birth, in his life, and in his death. Well, may God grant us the grace to follow with more docility the divine maxims of our new-born Lord Jesus Christ so that we will merit and enjoy his eternal glory.

Primer Día del Año [Circuncisión]

Epístola de día (Tito 2.11-12).

Es una costumbre establecida casi en todas las naciones a la ocasión del primer día de un año nuevo de desearse mutuamente prosperidades entre parientes, amigos y conocidos. Pues siendo así, me aprovecho de esta oportunidad del primer día de un año nuevo que guardamos como fiesta para consagrarla a Dios y así merecer de servirle con fidelidad los demás días del año y de toda nuestra vida. Sí, hermanos míos carísimos, me aprovecho de esta oportunidad para hablarles como un padre a sus hijos y desearles toda felicidad y prosperidad en lo temporal como en lo espiritual. Siendo nuestro santo ministerio por las cosas que miran al servicio de Dios, a la salvación de nuestra alma, hemos de decirles con el apóstol en la epístola de hoy, "La gracia de Dios ha aparecido a todos los hombres … enseñándonos a que, renunciando la impiedad y los deseos mundanos, vivamos sobria, justa y piadosamente en este siglo. Dios les conceda de / seguir estas reglas puestas por el grande apóstol. Lo que deseamos, lo que nos dará el mayor gusto es que se esfuerzan de observar fielmente estas reglas. Renunciando la impiedad, los deseos mundanos para tener una vida sobria, justa y piadosa, cumpliendo con todo eso los hijos de la Yglesia, tendríamos un cielo sobre la tierra; entonces se verían los parientes Cristianos criar, educar sus familias en el amor y temor de Dios; se verían los hijos obedecer a sus padres, honrarles y ser verdaderamente la gloria y el honor de sus parientes. No se verían aquellos escándalos que son el deshonor y el oprobio de las familias como de la sociedad. Guardándose así en los límites de la sobriedad y de la templanza, las familias y los miembros que las componen no seríamos testigos de tantas injusticias, fraudes, robos, engaños, maldades. Hubiera mas confianza entre los hombres, mas seguridad por las propiedades. Esta vida de moderación, de orden, nos merecería de Dios aquella virtud de devoción, de piedad que consiste en una inclinación un gusto grande para las cosas de Dios, para su gloria, para la salvación de nuestras almas inmortales. Al principiar este año pidamos todos a Dios que nos dé un corazón

L156 — The Circumcision of Jesus, Saturday 1 January 1859, Santa Fe; about 840 words on Titus 2.11-15; from AASF 1859 loose document # 34.

First Day of the Year [Circumcision]

Epistle of the day (Titus 2.11-12).

It is an established custom in nearly all nations on the occasion of the first day of the year to exchange wishes for prosperity among family members, friends, and acquaintances. This being the case, I take this opportunity on the first day of a new year, which we set apart as a feast day to consecrate it to God and thus deserve to serve him faithfully all the rest of the days of the year and of our whole lives. Yes, my beloved brethren, I take this opportunity to speak with you as a father to his children and to wish you all happiness and prosperity in temporal matters and in spiritual. Our holy ministry being for things that look to the service of God and to the salvation of our souls, we must say with the apostle in today's epistle, "The grace of God has appeared to all men, teaching us that by rejecting the impiety and desires of the world we may live soberly, justly, and devoutly in this age." May God grant you to / follow these rules laid down by the great apostle. What we desire, what will give us the most joy, is to make every effort to keep these rules faithfully. Renouncing godlessness, rejecting worldly desires so as to live a sober, just, and devout life, and by complying with all this, we children of the Church would build a heaven on earth; then Christian parents would find themselves raising and educating their families in the love and fear of God; children would find themselves obeying their parents, honoring them, and being truly their parents' honor and glory. There will be no scandals, which are the dishonor and the infamy of families as of society. Thus restraining themselves within the limits of sobriety and temperance, our families and we individual members who make them up would not witness such injustices, frauds, robberies, swindles, and evil deeds. There would be more confidence among men, more security of property. This life of moderation and order would merit from God the virtue of devoutness, of piety which consists in a great inclination and relish for the things of God and for his glory and for the salvation of our immortal souls.

As we begin this year, let us all ask God to give us a docile heart

dócil para seguir su santa ley, que nos guarde de orgullo, dureza y corazón impenitente que nos merecería / ira en el día de la revelación del justo juicio de Dios, él cual retribuirá a cada uno según sus obras (Romanos 2.3-6). Oh que pensamiento tan saludable al principio de este año nuevo de acordarnos de esta verdad eterna que Dios dará a cada uno lo que habrá merecido, que a los que habrán perseverado en hacer buenas obras, que habrán buscando la gloria, la honra, la inmortalidad, Dios les dará la vida eterna. Mas a los que no le rinden a la verdad pero que se entregan a la injusticia, a la iniquidad, al crimen, Dios los tratará con ira, con indignación, y los castigará por toda la eternidad. Tribulación y angustia sobre toda alma de hombre que obra mal. Así pues no hay mas que miseria para el pecador. Al contrario, gloria, honra y paz a todo [el] que hace el bien, a todos los que practican la virtud.

En la octava de la Natividad, que es hoy, celebramos también el misterio de la circuncisión del Señor. Se sujetó a este punto de la ley que era solamente para los pecadores,[24] pero fue para enseñarnos nuestra circuncisión espiritual que consiste a quitar, desechar todo lo que es malo, vicioso en nosotros, sea en nuestras palabras, acciones o pensamientos. Solamente las almas / cobardes y desagradecidas pueden rehusar de hacer esta circuncisión espiritual.

Siendo Cristianos, hemos de vivir de andar en Jesucristo según la expresión que hemos recibido, de él arraigados y sobreedificados en él y fortificados en la fe [Colosenses 2.6-7].

Pues, ¿que es vivir y andar en Jesucristo sino tomar la vida de Jesucristo por regla de la nuestra? Hablar como él hablabas, pensar como él pensaba, sufrir como él sufría, aguantar como él aguantaba, perdonar como él perdonaba, mortificarse como él se mortificaba, pues *"Cristus non sibi placuit* – él no complacía asimismo" [Romanos 15.3]. El no hacía su propia voluntad pero la de su Padre. Esto es vivir en Cristo y como Jesucristo arraigados en el, enraizado en el, pegados con el. Del mismo modo que una planta es unida y pegada con su raíz, de donde saca lo que la hace crecer lo que la hace fructificar. Creciendo en el, dice el apóstol, todo no parece difícil, y una tarea laboriosa, y lo es a la naturaleza; pero nuestro Señor, cuyo poder es igual a su bondad, cuya gracia hace todo fácil, nos dará los

to follow his holy law, to guard us from pride, cruelty, and an impenitent heart that will earn us / wrath in the day of the revelation of God's just judgment, when he will reward everyone according to his works (Romans 2.3-6). Oh what a salutary thought at the beginning of this new year to recall this eternal truth that God will give each one what he will have merited, that to all who will have persevered in doing good works and will have sought after glory, honor, and immortality, God will give everlasting life. But as for those who have never surrendered to the truth but have given themselves over to iniquity and crime, God will treat them with wrath and indignation and punish them for all eternity. Tribulation and anguish upon every human soul that works evil. So then there is nothing but misery for the sinner. By contrast, glory, honor, and peace [will come] to all who perform good works, to all who practice virtue.

Today on the octave of the Nativity, we celebrate also the mystery of the Circumcision of the Lord. He subjected himself to this point of the Law which was only for sinners[24] so as to teach us a spiritual circumcision that consists in quitting, in getting rid of whatever is evil and vicious in us, whether in our words, actions, or thoughts. Only cowardly and / ungrateful souls can refuse to undergo this circumcision of the spirit.

Being Christians, we should live by walking in Christ Jesus according to the expression we have received, in him rooted, built up in him, and confirmed in the faith [Colossians 2.6-7].

For what is it to live and walk in Christ Jesus except to take the life of Christ Jesus as a rule of our own, talking as he talked, thinking as he thought, suffering as he suffered, enduring as he endured, pardoning as he pardoned, mortifying ourselves as he mortified himself, for *"Christus non sibi placet* – he did not please himself" [Romans 15.3]. He did not do his own will but that of his Father. This it is to live in Christ and to live like Jesus Christ, established in him, rooted in him, and united with him. In the same way, a plant is attached and united to its root, from which it draws what makes it grow and what lets it bear fruit. Growing in him, says the apostle, nothing seems difficult or a tiring task, and that is according to nature; but our Lord, whose power is equal to his goodness, whose grace makes

medios y la fuerza de cumplir con estas obligaciones para seamos dignos de gozar de su gloria.

El Día de los Reyes

"Y entrando a la casa, hallaron al niño con María su madre, y postrados la adoraron, y abriendo sus cofres, le ofrecieron presentes de oro, incienso y mirra." Mateo 2.11.

En esta fiesta de la Epifanía hemos de considerar con el evangelista 1° la salida de los reyes, 2° su llegada a Jerusalem, 3° su vuelta en su patria.

1° La salida de los reyes. Llenaron mucha atención para considerar la nueva estrella y a saber lo que significaba. Muchos la vieron sin entender el misterio, y así sucede ahora que muchos por razón de su disipación [o] por falta de reflexión no conocen cuando Dios les habla por algunos acontecimientos que deberían ser para ellos como astros luminosos, las luces que Dios nos da harán nuestra condenación, si no nos aprovechamos de ellas para su servicio y nuestra salvación.

Luego los reyes conocieron la voz de Dios en esta estrella y se resolvieron a marcharse para Jerusalem con el deseo de informarse a donde podrían hallar al Rey recién nacido. Dios no nos enseña todo por si mismo, pero él nos da maestros depositarios de las Escrituras y interpretes de su verdadera sentido: nuestro deber es consultarlos. /

¿Qué ejemplos de fidelidad y de obediencia para todo que les pide Dios? No temen ni las fatigas, ni los peligros de un camino largo y penoso, no los discurso y burlas de los hombres. ¡Podemos decir que así obedecemos a Dios. Los reyes salen de su país sobre el testimonio de una estrella, mientras que por nuestra parte la palabra de Dios, su fuerza, su autoridad, su luz no pueden conseguir de nosotros el mas liviano sacrificio por nuestro Señor.

2° La llegada de los reyes a Jerusalem. Creían ellos de hallar

everything easy, will give us the means and the strength to fulfill these obligations so we may be worthy to enjoy his glory.

L119 – Epiphany, Saturday 6 January 1855, Santa Fe; about 885 words on Matthew 2.1-12; from AASF 1855 loose document # 12.

The Feast of the Kings

"And entering in to the house, they found the child with Mary his mother, and falling down they adored him, and opening their treasures, they offered him gifts, gold, frankincense, and myrrh." Matthew 2.11.

On this feast of the Epiphany we should consider with the evangelist the journey of the kings, their arrival at Jerusalem, and their return to their county.

1. The journey of the kings. They got a lot of attention through their interest in the new star and by knowing what it meant. Many people saw it without understanding the mystery, just as happens nowadays when many people, by reason of their lack of attention or by failing to reflect, do not know when God speaks to them by some events that ought to strike them like brilliant stars. The lights that God gives us will work our condemnation if we fail to profit by them unto the service of God and our own salvation.

As soon as the kings heard the voice of God in this star, they decided to get themselves to Jerusalem so they might learn where they could find the newborn King. God does not teach us everything himself, giving us instead teachers like trustees of the scriptures and interpreters of their true meaning, and our duty is to consult them. /

What examples of the fidelity and obedience that God asks of you! They weren't afraid of fatigue or of the dangers of a long, rough road or of the opinions and jests of men. Would that we could say we obeyed God like that! The kings set out from their land on the testimony of one star, while in our case the very word of God, its power, its authority, its light, cannot elicit from us the least sacrifice for our Lord.

Jerusalem llena de alegría por el nacimiento del nuevo Rey, pero ellos fueron los primeros a llevar la noticia. Lejos de tomar parte en el gozo de los reyes, Herodes y toda la ciudad se turban. Pero los santos reyes sin cuidar por la ambición del que reinaba sobre los Judíos declararon abiertamente lo que habían visto. Su intención [era] de buscar el Rey recién nacido para adorarle. Su constancia venció todos los obstáculos y dificultades. Habiendo recibido información que el Mesías había de nacer en Bethleem partieron luego para hallarle. No se pararon por el mal ejemplo de los que le enseñaban el / lugar del nacimiento de Cristo, y que no querían andar ni un paso para acompañarlos. Hemos de imitar a los santos reyes en este respecto. Cuando los que por su deber nos enseñan el camino de Dios, no quieren andar ellos mismos en este camino (no lo permita Dios) no tenemos excusa para dejar el servicio de Dios.[25]

3° La conducta de los santos reyes en Bethleem. Dios recompensó su perseverancia. Apenas había a partida de Jerusalem para Bethleem que les apareció la misma estrella, y les guía a su Salvador. Llenos de una viva fe que alumbraba su entendimiento, de un amor soberano que enardecía sus corazones, se postraron a los pies del divino recién nacido, quedándose bien recompensados con este tesoro de su viaje tan largo, y de las conveniencias que habían dejado en su tierra. Así suele Dios consolar a los que hacen algún sacrificio para ser fieles a su vocación, y corresponder a las luces y gracias que les da. "Abriendo sus cofres, le ofrecieron presentes de oro, incienso y mirra" [Mateo 2.11]. Lo que significan estos presentes .... [26] Lo que hemos de ofrecer nosotros en gratitud por nuestra vocación a la verdadera fe: oro de la caridad, del amor de Dios ... /

4° Su regreso en su patria. Una estrella les había conducido al Mesías; ahora por su fidelidad [y] obediencia merecen que Dios mismo les avise de volver por otro camino. Así también nosotros, después hallado a Dios, después de haber sido reconciliado con el, hemos de evitar la compañía de un mundo hipócrita que nos ha engañado, diciendonos que él vendrá también a adorar al Señor o servirle, mientras que en su corazón busca a destruir su santa ley. Busca a pedirle como haga el hipócrita Herodes. Hemos de tomar un camino diferente. Habíamos andado en las tinieblas, lo es preciso

2. The arrival of the kings in Jerusalem. They thought they would find Jerusalem filled with delight at the birth of their new King, but they themselves were the very first to bring the news. Far from sharing in the kings' happiness, Herod and the whole city were upset. But the holy kings, without caring about the ambition of him who reigned over the Jews, declared openly what they had seen. Their purpose was to seek out the newborn King so as to adore him. Their constancy overcame all obstacles and difficulties. Having received the information that the Messiah was to be born in Bethlehem, they set out at once to find him. They were undeterred by the bad example of the persons who told them / where the Christ was born but who didn't want to move an inch to accompany them. We ought to imitate the holy kings in this respect. When those who have a duty to do so teach us the way of God but do not wish to travel the road themselves (May God forbid it!), that is no excuse for us to abandon the service of God.[25]

3. The conduct of the holy kings in Bethlehem. God rewarded their perseverance. They had scarcely left Jerusalem headed for Bethlehem when the same star appeared to them and guided them to their Saviour. Filled with the living faith which enlightened their understanding, with a supreme love that warmed their hearts, they prostrated themselves at the feet of the divine newborn, feeling that this treasure rewarded them fully for their long journey and for the comforts they had left behind them in their own land. Thus it is that God always consoles persons who make any sacrifice so as to be faithful to their calling and to respond to the lights and graces he gives them. "Opening their treasures, they offered him gifts, gold, frankincense, and myrrh" [Matthew 2.11]. What these presents signify … .[26] What we ought to offer in gratitude for our vocation to the true faith: the gold of charity, of the love of God … /

4. Their return to their homeland. A star had led them to the Messiah; now for their fidelity and obedience, they deserve that God himself warn them to return by some other road. So it is with us: after having found God or after having been reconciled with him, we must avoid the company of a hypocritical world that has swindled us, telling us to go and adore the Lord or serve him, when

de andar en la luz. Habíamos andado en la desobediencia, es preciso de volver a la obediencia, a la fidelidad a la ley de Dios.

Estos reyes gentiles fueron las primicias de nuestra vocación a la fe, los primeras apóstoles de la religión.[27] Esta fiesta nos recuerda de esta gracia preciosa de la cual nos ha favorecido Dios con una predilección especial, aunque por nuestra indignidad hemos mirado muchas veces de perderla. Pero ahora la memoria de nuestra vocación a la fe será en adelante el motivo de nuestra gratitud la mas viva, y las máximas [y] obligaciones que no[s] imponer harán toda la regla de nuestra conducta.

Esa ha de ser nuestra disposición, así Dios no faltará de ayudarnos a corresponder a nuestra vocación a la fe.

Fiesta de San Juan Bautista

No puede haber cosa mas justa que de honrar y venerar a este santo, cuya fiesta guardamos hoy. A este santo de quien nuestro Señor Jesucristo ha dicho que entre los nacidos de mujeres no se levantó otro mas grande que Juan Bautista (Mateo 11.11). El era una antorcha que ardía y alumbraba, un ángel mandado para preparar el camino del Señor, un profeta y mas que un profeta, un mártir.

Ahora guardamos esta fiesta no solamente para dar a Dios las gracias por los favores y virtudes que han sido conferidas a este santo pero también para animarnos a la imitación de estas mismas virtudes. San Juan se distinguió por las tres virtudes de penitencia, de humildad y celo.

all the time in its heart it seeks to destroy his sacred law. It seeks to find him as the hypocrite Herod did. We must follow a different road. We used to walk in darkness, now we must walk in the light; we used to walk in disobedience, now we must return to obedience, to fidelity to the law of God.

These gentile kings were the first-fruits of our being called to the faith, the first apostles of religion.[27] Today's feast reminds us of the precious grace with which God has favored us by a special predilection, though by our unworthiness we have oftentimes looked for ways to lose it. But now the recollection of our calling to the faith will be from now on the most lively motive of our gratitude, the greatest obligations which will impose on us the entire rule of our conduct.

That must be our attitude; God will not fail to help us correspond to our calling to the faith.

L182 – Saint John the Baptist, Wednesday 24 June 1863, Santa Fe; about 1000 words on the preacher's patron saint; from the Loretto Archives. We can wonder if Lamy ends the sermon with an ideal self-portrait – "myself as I would like to become." Given the New Mexico emphasis on name-days, Lamy learned to spread himself a little on this day of the year. Much of this is drawn from previous John-the-Baptist sermons.

Feast of Saint John the Baptist

We cannot do anything more appropriate than to honor and venerate this saint whose feast we keep today, this saint of whom our Lord Jesus Christ said that among those born of women there has arisen none greater than John the Baptist (Matthew 11.11). He was a torch burning and illuminating, an angel sent to prepare the path of the Lord, a prophet and more than a prophet, a martyr.

Today we keep his feast not only to thank God for the favors and virtues conferred upon this saint but also to encourage ourselves to imitate these same virtues. Saint John distinguished himself for the three virtues of penitence, humility, and zeal.

1. To protect himself in his innocence, in the holiness he was

1° Para guardarse en la inocencia, en la santidad en la cual él había nacido por un milagro, se salió / todavía muy tierno para el desierto a donde pasó cerca de treinta años en la penitencia y la mortificación, y no salió de su retiro hasta que la voz del Dios le llamó. Era tan austera su vida que no llevara otra ropa sino una clase de vestido de pelo de camello, no probaba otra comida sino langostas y miel silvestre. Si no podemos nosotros reducirnos a una austeridad semejante, deberíamos que nos sirva este ejemplo para privarnos de muchas superfluidades en nuestro modo de vivir, de vestir, mortificar a lo menos nuestra vanidad, curiosidad y sensualidad.

2° Su humildad. El pueblo de Israel tenía la mas alta opinión del Bautista, en tal grado que le consideraban como el Mesías, pero él no se atribuyó ningún mérito, antes bien él declaró con franqueza que / él no era el Cristo, ni aun un profeta, y que ni tampoco él era digno de servir al Mesías hasta en el oficio el mas ínfimo, como de desatar las correas de sus zapatos. Oh dichosa humildad, que sola hace uno grande delante de Dios! Si las demás virtudes no se hallan fundadas sobre esta, mas bien degeneran en vicios.

3° Su celo para procurar la gloria de Dios, mantener la justicia y la verdad, sin respeto de personas. Para con los pecadores humillados, que querrían verdaderamente convertirse, el santo precursor era lleno de suavidad, de bondad. El privilegio de ser hijos de Abrahán les decía no podía salvarlos, solamente su obediencia a la ley de Dios. /

El le hablaba a todos con la libertad de un profeta, sobre sus deberes y obligaciones. El no sabía lisonjear a los ricos, a los grandes porque ellos tenían poder o influjo. Cuando ellos faltaban a sus deberes el hombre de Dios les decía sin temor *"non licet* — no es lícito" [Marcos 6.18].

Que el celo del santo precursor nos sirva para hacernos acordar de lo que le debemos a Dios, para que en todas las tentaciones resistamos al enemigo de nuestra salvación, diciendonos a nosotros mismos "No es lícito, no debo hacerlo." De este modo imitaremos el celo del Bautista y mereceremos participar a su gloria.

born in by a miracle, he went out / at a very tender age into the desert where he passed nearly thirty years in penitence and mortification, and he did not leave his retreat until God's voice called him. So austere was his life that he wore no garments other than a sort of dress of camel's hair, tasted no other food than locusts and wild honey. If we are unable to subject ourselves to a similar austerity, we should let this model help us to deprive ourselves of the many superfluous things in our manner of living, to mortify at least our vanity, curiosity, and sensuality.

2. His humility. The people of Israel had the highest opinion of the Baptist, so much so that they considered him the Messias, but he claimed no such merit and even stated frankly that / he was neither the Christ nor a prophet and that he was not worthy to serve the Messias even in the lowest office, loosening the latchet of his shoes. O fortunate humility, that by itself makes a man great in God's eyes! If the other virtues are not based on it, they soon degenerate into vices.

3. His zeal to advance the glory of God, to maintain justice and truth without respect of persons. Toward humble sinners who truly wished to change he was full of gentleness and goodness. He told them that the privilege of being sons of Abraham could not save them, only their obedience to God's law. /

He spoke to all men, with the freedom of a prophet, about their duties and obligations. He did not know how to flatter the rich and famous despite their power and influence. When they failed in their duties, the man of God fearlessly told them, "*Non licet* – It is not lawful" [Mark 6.18].

May the zeal of the holy precursor help us by making us consent to what we owe God so that in all temptations we will resist the enemy of our salvation, saying to ourselves, "*Non licet* – It is not lawful." In this way let us imitate the zeal of the Baptist, and we will deserve to share his glory.

La Natividad de María Santísima

"María de qua natus est Jesús qui vocatur Christus – María de la cual nació Jesús que se llama Cristo." Mateo 1.16 [todo = 1-16]

Este es el mas grande elogio de María santísima. La Yglesia celebra con alabanzas y acción de gracias la natividad o el nacimiento de María santísima, pues la bienaventurada virgen, la obra maestra de Dios, siendo distinguida por unas privilegios los mas especiales – ella vino al mundo no como los otros hijos de Adán, manchados con la contagión del pecado, sino pura, santa, hermosa, enriquecida con las mas preciosas gracias que debían adornar la dichosa criatura que había sido escogida para ser la madre de Dios, tan perfecta que el Espíritu Santo pudo decirle, "Tu eres toda hermosa, y en ti no hay mancha alguna" (Cánticos 4.7).

Para comprender el don tan grande que Dios hace al mundo, dándonos a / María santísima, hemos de considerar su dignidad sublime y los privilegios singulares que la distinguieron de las demás criaturas. Su dignidad de madre de Dios se halla expresada por el evangelista San Mateo (1.16) cuando él dice, "María de la cual nació Jesús." En la encarnación Cristo nuestro Señor tomó sobre si la naturaleza humana y se la unió de una manera tan íntima que las acciones hechas por esta naturaleza son las acciones de la naturaleza divina.[28] Del mismo modo que podemos decir con San Pablo que somos redimidos por la sangre de un Dios, así también podemos decir con la Yglesia que Dios nació de la bienaventurada virgen, que él padeció y murió en la cruz, todo lo cual Dios hizo en nuestra naturaleza humana que él tomó sobre sí de una manera tan milagrosa. En María santísima admiramos su eminente santidad, su privilegiada virginidad, tantas gracias que la adornaba, su / exaltación en los cielos sobre todos los santos, y los espíritus celestiales, pero su dignidad de madre de Dios sobrepuja todos estos privilegios. Al mismo tiempo, María santísima es madre y virgen sin mancha. Esta prerrogativa tan admirable pertenece a María santísima solamente y no será dado a ninguna otra criatura.

L185 – Nativity of Mary Most Holy, Thursday 8 September 1864, Santa Fe; about 1100 words concerning the virtues of the Virgin; from the Loretto Archives.

The Nativity of Mary Most Holy

"Maria de qua natus est Jesus qui vocatur Christus – Mary from whom was born Jesus called the Christ." Matthew 1.16.

This is the greatest praise of Mary most holy. The Church celebrates with praise and thanksgiving the birthday of Mary most holy, for the blessed virgin, God's masterwork, was distinguished for various most special privileges – she came into the world not as other children of Adam did, stained with the contagion of sin, but pure, holy, beautiful, enriched with the most precious graces appropriate for adorning the blest creature who had been chosen to be the mother of God, so perfect that the Holy Ghost could say of her, "Thou art all fair, and in thee there is no spot" (Canticle 4.7).

To comprehend the great gift that God made to the world by giving us / Mary most holy, let us consider her sublime dignity and the singular privileges that distinguished her from the rest of humanity. Saint Matthew expresses her dignity as Mother of God when he says (1.16), "Mary from whom was born Jesus." In the incarnation Christ our Lord took human nature upon himself and united it to himself so intimately that the actions done by that nature are the actions of the divine nature.[28] In the same way, we can say with Saint Paul that we are redeemed by the blood of a God, so we can say with the Church that God was born of the blessed virgin, that he suffered and died on the cross, all of which God did in our human nature which he took upon himself in a miraculous manner. In Mary most holy we admire her outstanding holiness, her privileged virginity, the many graces that adorned her, and her / exaltation in heaven above all the other saints and the heavenly spirits, but her dignity as mother of God surpasses all these privileges. At the same time, Mary most holy is mother and virgin without stain. This admirable prerogative pertains to Mary most holy solely and will never be given to another creature.

Her humility, her purity are the virtues we ought to imitate in her if we wish to assure her intercession and protection.

Su humildad, su pureza son las virtudes que hemos de imitar en ella si deseamos asegurarnos su intercesión, su protección.

Su nombre *María* significa Señora, reina, también estrella del mar.[29] Mientras vivimos en este mundo, navegamos en un mar-borrascoso, en medio de las tentaciones con peligro de ser arrastrados por su violencia. Pues no perdamos vista de este astro resplandeciente, no faltemos de acudir a María santísima, de invocar su poderosa protección. Ella es nuestra madre, mientras tendremos verdaderos sentimientos de hijos para con ella, mientras nos pondremos / bajo su intercesión con fervor y devoción no nos descaminaremos. Ella nos alentará, ella nos animará, ella nos conseguirá de su divino Hijo que nos perdones nuestras ofensas, y nos ayudará a perseverar fielmente en el servicio de Dios, y de este modo a merecer la corona de la gloria eterna.

Fiesta de Todos los Santos

La Yglesia nos da una prueba de la sabiduría divina en la división de sus fiestas y ceremonias, dándonos un compendio de toda la historia del genero humano. Las cuatro semanas de Adviento nos hacen acordar de los cuatro mil años durante los cuales fue esperado el Mesías. El tiempo que corre de la Natividad a la fiesta de Pentecostés nos enseña toda la vida privada, publica y gloriosa de nuestro Redentor. El intervalo que pasa desde la Pentecostés hasta la solemnidad de hoy nos representa la peregrinación de la Yglesia sobre la tierra. Ahora cuando llega el otoño, y que el labrador encierra su cosecha, fruto de su industria y de su trabajo, la Yglesia levanta la voz y dice a todos sus hijos de la tierra: levanten arriba sus ojos y sus corazones, y enseñándoles algunos rayos de la gloria que Dios reserva para los Santos. Les dice a todos, ricos y pobres, sabios y ignorantes, amos y sirvientes: estos bienes que amontonan no son mas que la figura de los bienes y gozos que os esperan en la otra vida.

Sembrad semillas de virtudes, y cosecharán méritos. Vivan como

The name "Mary" means Lady, queen, and star of the sea.[29] While we live in this world, we sail on a tempestuous ocean in the middle of temptations with the danger of being carried off by their violence. So we should never lose sight of this resplendent star, never fail to remember Mary most holy and to call on her powerful protection. She is our mother so long as we maintain the true attitudes of children toward her, and so long as we place ourselves / under her intercession with fervor and devotion we will never go astray. She will inspire us, she will encourage us, she will convince her divine Son to pardon our offenses, and she will help us persevere faithfully in God's service and in this way merit the crown of eternal glory.

L128 – All Saints, Saturday 1 November 1856, Santa Fe; about 1870 words on Apocalypse 7.2-12 and Matthew 5.1-12; from AASF 1856 loose document # 40. In the first paragraph, Lamy offers an intriguing allegorical reading of the liturgical cycle.

Feast of All Saints

The Church gives us a proof of divine wisdom in apportioning her feasts and ceremonies, giving us a compendium of the whole history of the human race. The four weeks of Advent remind us of the four millennia of waiting for the Messiah. The time from Christmas to the feast of Pentecost teaches us the whole private life, public life, and glorious life of our Redeemer. The interval that runs from Pentecost to today's solemnity represents the pilgrimage of the Church upon the earth. Today during autumn, when the farmer brings his harvest home, the fruit of his industry and his work, the Church raises her voice and says to all her children on earth, Lift up your eyes and your hearts, and point out to them some rays of the glory that God has in store for the saints. She says to all, rich and poor, wise and unlettered, masters and servants: These goods they pile up are no more than a suggestion of the goods and joys you hope for in the next life.

Sow the seeds of virtue and you will harvest merits. Live like Christians, like children of God, imitate the saints, and in recom-

Cristianos, como hijos de Dios; imiten a los santos, y el cielo con sus triunfos y coronas, el cielo con su / eternidad de gloria os será dado en recompensa.

En la epístola de esta solemnidad, para animar nuestra debilidad, la Yglesia nos dice que el cielo es poblado de personas de todos las naciones, que los Santos fueron lo que somos nosotros, frágiles, tentados y algunos pecadores antes de su conversión; pues si tenemos buena voluntad, podemos conseguir los que ellos han conseguido, podemos merecen la misma felicidad eterna.

El evangelio nos enseña cuales han de ser las condiciones necesarias para merecer el cielo. Es un consuelo grande que las mas humildes virtudes son otros tantos caminos que nos conducen a la felicidad.

La Fiesta de Todos los Santos es una fiesta universal que abrasa a todos los santos de todos los tiempos y lugares, una fiesta común de la gran familia de Dios, pues todos tenemos algunos parientes en el cielo. La Yglesia Militante, quiero decir, los miembros de la Yglesia que pelea las batallas de la fe, de la salvación, dirige hoy sus solemnes solicitaciones a la Yglesia Triunfante, así llamada porque ya llegó triunfante al puerto de la eternidad. Una voz unánime se eleva hoy de todos los puntos del universo. Teniendo la dicha de hacer parte de la grande comunión cristiana, participaremos también a este gozo / universal. Daremos gracias al Señor por la gloria y la felicidad que gozan. Nos animaremos a imitar sus virtudes y a obtener del cielo nuevos favores por la intervención de estos numerosos y poderosos intercesores. En esta ocasión, como en las demás fiestas de cada santo en particular, el culto supremo se da a Dios y a el solo la adoración. Damos a los santos la veneración y el respecto; honrarlos es honrar a Dios en ellos y por medio de ellos; en la fiesta de los santos honramos al Dios Padre que los crió, a Dios el Espíritu Santo que los santificó, a Dios Hijo que se hizo hombre por ellos y por el cual solo pudieron ellos merecer.

En la honra y la veneración que damos a los santos, no hemos de contentarnos con una admiración estéril. Los ejemplos de los santos han de animarnos, pues nosotros también somos llamados a ser santos, no solamente lo podemos, pero también es un deber, es

pense you will receive heaven with its triumphs and crowns, heaven with its eternity / of glory.

In the epistle of this solemnity, in order to strengthen our weakness, the Church tells us that heaven is filled with persons of all nations, that the saints were what we are, frail, tempted, some of them sinners before their conversion; for if we are of good will, we can attain what they have attained, we can merit the same everlasting happiness.

The gospel teaches us what the necessary conditions are for meriting heaven. It is a great consolation that the humblest virtues are merely other paths that lead us to happiness.

The Feast of All Saints is a universal feast which embraces all the saints of all times and places, a common feast of the great family of God, for all of us have some relations in heaven. The Church Militant – that is to say, the members of the Church still fighting the battles of faith and salvation – today directs its solemn petitions to the Church Triumphant, so called because it has already arrived triumphant at the gateway of eternity. A universal cry rises today from all points of the universe. Having the happiness of being part of the great Christian communion [of saints], we shall partake also in this universal / joy. Let us give thanks to the Lord for the glory and happiness they enjoy. Let us embolden ourselves to imitate their virtues and so obtain new favors from heaven by the intercession of these numberless powerful advocates. On this occasion, as on the other feast days of each individual saint, we give supreme homage to God and adoration only to him. We give the saints veneration and respect; to honor them is to honor God in them and by means of them; on the feast of the saints we honor God the Father who created them, God the Holy Spirit who sanctified them, and God the Son who became man for their sakes and by whom alone they are enabled to merit anything.

In giving honor and veneration to the saints, we should not stop with sterile admiration. The saints' example ought to animate us, for we also are called to be saints, and not only can we but we ought to, for it is our duty, our obligation. The God we serve is holy, and he wishes to be served by holy persons. So we have a duty to make

una obligación para nosotros. El Dios que servimos es santo, y es su voluntad de ser servido por santos. Pues nuestra obligación es de esforzarnos para imitar a los santos, santificarnos, como ellos lo hicieron.

Un primo motivo de animarnos en la virtud es que hay santos de todos edades, sexos, estado y condición, de todos los pueblos del mundo sin distinción de naciones, de civilizado o no civilizado.

Un segundo motivo de animarnos en la virtud es que los santos eran lo que somos / nosotros: hijos de Adán como nosotros, hechos de la misma materia que nosotros, sujetos a las mismas tentaciones y a las mismas miserias. Los medios de salvación que tenían los santos los tenemos nosotros en los sacramentos, en la oración, en la palabra santa, en la meditación de las verdades eternales.

¿Que nos impidiera pues de hacernos santos? No es una empresa arriba de nuestras fuerzas. La santidad, si lo queremos, estará con nosotros, a nuestro lado, día y noche, en nuestras palabras, en nuestros pensamientos, en nuestras acciones. Que cosa entonces es necesaria para ser santos? Hacer milagros? No – observar los mandamientos de Dios según dice nuestro Salvador. "Si quieres entrar en la vida, observa los mandamientos" [Mateo 19.17]. Conocemos bien estos mandamientos, no nos imponen un yugo duro y tiránico; el Dios que nos impone estos mandamientos quiere nuestra paz y felicidad que en su observación haciendo cada día lo que es de nuestra obligación, seremos santos. Porque nos dejaríamos espantar y creer que el servicio de Dios es imposible, que el cumplimiento de nuestros deberes es una cosa demasiado difícil, que es casi inútil de comenzar a hacer bien, que luego nos olvidamos de nuestros resoluciones, que teniendo tantas malas inclinaciones y tentaciones es como un martirio continuo de resistirlas. Pero tenemos la gracia de Dios para resistirlas; por eso nos dice el Señor en el evangelio, "Si uno quiere ser mi discípulo, que se niegue asimismo, lleve su cruz" [Mateo 16.24].

Que no podremos hacer lo que otros han hecho en las mismas circunstancias?

every effort to imitate the saints and to make ourselves holy as they did.

A main motive for pursuing virtue is that there have been saints of every age, sex, state and condition of life, of every people in the world without distinction of nation, civilized or uncivilized.

Another motive encouraging us toward virtue is that the saints were what we / are: children of Adam like ourselves, made of the same stuff as we, subject to the same temptations and the same woes. In the sacraments, prayer, holy conversation, and meditation on the eternal truths we have the means of salvation the saints had.

What then prevents us from becoming saints? There is no enterprise beyond our forces. Holiness, if we want it, will be ours, at our side, day and night, in our words, our thoughts, and our actions. What thing is needed to be saints? To work miracles? No – just to keep the commandments of God as our Saviour stated: "If you wish to enter into life, keep the commandments" [Matthew 19.17]. We know well these commandments, which do not impose on us any hard and tyrannical yoke; the God who imposes these demands on us seeks our peace and happiness, and in observing them day by day as is our duty we will become saints. For we could let ourselves become frightened and believe that the service of God is impossible, that the fulfillment of our duties is too difficult, that it is nearly useless to begin to do good, that we will shortly forget our good resolutions, that we have so many evil inclinations and temptations, that it is like a continual martyrdom to resist them. But we have the grace of God to resist them; here is what the Lord said in the gospel, "If anyone wishes to be my disciple, let him deny himself and take up his cross" [Matthew 16.24].

Can't we do what others have done in the same circumstances?

Autoridad de la Yglesia, Su Definición, Sus Notas o Caracteres.

1° Cuando nuestro Señor Jesucristo instituyó la Yglesia, le dio a San Pedro y a sus sucesores toda autoridad para gobernar esta misma Yglesia y para enseñar a los fieles. Acababa San Pedro de confesar la divinidad de su Maestro cuando Jesucristo le dijo, "Tu eres Pedro, y sobre esta piedra edificaré mi Yglesia, y las puertas del infierno no prevalecerán contra ella. Y a ti daré las llaves del reino de los cielos, y todo lo que atares sobre la tierra será también atado en los cielos, y todo lo que desatares sobre la tierra será también desatado en los cielos (Mateo 16.18-19). La facultad de atar y de desatar significa el supremo poder. La fe de San Pedro y de sus sucesores no puede faltar jamás. Su palabra será siempre el oráculo de la verdad. Esta sublime prerrogativa es fundada sobre lo que dijo el Señor a San Pedro, "Simón, Simón, mira que Satanás va tras de vosotros para cribaros como trigo. Mas yo he rogado por ti a fin de que tu fe no perezca, y tu cuando te conviertas confirma a tus hermanos" (Lucas 22.31-32). / ¿Cómo pudiera San Pedro confirmar a sus hermanos si él pudiera faltar en su fe? Para probar la infalibilidad de la Yglesia, este privilegio de no poder ser inducido en error ni de inducir en error a los fieles en su enseñanza, preguntaremos: 1° Si nuestro Señor Jesucristo es infalible? —Nadie lo duda. 2° Podía nuestro Señor Jesucristo comunicar su infalibilidad a los que él ha enviado para enseñar a los hombres? —Pues eso es claro, siendo Dios él puede todo. 3° Pero ¿habrá comunicado su infalibilidad a sus apóstoles y a sus sucesores? —Si, él lo ha hecho cuando él les dijo "Id, enseñad; y seré con vosotros hasta el fin de los siglos" (Mateo 28.20). 4° Debía él comunicarles esta infalibilidad? —Pues así lo debía. De otro modo no tendríamos ningún medio de conocer con certeza la verdadera religión. Y ahora sabemos que Dios quiere que conozcamos con certeza la verdadera religión, mirando que él manda bajo las penas de un castigo eterno que practiquemos esta religión y que seamos

L 175 – This 1861 instruction on Church authority is as academic and theoretical as Lamy ever gets; its 1700 words describe the power and structure of the Church in a sort of idealizing synopsis; from the Loretto Archives.

Authority of the Church, Its Definition, Its Notes or Characteristics.

1. When our Lord Jesus Christ founded the Church, he gave Saint Peter and his successors all authority to govern this very Church and to teach the believers. Saint Peter was just finishing confessing the divinity of his Master when Jesus Christ said to him, "Thou art Peter, and upon this rock I will build my Church, and the gates of Hell shall not prevail against it. And I will give to thee the keys of the kingdom of heaven, and whatever thou shalt bind upon earth shall be bound also in heaven, and whatever thou shalt loose upon earth shall be loosed also in heaven" (Matthew 16.18-19). The ability to bind and to loose signifies supreme power. The faith of Saint Peter and his successors cannot ever fail. His word will forever be an oracle of truth. This sublime prerogative is founded on what the Lord said to Saint Peter, "Simon, Simon, behold Satan hath come behind thee that he may sift thee like wheat, but I have prayed for thee that thy faith fail not, and thou, being once converted, confirm thy brethren" (Luke 22.31-32). / How could Saint Peter have confirmed his brothers if he could fail in his faith? To prove the infallibility of the Church, this privilege of being able neither to fall into error nor by its teaching to lead the faithful into error, we will ask first, is our Lord Jesus Christ infallible? –Nobody doubts it. Secondly, could our Lord Jesus Christ communicate his infallibility to those he has sent to teach the faithful? –Clearly so; being God, he can do everything. Thirdly, has he communicated his infallibility to his apostles and to their successors? –Yes, he did it when he told them, "Go and teach; I will be with you until the end of time" (Matthew 28.20). Fourthly, ought he to have communicated this infallibility? So he should, for otherwise we would have no means of knowing the true religion with certainty. And now we know that God wishes us to know the true religion for sure, seeing that he commands under

prontos a perder la vida antes que de revocar en duda ninguna de las verdades que nos enseña esta religión.

2° ¿Qué es la Yglesia? Es la sociedad de todos los fieles, reunidos por la profesión de una misma fe, por la participación a los mismos sacramentos y por la sumisión / a sus pastores legítimos, principalmente al sumo pontífice. La Yglesia se llama también la casa de Dios, porque es como una grande familia gobernada por un solo jefe y en cual todos los bienes espirituales son comunes; también se llama la esposa de Jesús porque es en esta santa sociedad que nacen los hijos de Dios. En fin se llama el cuerpo de Jesucristo porque él es la cabeza, el jefe de este cuerpo, todos los fieles son sus miembros, animados de su Espíritu, viviendo de su vida, obedeciendo a su voluntad. La reunión *de todos los fieles*: Esta sociedad reunida en Jesucristo tiene tres partes que son la Yglesia del cielo, llamada triunfante porque los ángeles y los bienaventurados que la componen gozan de la beatitud eterna, recompensa de sus triunfos. La Yglesia del Purgatorio, llamada padeciendo, porque la justicia de Dios los detiene por algún tiempo en padecimientos por algunas faltas antes de hacerlos participantes de su gloria. En fin, la Yglesia militante así llamada porque tiene que sostener en esta vida una guerra continua contra el mundo, la carne y el demonio.[30] Estas tres Yglesias no son mas que una sola y misma Yglesia, compuesta de tres partes, existentes en estados y lugares diferentes. Una ha precedencia / de las dos otras en la patria celestial, pero llegará el día feliz en el cual no formarán mas que una Yglesia enteramente triunfante. *Reunidos por la profesión de una misma fe* porque creen en una misma manera todas las verdades enseñadas por Jesucristo. *Por la participación a los mismos sacramentos*: de este modo los fieles son incorporados con Jesucristo. Son unidos entre si, y componen una sociedad exterior. *Por la sumisión a sus pastores legítimos y al sumo pontífice*: no puede existir ninguna sociedad sin autoridad por una parte y sin obediencia por otra parte. Para pertenecer a la Yglesia, dos cosas son necesarias. La primera es ser bautizado, pues nuestro Señor Jesucristo ha dicho que los que no son regenerados en las aguas del bautismos no entrarán en el reino de los cielos.[31] La segunda es de no ser excluido de esta santa sociedad como hijo rebelde y desobediente porque

pain of eternal punishment that we practice this religion and be ready to die before we call into doubt any of the truths this religion teaches us.

2. What is the Church? It is the society of all the faithful, united by the profession of the same faith, by participation in the same sacraments, and by submission / to their lawful pastors, especially the supreme pontiff. The Church also calls itself the House of God because it is like a great family governed by one leader and in which all spiritual goods are commonly owned. It is also the Bride of Christ because in this holy society the children of God are born. Finally it is the Body of Christ because he is its head, the chief of this body, all the faithful are his members, vivified by his Spirit, living his life and obedient to his will.

The union of all the faithful: This society united in Christ Jesus has three parts which are the Church of heaven, called triumphant because the angels and the blessed who compose it enjoy eternal beatitude, the reward of their victory; the Church of purgatory, called suffering, because God's justice detains them for a certain time to suffer for certain faults before they partake of his glory. And lastly, the Church militant, so called because in this life it must maintain a constant warfare against the world, the flesh, and the devil.[30] These three churches are nothing other than one unique Church, composed of three parts and existing in different times and conditions. The one has precedence / over the two others in the heavenly homeland, but the happy day will come when they will form no more than the one totally triumphant Church.

United by the profession of the same faith because they believe in the same manner all the truths taught by Jesus Christ. By participation in the same sacraments: in this way the faithful are incorporated with Christ Jesus. By submission to their lawful pastors and the supreme pontiff: no society can exist without authority on one side and obedience on the other.

To belong to the Church, two things are necessary. The first is being baptized, for our Lord Jesus Christ has said that those who are not reborn in the waters of baptism will not enter into the kingdom of heaven.[31] The other is not being excluded from this holy society

nuestro Señor ha dado a su Yglesia el poder de echar fuera de su sociedad los que rehúsan de someterse a su autoridad. ¿Qué agradecidos deberíamos quedar de ser hijos de la Yglesia, de haber recibido tantos favores espirituales por el medio de la Yglesia. Como el profeta real, hemos de decir, "Oh Yglesia mi madre, si me olvidaré de ti olvídese mi mano derecha. Pegada quede al paladar mi lengua si no me acordaré de ti, si no me prepusiera a ti por el primer objeto de mi alegría" (Salmo 136.5-6).

A la ocasión de la bendición de este campo santo les haré unas pocas reflecciones prácticas.

Si todas las naciones han tenido mucho respeto por los muertos, los Cristianos por razón de su fe en la futura resurrección han de tener un mas grande respecto todavía por aquellos cuerpos que han sido santificados por los sacramentos. Estos cuerpos animados por unas almas inmortales, y separados de ellas por la muerte, volverán un día a juntarse con estas mismas almas cuando Dios lo determinará; y es por eso que esos restos mortales son depositados en un lugar consagrado por ceremonias santas, por la oración y la palabra de Dios.

Esta creencia en el dogma de la resurrección nos anima a la practica de la virtud, a la obediencia de la ley de Dios y al cumplimiento de nuestros deberes, acordándonos de lo que dijo nuestro Señor Jesucristo en el capítulo 5° del apóstol San Juan, / versículo 28: "Pues vendrá tiempo en que todos los que están en los sepulcros oirán la voz del Hijo de Dios, (29) y saldrán los que hicieron buenas obras a resucitar para la vida eterna, pero los que hicieron malas, resucitarán para ser condenados." La certidumbre de la resurrección futura debe ser pues para todo hombre sensato y que

as a rebellious and disobedient child, for our Lord has given the Church the power to expel from its membership those who refuse to submit to its authority. How thankful we ought to be to remain children of the Church, to have received so many spiritual favors by means of the Church. We ought to say with the royal prophet, "O Church my mother, if I forget thee, let my right hand be forgotten. Let my tongue cleave to the roof of my mouth if I do not remember thee, if I do not make thee the first object of my joy" (Psalm 136.5-6).

L206 – Cemetery Blessing, perhaps spoken at the 1870 consecration of the National Cemetery in Santa Fe; about 1030 words; from AASF 1876 loose document # 14F. The talk sounds quite ecumenical, particularly with its references to "Christians" rather than "Catholics" and its citing Job rather than merely the Greek scriptures.[32]

On the occasion of the blessing of this cemetery I will make a few remarks of an expedient nature.

If all nations have respected the dead, Christians by reason of their faith in the future resurrection have to have a very great respect at all times for such bodies as were hallowed by the sacraments. These bodies, animated by immortal souls and separated from them by death, will return one day to join themselves to the same souls when God chooses; and it is for this reason that those mortal remains are buried in a place consecrated by holy rituals, by prayer, and by the word of God.

This belief in the dogma of the resurrection encourages us in practicing virtue, in obeying the law of God, and in fulfilling our duties, reminding us of what our Lord Jesus Christ said in the fifth chapter of the apostle Saint John, / verses 28-29: "For the time cometh when all that are in the graves shall hear the voice of the Son of God and those who have done good things shall come forth unto the resurrection of life eternal, but those who have done evil shall rise to be condemned." The certainty of the future resurrection ought therefore to be, for every sensible man who has any faith, a sufficiently strong motive to arouse him to the exercise of the vir-

tiene algo de fe, un motivo bastante poderoso para llevarle al ejercicio de la virtudes que enseña el Cristianismo, como también no ha freno mas enérgico contra el vicio que este dogma, eminentemente moralizada, que espantó a un Félix en el crimen, quien oyendo a San Pablo predicando el juicio venidero, le mando luego de pararse porque no le gustaba esta doctrina [Hechos 24.25]. Pero si por una parte el dogma de la resurrección hace temblar a los que desprecian a su Criador y Salvador porque quieren entregarse a sus inclinaciones malas, por otra parte esta saludable doctrina constituye un motivo grande. /

Para consolar uno en sus esfuerzos para hacer el bien y guardar la obediencia y la fidelidad que le debe a Dios, es cierto que resucitarán nuestros cuerpos; lo prueba la escritura sagrada casi en cada página de la manera la mas formal. Que nos baste el testimonio del santo patriarca Job (19.23-27): "¿Quién me diera," dice, "que mis palabras se escribirán? ... que con punzón de hierro se esculpieran en planchas de plomo, o con el cincel se grabasen en la piedra?" Y cual es este asunto tan importante? Pues es el dogma de la resurrección. "Porque yo sé," añade Job, "que vive mi Redentor, y que he de resucitar en el último día, he de salir de la tierra y que de nuevo he de ser revestido de esta mi piel, y he de ver a mi Dios en mi propia carne, le he de ver yo mismo con mis propios ojos; *reposita est haec spes mea in sinu meo* – esta es la esperanza que tengo aguardada en mi pecho." Tal es también, hermanos míos carísimos, la esperanza de los que dóciles a la voz de Dios, guardándole la fidelidad que le deben, merecerán de contemplarle en el gozo de su gloria eterna.

tues that Christianity teaches, as also there is no more effective bridle against vice than this eminently moral dogma which frightened Felix in his sinfulness when he heard Saint Paul preach the judgment to come and ordered him to stop immediately because he had no taste for this doctrine [Acts 24.25]. But if on the one hand the dogma of the resurrection makes those tremble who undervalue their Creator and Saviour because they want to give themselves over to their evil tendencies, on the other hand this salutary doctrine offers a great motive. /

To console someone in his endeavors to do good and maintain the obedience and faithfulness he owes God, it is certain that our bodies will rise again; holy scripture proves this on almost every page in a very formal manner. The testimony of the holy patriarch Job is enough for us (19.23-27): "Who will grant me that my words will be written ... with an iron pen and in a plate of lead, or else graven with an instrument in the rock?" And what topic is this that is so important? It is the dogma of the resurrection. "For I know," Job adds, "that my Redeemer liveth, and in the last day I shall rise out of the earth, and I shall be clothed again with my skin, and in my flesh I shall see my God in my own flesh, for I must see him with my own eyes; *reposita ista haec spes mea in sinu meo* – this hope is laid up in my bosom." Such, my beloved brethren, is also the hope of those who respond to God's voice, maintain the fidelity they owe him, and will deserve to contemplate him in the joy of his eternal glory.

Algunas reflexiones dirigidas a las hermanas a la ocasión de su retiro espiritual en su capilla nueva, por el Ilustrísimo Señor Arzobispo.

Hermanas carísimas en Dios: Hace veinte y seis años que cuatro Hermanas de Loretto llegaron a Santa Fe después de un viaje de tres meses, y un viaje penoso y muy peligroso.[33] Hemos de bendecir la divina Providencia de habernos prestado vida para ver la prosperidad de aquella primera comunidad tan pequeña al principio, tan débil, tan sin recursos, no teniendo otro recurso, sino su fe y confianza grande en aquel Dios que no se olvida de dar su alimento al ser el mas mínimo de la creación. Dios las ha prosperado y multiplicado pues hay ya nueve establecimientos en la provincia de Santa Fe.[34] / Qué gusto para nosotros de ser testigo de un numero tan grande de hermanas que se han reunido en esta capilla hermosa para hacer su retiro todas juntas y con el fin de animarse y renovarse en el espíritu de su santa y sublime vocación. He hecho mención de su hermosa capilla y me alegro de tener esta ocasión para decir una palabra con respecto a esta fábrica. Todos los que la han visitado, y entre ellos muchas personas que habían visto fábricas hermosas, han declarado que esta capilla seria un monumento, un adorno en cualquiera ciudad del mundo.[35]

Ahora, las hermanas que han dado su patrimonio para levantarla tienen el consuelo de haber contribuido a una / obra buena, a una casa de Dios, pudiéramos decir, casi digna de la majestad divina, en cuanto puede el hombre alcanzar con sus débiles recursos; si han contribuido a esta buena obra, a la construcción de esta noble capilla, ellas tendrán una participación mas abundante a los santos sacrificios, a las oraciones, que se ofrecen y se ofrecerán en ella.

Ayudando para el culto de Dios en esa demos a Dios una prueba

L231 – The New Loretto Chapel, Saturday 8 September 1878, in the Loretto nuns' chapel in Santa Fe; about 900 words of Archbishop Lamy's reminiscences twenty-six years after the first nuns' September arrival, plus some comments on Matthew 25.1-13 and the five prudent and five foolish virgins, points for meditation during the sisters' annual eight-day retreat. The text comes from New Mexico State Records and Archives.

Some reflections addressed to the Sisters on the occasion of their Spiritual Exercises in their new chapel.

My most dear Sisters in Christ: Twenty-six years ago, four Sisters of Loretto arrived in Santa Fe after a journey of three months, a difficult and very dangerous trip indeed.[33] We must bless divine Providence for having sustained us in life to be able to see the present prosperity of that original community, so small at first, so weak, so lacking in resources – having no other reliance except its faith and its great trust in that God who will never fail to give his sustenance to the most insignificant creature in the whole world. God has made them prosper and multiply, for now there are nine establishments in the Province of Santa Fe.[34] / What a joy to our heart to witness so great a number of Sisters who have gathered in this beautiful chapel to make their retreat together, with the purpose of animating themselves and renewing in the Spirit their sacred and sublime vocation. I have introduced the topic of your beautiful chapel, and I am delighted to take this occasion to say a word in reference to this building. Everyone who has visited it, and among them many persons who are familiar with beautiful architecture, have declared that this chapel would stand as a monument, an adornment, of any city in the world.[35]

Today, the sisters who have donated their patrimony to raise it have the consolation of having contributed to a / good work, to a house of God, to what we can even call a home worthy of the divine majesty insofar as is possible to man with his limited abilities. If they have contributed to this good work, to the construction of this noble chapel, they will participate most abundantly in the holy Sacrifices [of the Mass] and in all of the prayers now offered and yet to be offered in it.

de nuestra fe, de nuestra religión, y de este modo enseñamos que apreciamos mas las cosas de Dios, su Santa Casa que cualquiera otra cosa del mundo. Pero basta lo poco que he dicho con respecto a esta capilla que es y que será el adorno de la humilde capital de nuestro territorio. /

Dirigiremos ahora una palabra a las hermanas aquí presentes que acaban de hacer su retiro, y entre las cuales algunas van a hacer sus votas y otras tomar el hábito.

"Oh qué hermosa la generación casta con claridad," dice el Sabio inspirado por el Espíritu Santo (Sabiduría 4), "pues es inmortal su memoria, por cuanto es conocida delante de Dios, y delante de los hombres."[36] Sí, hermanas mías carísimas en Dios, no solamente la virginidad es hermosa, pero es una belleza con claridad; su memoria durará para siempre, Dios no se olvidará de premiarla, y los hombres, aunque pocos la practiquen, la admirarán y la aplaudirán. /

Imitad por su parte a las vírgenes prudentes mencionadas por nuestro Señor mismo que tuvieron sus lámparas bien surtidas de aceite, eso quiere decir sus almas bien preparadas y adornadas de virtudes para encontrar a su divino Esposo y acompañarle en el banquete eterno. Cuando el Señor nos habla de cinco vírgenes prudentes y de cinco necias, El nos da a entender que hay almas verdaderamente buenas y piadosas, y otras que no tienen mas que la apariencia de virtud. Una señal infalible para distinguir las vírgenes, las almas necias, es que todas estas faltan de caridad en donde no se ve una tierna compasión, aquella mansedumbre y bondad que sabe perdonar, aquella severidad por si mismo / y indulgencia por los demás. Sean lo que fueran las apariencias, allí no hay virtud. Aquellas vírgenes infelices se hallan adornadas a lo exterior como las prudentes. Llevarán sus lámparas pretenden ir al mismo banquete al encuentro del mismo esposo; a lo exterior no hay diferencia entre ellas y las prudentes o buenas. Pero luego por falta de aceite en sus lámparas o de caridad, de verdadera virtud en sus almas; quedan desechadas del banquete del Cordero de Dios.[37]

Strengthened by the cult of God in this chapel, let us give God a proof of our faith, of our religion, and in this manner we show that we value the things of God, the house of God, more than anything else in the world. But the few words I have said are enough about this chapel, which is and will be such an adornment of the humble capital of our Territory. /

Let us now direct a word to the sisters here present who have come to the end of their retreat, and among them those who are going to pronounce their vows and those who are to take the religious habit.

"Oh how beautiful the chaste generation in its renown," says the wise man inspired by the Holy Spirit (Wisdom 4:1), "for its memory is immortal, since it is known to God as well as to men."[36] Yes, my most beloved sisters in the Lord: not only is virginity beautiful, but it is a beauty with renown, its remembrance will endure forever. God will not forget to reward it, and although few men may practice it, they admire it and applaud it. /

For your part, imitate the prudent virgins mentioned by our Lord, those that kept their lamps well supplied with oil, that is to say their souls well prepared and adorned with virtues, when they went to meet their divine Bridegroom and accompany him into the eternal wedding-banquet. When the Lord speaks to us about the five prudent virgins and the five foolish ones, he gives us to understand that there are souls truly good and devout and others with no more than the appearance of virtue. An infallible sign for distinguishing the devout and the foolish souls is that all the foolish ones lack charity, do not demonstrate tender compassion, and fail to attain tender compassion, the gentleness and goodness that knows how to forgive, severity toward itself, / or leniency toward others. Whatever the appearances might be, there is no virtue there. Those wretched virgins show themselves adorned externally like the prudent ones. They will take up their lamps and expect to arrive at the same wedding-banquet and to meet with the same Spouse. From the outside, there is no difference between them and the prudent and good ones. But presently, because of the lack of oil in their lamps – lack of charity or of true virtue in their souls – they find themselves barred from the wedding-feast of the Lamb of God.[37]

Hermanas carísimas, han renunciado Vds para siempre a lo que las otras mujeres desean con mas anhelo, quiero decir la fortuna y los placeres; y todavía han hecho un sacrificio mas grande que es de renunciar a su propia voluntad.[39] /

Pero lo han hecho libremente por el amor de su Dios, y se ve por su semblante que ya el divino Salvador a quien se han consagrado les ha recompensado con un gran consuelo espiritual en esta vida, y pueden quedar seguras que perseverando fieles a su santa vocación serán admitidas en el banquete de su gloria eterna y es la gracia que les deseo a todas. /

Lo que les ayudará mucho para perseverar en el servicio de Dios y adelantar en el camino de la perfección religiosa es de acordarse de las palabras de nuestro Señor. "El que deja casa, parientes, hermanos hermanas etc. por mi amor, recibirá cien veces mas en este mundo, y la vida eterna en el otro" [Marcos 10:29-30].[39]

Salvación – para los de retiro.

"Ecce nunc dies salutis" 2 Corintios 6.2.

Todos los días son días de salvación. Juzgados al valer de la vida recompensados o castigados para la eternidad. "Locura de los que no lo piensan" [1 Corintios 2.14], mas grande en los sacerdotes, mas inescapable porque lo predican y lo conocen mejor que los del mundo. Si no trabajan a su salvación como trabajaran a la salvación de los demás. Si se han olvidado de su salvación deben meditar de la necesidad de procurarla para si primero y para los demás después. Como hace de trabajar *viriliter* [Salmo 26.14] *et* con confianza de Dios.

Su necesidad: ¿Cuántas veces el sacerdote sirviéndose de la muerte que lo destruye todo y del juicio que sigue la muerte ha predicado con elocuencia y fuerza invencible la necesidad de trabajar uno a su salvación?

My most beloved sisters, you have renounced forever what other women desire with great longing: I mean of course wealth and pleasure. Yet you have made an even greater sacrifice, which is the renunciation of your own will.[38] /

But you have done so freely, out of your love for God, and judging by the look on your faces, it seems that the divine Saviour to whom you have consecrated yourselves has already rewarded you with great spiritual consolation in this life, and you can rest assured that after faithfully persevering in your holy vocation you will be admitted to the banquet of His eternal glory, and that is the grace I pray for on behalf of all of you. /

The thing that will help you a great deal toward perseverance in the service of God and will move you along the path of religious perfection is to remember the words of Our Lord, "Whoever has left home, relatives, brothers, sisters, etc., for love of me, will receive a hundred times in this world, and in the other world eternal life" [Mark 10:29-30].[39]

L234 – Retreat Talk to Priests on Their Own Salvation, about 1880, Santa Fe; about 1340 words; AASF 1876 loose documents 15A.

Salvation – for those in retreat

"Ecce nunc dies salutis – Behold, now is the day of salvation" 2 Corinthians 6.2.

All days are days of salvation. [We will be] judged on the value of our life, recompensed of punished for eternity. "It is foolishness to those who do not understand" [1 Corinthians 2.14], even more so in priests, more culpable because they preach it and know it better than persons of the world. If they do not work out their salvation [Philippians 2.12] as they work for the salvation of others, if they have forgotten about their salvation, they ought to meditate upon the necessity of gaining it – for themselves first of all and for others thereafter, as they must work at it in a manly manner [Psalm 26.14] and with confidence in God.

Its necessity: How often has a priest, while preaching about death

Nada después de la muerte y del juicio sino el cielo o el infierno o la gloria inmensa et interminable o un castigo terrible y que no se acaba.

Nada mas necesario para un sacerdote que responde y de su salvación y la salvación del pueblo. Los sacramentos que el administra son para este fin. Y todo lo que Dios hizo en la redención fue para este fin. La redención de nuestra, la necesidad extrema que hay para nosotros de la salvación. Si un Dios da un Dios para redimirnos, es prueba del mal infinito que nos es por la perdida de nuestras almas. Debe ser infinito el mal contra el cual se usa en su sabiduría infinita un remedio de valor infinito, infinito había de ser la necesidad de este remedio. La salvación es la cosa únicamente necesaria para nosotros.

No es necesario que sea rico, sabio, pero que me salvo es de necesidad única. Si no me salvo caigo en el fuego eterno. O el cielo o el infierno: *"Quid prodest homini si mundum universum lucretur, animae vere suae [detrimentum patiatur]"* [Mateo 16.26].

La salvación [es] todo lo necesario, todo lo demás es como nada comparado con la salvación, todo se vuelve nada.

Necesidad pues [es] de lograr este retiro para salir del pecado. Si yo sé ciertamente que estoy en pecado o si yo dudo, un examen franco, sincero, confesión llena de humildad, arrepentimiento y buen propósito, la verdadera penitencia es la satisfacción de la necesidad extrema en que estemos de salvarnos, la reparación de lo pasado.

Manera de trabajar a nuestra salvación: Como hemos de trabajar a nuestra salvación con energía y confianza en Dios:

1° Con energía, *"viriliter agite et confortetur cor vestrum"* [Salmo 26.14]. La palabra "salvación" indica de por si lo que nuestro Señor dice, *"Quam arcta via est quae ducit ad vitam; pauci intrant per illum"* [Mateo 7.13-14]. Peligro de no escapar; es un naufragio, o una guerra, o una quemazón.

Trabajo: Si hay trabajo para los del mundo, lo hay mas para nosotros. Dificultades que vencer de parte de nosotros, de nuestras pasiones, nuestra flaqueza, siendo las mismas que las de los otros hombres y nuestras obligaciones a la santidad mucho mas estrictas

that brings everything to destruction and about the judgment that
follows death, spoken eloquently and with invincible force about
the need for everyone to work out his salvation?

There is nothing after death and judgment except heaven or
hell, infinite and interminable glory or a terrible punishment – and
one that will never end.

There is nothing more necessary for a priest than his responsibil-
ity both for his own salvation and for the salvation of the people.
The sacraments he administers are for this end, and all that God did
in the redemption was for this end. The redemption presents us
with the extreme necessity that is our own in regard to salvation. If
a God sends a God to redeem us, it proves that an infinite evil is the
cause of the loss of our souls. It must be an infinite offense against
himself that makes him employ in his wisdom an infinite remedy
of an infinite value, and the need of this remedy must be infinite.
Salvation is our uniquely necessary need.

It is not necessary that I be rich or wise, but that I save myself is
of utmost necessity. If I do not save myself I fall into the eternal fire.
Either heaven or hell: *"Quid prodest homini si mundum universum lucretur,
animae vere suae [detrimentum patiatur]? –* What doth it profit a man if he
gain the whole world and suffer the loss of his own soul?" [Matthew
16.26]. Salvation is all that is necessary, and everything else is of no
account compared with salvation – it all comes to nothing.

It is necessary, then, to make use of this retreat to escape from the
[state of] sin. If I know for certain that I am in the state of sin or if I
even suspect it, an honest, sincere examination [of conscience], a
confession in full humility, repentance and a good purpose [of
amendment]: true penitence satisfies the extreme need we have to
save ourselves and make reparation for the past.

The method of working for our salvation: How we must work
out our salvation with effort and confidence in God:

1° With effort: *"Viriliter agite et confortetur cor vestrum –* Do manfully,
and let your heart take courage" [Psalm 26.14]. The word "salvation"
indicates in itself what our Lord says, *"Quam arcta via est quae ducit ad
vitam; pauci intrant per illam –* How narrow the way is that leads to life;

y graves, nuestras faltas serán mas graves.

El demonio hace mas fuerza para derribarnos porque las consecuencias de nuestras caídas son mas deplorable.

few enter through it" [Matthew 7.13-14]. The danger of not escaping – it is a shipwreck, or a war, or a conflagration.

Work: If there is work for worldlings, there is even more for us. There are difficulties that we must overcome – our passions, our frailty being the same as those of other men. And as our obligations to be holy are much more strict and serious, so our failures will be much more serious.

The devil exerts more power to overcome us because the consequences of our failings are more lamentable.

Endnotes

[1]   William Howlett, *Life of Bishop Machebeuf* (Denver: Regis College, 1987), pp. 180-81, 189; Paul Horgan, *Lamy of Santa Fe* (New York: Farrar, Straus, and Giroux, 1975), pp. 153-60, 164-65; Lynn Bridgers, *Death's Deceiver* (Albuquerque: University of New Mexico Press, 1997), p. 100.

[2]   The Friday before Good Friday is the lunar feast of the Lady of Sorrows; September 15 is the solar feast, useful for celebrating parish-church and placita-chapel fiestas. Nuestra Señora de los Dolores arose about 1390, apparently when the "mourning figure" of Mary from a sculptured Calvary scene became detached and began to be venerated by herself; see William Wroth, *Images of Penance, Images of Mercy* (Norman: Oklahoma University Press, 1991), p. 75. The 15 September feast, removed from the liturgical calendar by the Council of Trent in the sixteenth century, was restored in 1727, and the sequence "Stabat Mater" was restored to the Mass.

[3]   This is nineteenth-century "Maximalist Mariology," an interpretation of Mary's place in the scheme of things that resulted from Mariology becoming divorced from Christology and ecclesiology to such a degree that it created for Mary the roles of active co-redemptrix and mediatrix of all graces. As it turned out, *"Nil nimis de Maria* – It is impossible to say anything exaggerated about Mary" was not a sound principle. Vatican II placed the preliminary schema on Mary into the schema on the Church, thereby relating Marian theology to the rest of theology, especially to the theology of *being*-redeemed.

[3]   The Latin hymn "Stabat Mater" is traditionally attributed to Jacopone da Todi, a Franciscan who lived in the late thirteenth century, about fifty years after Francis of Assisi and about a century and a half after Bernard of Clairvaux. In the original Latin:

> Quis non posset contristari
> Christi matrem contemplari
> Dolentem cum Filio?

> (Who could be unable to sympathize
> when contemplating the mother of Christ
> suffering with her Son?)

In a widespread Spanish version:

> ¿Quién será aquel que no llora
> Contemplando a esta Señora
> En tan grande suplicio?

In another Spanish version by Father Jean Baptiste Rallière of Tomé:

> ¿Quién no puede enternecerse,
> Viendo a esta Madre dolerse
> Con su Unigénito?

And in the familiar English translation:

> Who could see, from tears refraining,
> Christ's dear mother uncomplaining
> In so great a sorrow bowed?

[5]   Lamy gets very elliptical here. The very difficulties that Jesus' disciples had in believing in his resurrection come to serve as proofs once the disciples have actually experienced the risen Lord.

[6]   As a gloss upon Psalm 22.6, Lamy seems to cite Psalm 102.17-18: "The mercy of the Lord is from eternity to eternity upon those that fear him, ... such as keep his covenant and are mindful of his commandments to do them."

[7]   Pentecost in the Old Covenant was a harvest feast fifty days after the Passover, the end of the barley and the beginning of the wheat harvest, and as Lamy notes, it also commemorates God's giving of the Ten Commandments.

[8]   Lamy began this scrambled quotation by copying the first line (the working title or *incipit*) of a famous hymn to the Holy Spirit that he would recite as the Sequence of the Mass for Pentecost a few minutes before he would begin to read the sermon. He next translated it into Spanish. He next wrote line 14 of "Veni, Sancte Spiritus," then scratched most of it out and replaced it with line 2 of "Veni, Creator Spiritus," a hymn from the Roman Breviary (the priest's daily office) for Pentecost; he then paraphrased lines 2 to 4 of the first stanza of "Veni, Creator."

The *"potencias* – mental powers" in Lamy's paraphrase are the memory, understanding, and will of each human being. See Felipe Mirabal, "Las Tres Potencias: Images of Memory, Judgment, and Will in Spanish Colonial New Mexico," *Tradición Revista* 1 # 1 (Spring 1996), 20-21.

[9]   Lamy returns here to "Veni Sancte Spiritus" to quote lines 4 to 6 of the third stanza, which literally translate as "Without thy divinity, Nothing is in man, Nothing is harmless"; then he makes his third trip into "Veni Sancte Spiritus" to quote the first four lines of stanza 4 in a very free translation: *"Lava quod est sordidum, Riga quod est aridum, Sana quod est saucium, Flecte quod est rigidum"* translates literally as "Cleanse what is base, Moisten what is dry, Heal what is wounded, Soften what is rigid."

[10]   Guadalupe at Agua Fria (the old Camino Real) and Guadalupe Street, San

Miguel south of the Santa Fe River along the Old Santa Fe Trail, and Our Lady of Light on the south side of the Plaza were three chapels in the Cathedral parish. The Rosario Chapel north of the Plaza area and San Isidro in Agua Fria were others close by, and the priests in Santa Fe probably also served Tesuque, Cerrillos, and Galisteo. The High Mass was doubtless sung by priest and choir in the Cathedral Church of San Francisco just east of the Plaza.

The priests at the parish were Bishop Lamy and Father Charles Brun.

[11] The translation "I will know fully, just as I am known" requires three comments. First, scripture's "theological passive" normally means that God is the agent of the passive verb – "just as God will see and know me." Secondly, we must necessarily attribute the apparent suggestion of equality between God's and a human person's acts of knowing to hyperbole. Granted that in heaven we will comprehend vastly more of the divine than we presently do on earth, the human intellect, despite whatever in the way of divinization accrues to it, will remain intrinsically created and limited forever. The infinite will not fit into the finite, no matter how much the finite achieves or approaches transfinity. Thirdly, Christian *faith* is largely propositional in character; it is not merely the trusting faith of the Old Testament, for it includes intellectual truths of which we must let ourselves be persuaded. But the knowing of which Paul speaks in 1 Corinthians 13.12 will be not the propositional knowing of verbalized truths but the immediate communion that goes beyond faith and hope and moves altogether into the realm of love and connatural interpersonalism, Paul's topic in this sublime chapter. Bultmann in *Theological Dictionary of the New Testament* expertly differentiates practical Christian love-knowing from Gnostic head-knowing (eds. Kittel and Friedrich, Grand Rapids: Eerdmans, 1964 [original 1948]), 1:710).

[12] Lamy must have gotten carried away by his own rhetoric. Neither scripture nor moral theology would back him up on this.

[13] Faith is termed a theological or infused virtue because it is a share of God's own knowing that derives solely from the divine nature and is "poured into us" by the divine Persons; it does not originate or arise in any way from within our human nature or our human personhood. The most we can claim is that under the liberating influence of God's grace we "let ourselves be persuaded" of the truths of revelation; see James L. Kinneavy, *The Greek Rhetorical Origins of Christian Faith* (New York: Oxford University Press, 1987).

[14] Many of the foundation stones of the Temple built by Herod the Great still remain as the Wailing Wall, but in 70 A.D. the Romans destroyed the upper or "working" part of the Temple completely.

[15] Lamy here suggests that Protestants would consider the Roman Catholic Church respectable if more Catholics learned to behave.

[16] Leszek Kolakowski's *God Owes Us Nothing* (Chicago: University of Chicago Press, 1995), is a defense of Jansenism, and the very title suggests the Jansenist tilt of Lamy's statement. With the advent of Calvinism, the development of Catholic

doctrine made it clear that Augustinianism was no longer a suitable or even tenable theology.

[17]   As was the custom in Jesus' day, both men stood and prayed aloud. The Pharisee went to the front, stood tall, raised his hands, and looked up to heaven, while the publican remained in the back, leaned forward, beat his breast, and cast his eyes down. Kneeling in prayer and silent ("mental") prayer were later inventions.

[18]   In Psalm 81.6, God speaks to properly-appointed judges on earth and says to them, "Ye are gods" – meaning that they exercise a strictly divine function and reminding them that he will judge the judges. Anyone not appointed a judge should beware of usurping God's prerogative (see John 10:34-35).

[19]   After the first sentence, that is not God talking but Lamy.

Note that Lamy omits the senses of smell (perhaps not suitable for the Cathedral) and of touch (thereby neglecting the standard fire-and-brimstone component of "four-last-things" preaching).

[20]   If Lamy had read the remainder of the scene in Matthew 25, he would have learned what Jesus mandated for us to do so that we would have assurance on the day of judgment: feed the hungry, give drink to the thirsty, shelter the homeless, clothe the naked, and visit the sick and the imprisoned. In Lamy's defense, I must add that this is as much of a Jonathan Edwards "Sinners in the Hands of an Angry God" imitation as he ever does, and I am quite certain that he did this performance not because he enjoyed doing it but because he thought it was his duty.

[21]   Participation (*méthexis*) is a key concept in Platonic and Neoplatonic thought: the sharing of a lesser entity in the being of a greater, as of a particular horse in the Idea of horse that exists in the world of Ideas – or in God the Father's memory, as Saint Augustine and other Christian Platonists would have it, or in the archetypes, as Carl Jung would say. Mircea Eliade wrote that Plato raised an archaic religious insight to the philosophical level; see *The Myth of the Eternal Return* (Princeton: Princeton University Press, 1965), pp. 6, 32, 34-35.

[22]   First, by "sin" Lamy might have meant Original Sin, personal sins, or any combination of the two. Secondly, "referring," here used twice, is pretty much the equivalent of "contextualizing" – living *mentally* either in a world that is centered on self or in a world that is centered on God.

[23]   A slight echo of Ignatius Loyola's "tantum-quantum" from the "Principle and Foundation" of the *Spiritual Exercises*, which had become a staple of Christian spirituality: "El hombre tanto ha de usar ellas quanto le ayudan para su fin, y tanto debe quitarse dellas quanto para ello impiden – a man ought to use [the things on the face of the earth] in so far as they help him to his end [of praising, reverencing, and serving God and thereby saving his soul], and he ought to reject them in so far as they prevent him from doing so."

Granted that evil inclinations are not a valid criterion, but as Lear points out (2.4.260-71), need in the limited sense is not a valid criterion either.

[24] It is hard to guess what Lamy meant by saying that circumcision was only for sinners. As far as anyone knew, who else was there? The foreskin may have originally been associated with ritual impurity (which is not sin), or it may have been the near-identification with the Old Law that enabled circumcision to unite Christ with sinners so that he might take their sins upon himself and away from us. Thus it might form a very close parallel to Christ's acceptance of John the Baptist's ur-sacrament of baptism and his institution of the Eucharist before he suffered.

[25] Lamy's confusing parenthetical remark "May God forbid it" refers only to God's keeping Herod and his goons from finding and killing the Christ Child. His main assertion is that even when the person who tells us God's will does not obey God's will, *we* should obey it.

[26] In Lamy's mind, the symbolism of the three gifts probably went like this: gold, the king of metals, represented Christ's royalty as Son of David; the incense betokened his divinity as the Second Person of the Trinity; and the myrrh, a spice used in embalming, denoted his mortality as Son of Mary.

[27] For Lamy, the calling of the gentile Magi prophesied the calling of the gentile nations, since they themselves first became believers and then spread their belief to others.

[28] An old Latin dictum will help us to sort out the mess that Lamy makes of Christology here: "*Actiones sunt suppositorum* – Actions pertain to supposits," that is to say to substances, here the divine Person, the Son or Word. Natures don't do actions, persons (or impersonal substances like dogs and dahlias) do them. If the actions done in and by the powers of Christ's human nature had pertained to the divine nature, then the Father and the Spirit would have performed them equally with the Son – a clear slip into Patripassionism and Trinitarian Modalism, two heresies that Christian theologians got over about sixteen hundred years ago.

For the reference to redemption "by the blood of a God – por la sangre de un Dios," see Ephesians 1.7 and Colossians 1.14, 20; Lamy stretches the meaning a little.

[29] There is no merit in the three folk etymologies – one of them from Latin, which wasn't even spoken when Moses' sister Miriam bore the name for the first recorded time. If the name was Egyptian, it may have meant "rebellious," as anyone familiar with the "Magnificat" might have guessed.

[30] This phrase from the Anglican *Book of Common Prayer* must have become part of Lamy's repertoire of formulas during his time in the States.

[31] The doctrine is all right, but Lamy does not do a very good logical job of dividing and subdividing his topic. Baptism (and probably also its contrary, not being expelled for rebelliousness or disobedience) ought to be part of the previous "sacraments" section of the definition.

[32] Louis H. Warner, *Archbishop Lamy, an Epoch Maker* (Santa Fe: Santa Fe New Mexican Publishing, 1936), p. 163, reports that in 1870 Bishop Lamy blessed the

National Cemetery in Santa Fe, and the non-confessional tone of this short sermon suggests that it might have been written for that occasion. On p. 276, Warner mentions an 1868 blessing of a family cemetery, but I do not feel that this talk belonged at that ceremony.

[33]   The best account of the trip across the plains in 1852 is to be found in Sister Richard Barbour, S.L., *Light in Yucca Land* (Santa Fe: Loretto Academy of Our Lady of Light, 1952), pp. 29-31; the sisters arrived in Santa Fe on 26 September 1852. See also W.J. Howlett, *Life of Bishop Machebeuf* (Denver: Regis College, 1987 [orig. 1908]), pp. 186-91; Paul Horgan, *Lamy of Santa Fe* (New York: Farrar, Straus and Giroux, 1975), pp. 160-65; Mary Straw, *The Chapel of Our Lady of Light* (Santa Fe: Chapel of Our Lady of Light, 1984), pp. 21-26.

[34]   The Province in question, whether Lamy is identifying it from the Sisters' point of view or his own, was made up of the Archdiocese of Santa Fe and the suffragan vicariates-apostolic of Arizona and Colorado. The Sisters' nine houses were in Santa Fe, Taos, Mora, Las Vegas, and Bernalillo in the Santa Fe Archdiocese; in Las Cruces in the Arizona Vicariate; and in Denver, Conejos, and Pueblo in the Colorado Vicariate.

[35]   The Chapel of Our Lady of Light was begun on 25 July 1873, and it was dedicated on 25 April 1878; Barbour, p. 38; Straw, passim.

The Sisters of Loretto school was named for Our Lady of Light because much of its early funding came from the sale of the chapel building on the south side of the Santa Fe Plaza originally built as the quarters of a chapter of the confraternity of Nuestra Señora de la Luz. Governor Francisco Marin del Valle and the elite of Santa Fe constructed it in 1759-61; Lamy saved the stone altar screen, a major monument of provincial baroque which can be seen today in the Church of Cristo Rey at the head of Canyon Road.

In Lamy's mind, adobe buildings seldom qualified as beautiful architecture, so he here refers to the positive reactions of Anglos familiar with acceptable religious buildings in Europe and the States – Classical, Romanesque, and Gothic structures particularly.

[36]   "Childlessness is better, so long as one is virtuous, for immortality abides in the remembrance of virtue, which is recognized both by God and by men." The writer here is talking about the effect of sterility rather than that of chastity; Saint Jerome seems to have "read in" the meaning that he enshrined in the Latin Vulgate that Lamy relied on.

Though the New Testament quotes it, the Wisdom of Solomon ranks among the Apocrypha (deuterocanonical books) since it exists only in a Greek text; it derives from the Hellenistic world, written perhaps in Alexandria of the first century B.C., perhaps as late as the reign of the dreadful Emperor Caligula (37-47 A.D.). In this highly Platonic-Manichaean writing, the pre-existent soul "falls" into the evil body, but if it behaves itself it earns a subsequent immortality as a separated soul; there is no hint of a belief in the resurrection of the body. It seems to echo

Plato's *Symposium* 208E and Xenophon's *Memorabilia of Socrates* 2.1.33 as well as some Hebrew wisdom literature and Qumran. It shares the ethical use of *arete* with 2-4 Maccabees, a sense that never appears in the Septuagint Greek translation of books with a canonical Hebrew original.

[37]   Though the allegorical application is Lamy's own invention, the parable of the wise and foolish virgins (Matthew 25:1-13) occurred as the gospel of one of the special masses to be said on the occasion of the taking of religious vows.

The Wedding of the Lamb is the concluding episode of the apocalyptic Book of Revelations at the end of the New Testament; the Eucharistic banquet symbolism (God and humans united by sharing a meal) reinforces the symbolism of wedding (God and humans forever united in marriage).

[38]   In mentioning the renunciations of wealth, pleasure, and will, Lamy refers to the vows of poverty, chastity, and obedience.

[39]   The sermon originally seems to have ended prior to this brief paragraph, for the remainder appears in Lamy's handwriting on a separate, unnumbered page of slightly different paper, torn neatly from a larger piece. It may well have been Lamy's afterthought, but it could possibly have come loose from a different sermon altogether. The Spanish of this last paragraph does not appear in the version printed in the Albuquerque *Review* 3 # 19 (14 September 1878), p. 3.

Example of Lamy's handwriting in one of his sermons in Spanish. Sermon for
Viernes de Dolores, 1868 (L.202).

Afterword

There have been many books and articles written about the Most Reverend Jean Baptiste Lamy, the first Archbishop of Santa Fe. I doubt that this zealous pioneer bishop of French origins, who was a practical man of modest theological talents, ever thought so much would be written about him by historians and others. As the eleventh Archbishop of Santa Fe I am privileged to sit in the same chair that he once sat in and to lead the Church from the Cathedral that he built. Lamy left a great legacy in that he established the long sought after Archdiocese for the territory of New Mexico and saw it flourish.

For almost thirty-five years he administered the Church, establishing the first schools and first hospital as we know them today. He brought in priests, brothers, and sisters, promoted local vocations, and built up the Church in many ways. He was a leading citizen of the territory, an energetic and pastoral man with a sense of vision for the Catholic faith in the area entrusted to him by his superiors.

He is clearly not the Archbishop Willa Cather writes about in *Death Comes to the Archbishop.* That book, most agree, is more fiction than history and is excessive in praise of him, even though a very successful, well written book. Paul Horgan's excellent book *Lamy of Santa Fe* is much more accurate historically but still misses the mark in terms of a balanced picture of the first Archbishop of Santa Fe.

Father Steele has approached Lamy from a most creative angle – through a study of approximately 250 of his sermons and talks. Through his sermons, Steele has constructed a psychological profile of the Archbishop using the Myers-Briggs Type Indicator, saying that he was an Extrovert, Sensor, Thinker, and Judger – the most

common profile among American males. He has truly plowed fresh ground in his study of the sermons. (I shudder to think of someone later on trying to make sense of all my homilies and sermons and creating a psychological profile of me!)

It is clear that Archbishop Lamy worked hard on his sermons and that a rough draft probably always preceded the final copy. The fact that he saved, reviewed, and revised them doubtless points to his being at least somewhat satisfied with them. He translated sermons from his Ohio and Kentucky days into Spanish and used them here in New Mexico.

The background material of this book helps us to see Archbishop Lamy as a man of his time so that we can understand him accurately and fairly. As we would not like to be judged by the unknown standards of the twenty-first century, so we should not judge Lamy merely by the standards of our time. He was in many ways, Father Steele says, a typical preacher of the day, especially one trained in French seminaries. Lamy shows himself to be clearly a teacher in his sermons, which are rooted in the Bible and structured in the manner of his time. He seeks to give strong moral guidance to his people. One looks long and hard for any signs of humor or the use of stories to illustrate a point. He followed the traditional theological teachings in which he was formed as a seminarian in France. He shows a strong loyalty to the Pope as the successor of Peter and seeks to instill these values into his hearers through his sermons.

I believe that Father Steele has made significant contribution to the memory of Archbishop Lamy and provided an accurate picture of the type of preaching that was common in the Church during the latter half of the nineteenth century.

The book reminds me how grateful we must be for those who have gone before us bringing the light of the Gospel to the people of New Mexico.

Most Rev. Michael J. Sheehan
Eleventh Archbishop of Santa Fe

Appendix

SERMONS IN LITURGICAL-CALENDAR ORDER

NMSRO = published in Steele, *New Mexican Spanish Religious Oratory.*

———————— SUNDAYS, XMAS, EPIPH, ETC) ———

1ST OF ADVENT	L066	02 DEC 49
2ND OF ADVENT	L067	09 DEC 49
3RD OF ADVENT	L121	16 DEC 55
CHRISTMAS	L122	25 DEC 55
	L129	25 DEC 56
	L137	25 DEC 57
(Midnight?)	L154	25 DEC 58
(definitely Dawn)	L155	25 DEC 58
	L174	25 DEC 61
(Spanish)	L198	25 DEC 65 – published in *NMSRO*
(English)	L199	25 DEC 65 – published in *NMSRO*
	L205	25 DEC 68
CIRCUMCISION	L117	01 JAN 54
	L149	01 JAN 58
	L156	01 JAN 59
EPIPHANY	L119	06 JAN 55
1 AFT EPIPH - Holy Fam	L068	13 JAN 50
1 AFT EPIPH - Holy Fam	L150	10 JAN 58
3RD AFT EPIPHANY	L087	26 JAN 51
(Centurion's Faith)	L157	23 JAN 59
	L177	26 JAN 62
SEPTUAGESIMA SUN	L040	04 FEB 49
	L158	20 FEB 59
	L179	16 FEB 62
SEXAGESIMA SUN	L001	26 JAN 45
	L041	11 FEB 49
	L069	27 JAN 50
	L090	30 JAN 53
QUINQUAGESIMA SUN	L026	05 MAR 48
	L042	18 FEB 49
	L091	06 FEB 53
1ST OF LENT	L043	25 FEB 49
	L070	17 FEB 50
	L120	25 FEB 55
(Commandments)	L134	01 MAR 57
	L151	21 FEB 58
	L159	13 MAR 59

2ND OF LENT	L044	04 MAR 49
	L071	24 FEB 50
	L088	16 MAR 51
(vs Impurity)	L135	08 MAR 57
SAT 2 SUN LENT/PROD SON	L027	25 MAR 48
3RD OF LENT	L045	11 MAR 49
	L072	03 MAR 50
	L089	14 MAR 52
	L180	23 MAR 62
4TH OF LENT	L046	18 MAR 49
	L073	10 MAR 50
PASSION SUNDAY	L016	21 MAR 47
	L028	09 APR 48
	L047	25 MAR 49
	L074	17 MAR 50
VIERNES/DOLORES	L202	03 APR 68
PALM SUNDAY	L029	16 APR 48
	L049	01 APR 49
HOLY THURSDAY	L160	21 APR 59
GOOD FRIDAY	L030	21 APR 48
EASTER SUNDAY	L031	23 APR 48
	L050	08 APR 49
	L092	27 MAR 53
	L136	12 APR 57
	L169	08 APR 60
	L203	12 APR 68
1ST AFT EASTER	L032	30 APR 48
2ND AFT EASTER	L033	07 MAY 48
	L075	14 APR 50
	L093	10 APR 53
	L161	08 MAY 59
3RD AFT EASTER	L034	14 MAY 48
	L051	29 APR 49
	L076	21 APR 50
	L126	13 APR 56
4TH AFT EASTER	L077	28 APR 50
	L095	24 APR 53
	L162	22 MAY 59
5TH AFT EASTER	L017	09 MAY 47
	L078	05 MAY 50
	L118	28 MAY 54
ASCENSION THURSDAY	L079	09 MAY 50
SUNDAY BEFORE PCOST	L163	05 JUN 59
PENTECOST	L018	23 MAY 47
	L035	11 JUN 48
	L052	27 MAY 49

	L080	19 MAY 50
	L164	12 JUN 59
TRINITY SUNDAY	L003B	07 JUN 46
	L019	30 MAY 47
	L081	26 MAY 50
	L097	22 MAY 53
	L153	30 MAY 58
CORPUS CHRISTI	L020	27 MAY 47
SUN IN OCTAVE /CORP XTI	L053	10 JUN 49
	L098	29 MAY 53
SACRED HEART	L197	23 JUN 65
3RD AFT P'COST	L021	13 JUN 47
	L054	17 JUN 49
4TH AFT P'COST	L022	20 JUN 47
	L099	12 JUN 53
5TH AFT P'COST	L004	05 JUL 46
	L023	27 JUN 47
	L056	01 JUL 49
7TH AFT P'COST	L005	19 JUL 46
	L057	15 JUL 49
8TH AFT P'COST	L006	26 JUL 46
(8th, cont'd)	L058	22 JUL 49
	L184	10 JUL 64
9TH AFT P'COST	L007	02 AUG 46
	L101	17 JUL 53
10TH AFT P'COST	L059	05 AUG 49
	L102	24 JUL 5
12TH AFT P'COST	L060	19 AUG 49
	L082	11 AUG 50
	L103	07 AUG 53
13TH AFT P'COST	L061	26 AUG 49
14TH AFT P'COST	L008	06 AUG 46
	L104	21 AUG 53
15TH AFT P'COST	L083	01 SEP 50
17TH AFT P'COST	L085	15 SEP 50
	L105	11 SEP 53
18TH AFT P'COST	L086	22 SEP 50
19TH AFT P'COST	L010	11 OCT 46
20TH AFT P'COST	L063	14 OCT 49
21ST AFT P'COST	L107	09 OCT 53
22ND AFT P'COST	L064	28 OCT 49
23RD AFT P'COST	L173	27 OCT 61
4TH LEFTOVER/EPIPH	L108	30 OCT 53
5TH LEFTOVER/EPIPH	L110	06 NOV 53
6TH LEFTOVER/EPIPH	L111	13 NOV 53
LAST SUN AFT P'COST	L065	25 NOV 49
	L112	20 NOV 53

```
––––––––– SAME DAY OF SAME MONTH EVERY YEAR –––
```

CONVERSION OF St PAUL	L003A	25 JAN 46
	L133	25 JAN 57
PURIFICATION (Sunday)	L178	02 FEB 62
SAN JOSÉ	L152	19 MAR 58
ANNUNCIATION (Monday!)	L048	26 MAR 49
PATRONAGE OF St JOSEPH	L094	17 APR 53
SS FELIPE Y JACOBO	L096	01 MAY 53
MONTH OF MARY	L170	01 MAY 60
San JUAN BAUT (Namesday)	L055	24 JUN 49
	L100	24 JUN 53
	L182	24 JUN 63
	L183	24 JUN 64
	L201	24 JUN 66
Sts PETER & PAUL	L036	29 JUN 48
SANTIAGO	L165	26 JUL 59
NATIVITY OF BVM (Sunday)	L084	08 SEP 50
(to nuns)	L127	08 SEP 56
	L185	08 SEP 64
EXALTATION/CROSS	L037	14 SEP 48
(Friday)	L062	14 SEP 49
GUARDIAN ANGELS	L009	02 OCT 46
(Sunday)	L106	02 OCT 53
ALL SAINTS	L002	01 NOV 45
	L109	01 NOV 53
	L128	01 NOV 56
STANISL KOSTKA (to nuns)	L232	14 NOV 79
CONCLUSION OF THE YEAR	L038	31 DEC 48

```
––– NON-LITURGICAL-CALENDAR TALKS (Instructions etc) ––
```

	English	
CEREMONIES OF THE MASS	L011	
SMALL NUMBER OF ELECT	L012	
ON JUDGMENT	L013	
PRECIOUS...DEATH /STS	L014	
FUNERALS	L015	
ON CHRISTIAN PEACE	L024	
REAL PRESENCE	L025	
MARRIAGE	L039	
FAREWELL ADDRESS	L245	26 AUG 85

	Spanish	
SAC/PENANCE	L113	
PARTS/PENANCE	L114	
EUCHARIST	L115	
FOR SISTERS	L116	
PRODIGAL SON	L123	
SACRAMENTS	L124	
FIRST COMMUNION	L130	
THIRD COMMANDMENT	L132	
FIRST COMMANDMENT	L161	
HOPE [perh. two]	L162	
AUTHORITY OF THE CHURCH	L165	
FOUR MARKS OF THE CHURCH	L166	
BLESSING OF CAMPOSANTO	L184	
CONCURSUS NS Luz Acad	L185	
ADDRESS IN MORA CHURCH	L187	30 MAY 78
LORETTO NUNS' HISTORY	L188	08 SEP 78
FAREWELL ADDRESS	L244	26 AUG 85
RETREAT OUTLINE	L204, L246	
INTRODUCTION TO RETREAT	L139, L147, L187, L207, L237	
TEMPTATION	L167, L217	
SIN	L140	
MORTAL SIN	L143, L235	
VENIAL SIN	L194, L236	
DEATH	L141, L223	
JUDGMENT	L142	
HEAVEN	L145, L196, L224, L225 [Latin quotes]	
PERSEVERANCE	L146, L220	
SALVATION	L234	
HELL	L125 [fragment], L144	
RELIGIOUS STATE, VOWS	L188, L232, L240	
ADVANTAGES/RELIG. LIFE	L214, L215, L216, L217, L221, L227	
POVERTY	L189, L218	
CHASTITY	L190, L220	
OBEDIENCE	L191, L208, L209, L213	
TEACHING GIRLS	L192	
CHARITY	L193, L210	
PASSION OF CHRIST	L195, L226, L228	
MARY'S SORROWS & PAINS	L222, L238	
RESURRECTION	L138, L181	
PRAYER	L131, L233, L241, L242	

SERMONS IN CHRONOLOGICAL ORDER

AASF = Archives of the Archdiocese of Santa Fe
LNER = Archives of Loretto at Nerinx, Kentucky
NMHR = *New Mexico Historical Review*
N.MRA = New Mexico State Records Center & Archives
NMSRO = published in Steele, *New Mexican Spanish Religious Oratory.*

Bold entries are contained in this book and can be found at the page number referenced.

1845			*AASF #*	*Page #*
L001EN-S.F15	26 JAN	SEXAGESIMA SUN	4515	
L002EN-S.F16	01 NOV	ALL SAINTS (SAT)	4516	
1846				
L003AENS.F4D	**25 JAN**	**CONVERSION OF SAINT PAUL**	**7614D**	**111**
L003BENS.F3J	07 JUN	TRINITY SUNDAY	7613J	
L004EN-S.F3M	05 JUL	5TH AFT P'COST	7613M	
L005EN-S.F3N	19 JUL	7TH AFT P'COST	7613N	
L006EN-S.F3o	26 JUL	8TH AFT P'COST	7613O	
L007EN-S.F08	02 AUG	9TH AFT P'COST	4608	
L008EN-S.F3P	06 AUG	14TH AFT P'COST	7613P	
L009EN-S.F10	02 OCT	GUARDIAN ANGELS (FRI)	4610	
L010EN-S.F3Q	11 OCT	19TH SUN AFT P'COST	7613Q	
L011EN-S.F4B		INSTRUCTION CEREMONIES OF THE MASS	7614B	
L012EN-S.F09		INSTRUCTION SMALL NUMBER OF ELECT	4609	
L013EN-S.F4C		INSTRUCTION ON JUDGMENT	7614C	
L014EN-S.F4I		INSTRUCTION PRECIOUS...DEATH /STS	7614I	
L015EN-S.F4J		INSTRUCTION FUNERALS	7614J	
1847				
L016EN-S.F3C	21 MAR	PASSION SUNDAY	7613C	
L017EN-S.F06	09 MAY	5TH AFT EASTER	4706	
L018EN-S.F3F	23 MAY	PENTECOST	7613F	
L019EN-S.F3I	30 MAY	TRINITY SUNDAY	7613I	
L020EN-S.F3E	27 MAY	CORPUS CHRISTI	7613E	
L021EN-S.F3K	13 JUN	3RD AFT P'COST	7613K	
L022EN-S.F3L	20 JUN	4TH AFT P'COST	7613L	
L023EN-S.F07	27 JUN	5TH AFT P'COST	4707	
L024EN-S.F4E		INSTRUCTION ON CHRISTIAN PEACE	7614E	
L025EN-S.F4H		INSTRUCTION REAL PRESENCE	7614H	
1848				
L026EN-S.F11	05 MAR	QUINQUAGESIMA S	4811	
L027EN-S.F12	25 MAR	PROD SON/SAT 2 SUN LENT	4812	
L028EN-S.F13	09 APR	PASSION SUN	4813	
L029EN-S.F10	16 APR	PALM SUNDAY	4810	
L030EN-S.F05	21 APR	GOOD FRIDAY	4805	
L031EN-S.F06	23 APR	EASTER SUN	4806	
L032EN-S.F07	30 APR	1ST AFT EASTER	4807	
L033EN-S.F08	07 MAY	2ND AFT EASTER	4808	
L034EN-S.F09	14 MAY	3RD AFT EASTER	4809	
L035EN-S.F3G	11 JUN	PENTECOST	7613G	
L036EN-S.F3S	29 JUN	SAINTS PETER & PAUL	7613S	
L037EN-S.F3A	14 SEP	EXALTATION OF H CROSS	7613A	
L038EN-S.F4K	31 DEC	CONCLUSION OF THE YEAR	7614K	
L039EN-S.F04		**INSTRUCTION MARRIAGE**	**4804**	**115**

1849

L040EN-S.F08	04 FEB	SEPTUAGESIMA S	4908	
L041EN-S.F09	11 FEB	SEXAGESIMA S	4909	
L042EN-S.F07	18 FEB	QUINQUAGESIMA S	4907	
L043EN-S.F12	25 FEB	1ST OF LENT	4912	
L044EN-S.F18	**04 MAR**	**2ND OF LENT**	**4918**	107
L045EN-S.F19	11 MAR	3RD OF LENT	4919	
L046EN-S.F13	18 MAR	4TH OF LENT	4913	
L047EN-S.F3D	25 MAR	PASSION SUNDAY	7613D	
L048EN-S.F10	26 MAR	ANNUNCIATION (MON!)	4910	
L049EN-S.F14	01 APR	PALM SUNDAY	4914	
L050EN-S.F15	08 APR	EASTER SUNDAY	4915	
L051EN-S.F16	29 APR	3RD AFT EASTER	4916	
L052EN-S.F20	27 MAY	PENTECOST SUN	4920	
L053EN-S.F17	10 JUN	SUN IN OCTAVE /CORP XTI	4917	
L054EN-S.F21	17 JUN	3RD AFT P'COST	4921	
L055EN-S.F22	24 JUN	SAN JUAN BAUTISTA	4922	
L056EN-S.F23	01 JUL	5TH AFT P'COST	4923	
L057EN-S.F24	15 JUL	7TH AFT P'COST	4924	
L058EN-S.F25	22 JUL	8TH AFT P'COST	4925	
L059EN-S.F26	05 AUG	10TH AFT P'COST	4926	
L060EN-S.F27	19 AUG	12TH AFT P'COST	4927	
L061EN-S.F28	26 AUG	13TH AFT P'COST	4928	
L062EN-S.F11	14 SEP	EXALTATION OF CROSS (FRI)	4911	
L063EN-S.F3R	14 OCT	20TH AFT P'COST	7613R	
L064EN-S.F29	28 OCT	22ND AFT P'COST	4929	
L065EN-S.F30	25 NOV	LAST SUN AFT P'COST	4930	
L066EN-S.F31	**02 DEC**	**1ST OF ADVENT**	**4931**	88
L067EN-S.F32	**09 DEC**	**2ND OF ADVENT**	**4932**	91

1850

L068EN-S.F46	**13 JAN**	**1ST AFT EPIPHANY**	**5046**	95
L069EN-S.F44	27 JAN	SEXAGESIMA SUN	5044	
L070EN-S.F48	**17 FEB**	**1ST OF LENT**	**5048**	103
L071EN-S.F49	24 FEB	2ND OF LENT	5049	
L072EN-S.F50	03 MAR	3RD OF LENT	5050	
L073EN-S.F51	10 MAR	4TH OF LENT	5051	
L074EN-S.F43	17 MAR	PASSION SUNDAY	5043	
L075EN-S.F52	14 APR	2ND AFT EASTER	5052	
L076EN-S.F53	21 APR	3RD AFT EASTER	5053	
L077EN-S.F54	28 APR	4TH AFT EASTER	5054	
L078EN-S.F55	05 MAY	5TH AFT EASTER	5055	
L079EN-S.F45	09 MAY	ASCENSION (THU)	5045	
L080EN-S.F3H	19 MAY	WHITSUNDAY (P'COST)		
L081EN-S.F41	26 MAY	TRINITY = 1ST AFT P'COST	5041	
L082EN-S.F56	11 AUG	12TH AFT P'COST	5056	
L083EN-S.F59	01 SEP	15TH AFT P'COST	5059	
L084EN-S.F42	08 SEP	NATIVITY OF BVM (SUN)	5042	
L085EN-S.F57	15 SEP	17TH AFT P'COST	5057	
L086EN-S.F58	22 SEP	18TH AFT P'COST	5058	

1851

L087EN-S.F21	26 JAN	3RD AFT EPIPHANY	5121	98
L088EN-S.F20	16 MAR	2ND OF LENT	5120	

1852

L089ES-LNER	14 MAR	3RD OF LENT	

1853

L090ES-S.F23	30 JAN	SEXAGESIMA	5323	
L091ES-S.F24	06 FEB	QUINQUAGESIMA	5324	
L092ES-L.NER	**27 MAR**	**EASTER SUNDAY**		136
L093ES-L.NER	**10 APR**	**2ND AFT EASTER**		140
L094ES-L.NER	17 APR	PATROCINIO DE SAN JOSÉ		
L095ES-L.NER	**24 APR**	**4TH AFT EASTER**		144
L096ES-L.NER	01 MAY	SS. FELIPE Y JACOBO		
L097ES-L.NER	**22 MAY**	**TRINITY SUN**		154
L098ES-L.NER	**29 MAY**	**SUNDAY /OCTAVE CORP XTI**		156
L099ES-L.NER	**12 JUN**	**4TH AFT P'COST**		164
L100ES-L.NER	24 JUN	JUAN BAUT (FRI) NAMESDAY		
L101ES-L.NER	**17 JUL**	**9TH AFT P'COST**		170
L102ES-L.NER	**24 JUL**	**10TH AFT P'COST**		174
L103ES-L.NER	07 AUG	12TH AFT P'COST		
L104ES-L.NER	21 AUG	14TH AFT P'COST		
L105ES-L.NER	11 SEP	17TH AFT P'COST		
L106ES-L.NER	02 OCT	GUARDIAN ANGELS (SUN)		
L107ES-L.NER	**09 OCT**	**21 AFT P'COST**		180
L108ES-S.F20	30 OCT	4TH LEFTOVER/EPIPH	5320	
L109ES-S.F22	01 NOV	ALL SAINTS (TUES)	5322	
L110ES-L.NER	06 NOV	5TH LEFTOVER/EPIPH		
L111ES-L.NER	13 NOV	6TH LEFTOVER/EPIPH		
L112ES-L.NER	**20 NOV**	**LAST SUN AFT P'COST**		186
L113ES-L.NER		INSTRUCTION-SAC/PENANCE		
L114ES-L.NER		INSTRUCTION-PARTS/PENANCE		
L115ES-L.NER		INSTRUCTION EUCHARIST		
L116EN-S.F21		INSTRUCTION FOR SISTERS	5321	

1854

L117ES-S.F17	01 JAN	CIRCUMCISION	5417	
L118ES-L.NER	28 MAY	5TH SUN AFT EASTER		

1855

L119ES-S.F12	**06 JAN**	**EPIPHANY**	5512	200
L120ES-S.F15	25 FEB	1ST SUN OF LENT	5515	
L121ES-N.MRA	16 DEC	3RD SUN OF ADVENT	NMRA	
L122ES-S.F14	25 DEC	CHRISTMAS	5514	
L123ES-L.NER		INSTRUCTION PRODIGAL SON		
L124ES-L.NER		INSTRUCTION SACRAMENTS		
L125ES-L.NER		FRAGMENT OF INSTRUCTION HELL		

1856

L126ES-L.NER	13 APR	3RD SUN AFTER EASTER		
L127ES-L.NER	08 SEP	NATIVITY OF BVM (to nuns)		
L128ES-S.F40	**01 NOV**	**ALL SAINTS**	5640	210
L129ES-L.NER	25 DEC	CHRISTMAS		
L130ES-L.NER		INSTRUCTION FIRST COMMUNION		
L131ES-L.NER		INSTRUCTION ON PRAYER		
L132ES-L.NER		INSTRUCTION THIRD COMMANDMENT		

1857

L133ES-S.F29	25 JAN	CONVERSION OF ST PAUL	5729	
L134ES-L.NER	01 MAR	1ST SUN LENT; 6TH-9TH COMMTS		
L135ES-L.NER	08 MAR	2ND SUN LENT; AGAINST IMPURITY		
L136ES-L.NER	12 APR	EASTER		
L137ES-L.NER	**25 DEC**	**CHRISTMAS**		190

L138ES-S.F28	INSTRUCTION RESURRECTION		5728
L139ES-S.F6A	INSTRUCTION INTRO TO RETREAT		5726
L140ES-S.F6B	MEDITATION 1 PECADO		5726
L141ES-S.F6C	2 MUERTE		5726
L142ES-S.F6D	3 JUICIO	5726	
L143ES-S.F6E	3a PECADO MORTAL		5726
L144ES-S.F6F	4 INFIERNO	5726	
L145ES-S.F6G	5 GLORIA	5726	
L146ES-S.F6H	6 PERSEVERANCIA		5726
L147ES-S.F27	NECESIDAD DE EJERCICIOS		5727

1858

L148ES-S.F22	01 JAN	CIRCUMCISION	
L149ES-S.F21	10 JAN	HOLY FAMILY	
L150ES-S.F04	14 FEB	QUINQUAGESIMA	
L151ES-L.NER	21 FEB	1ST SUN OF LENT	
L152ES-L.NER	19 MAR	SAN JOSÉ (FRI)	
L153ES-L.NER	30 MAY	TRINITY	
L154ES-L.NER	25 DEC	CHRISTMAS (maybe MIDNIGHT?)	
L155ES-L.NER	25 DEC	CHRISTMAS (definitely DAWN)	

1859

L156ES-S.F34	**01 JAN**	**FIRST DAY OF YEAR (SAT)**	**196**
L157ES-S.F33	23 JAN	3RD SUN AFT EPIPH; FAITH/CENTURION	
L158ES-L.NER	20 FEB	SEPTUAGESIMA	
L159ES-S.F35	13 MAR	1ST SUN OF LENT	
L160ES-L.NER	**21 APR**	**HOLY THURSDAY**	**130**
L161ES-L.NER	08 MAY	2ND SUN AFTER EASTER	
L162ES-L.NER	22 MAY	4TH SUN AFTER EASTER	
L163ES-L.NER	05 JUN	SUNDAY BEFORE P'COST	
L164ES-L.NER	**12 JUN**	**PENTECOST**	**150**
L165ES-L.NER	25 JUL	SANTIAGO (MONDAY)	
L166ES-S.F32	INSTRUCTION RELIGOUS PROFESSION		
L167ES-L.NER	INSTRUCTION TEMPTATION		

1860

L168ES-N.MRA	30 MAR	RELIGIOUS PROFESSION	*NMSRO*
L169ES-L.NER	08 APR	EASTER	
L170ES-L.NER	01 MAY	MONTH OF MAY (TUESDAY)	
L171ES-L.NER	INSTRUCTION FIRST COMMANDMENT		
L172ES-L.NER	INSTRUCTION HOPE [perh. two instructions?]		

1861

L173ES-L.NER	27 OCT	23RD SUNDAY AFT P'COST	
L174ES-S.F24	25 DEC	CHRISTMAS (WEDNESDAY)	
L175ES-L.NER	**INSTRUCTION AUTHORITY OF THE CHURCH**		**216**
L176ES-L.NER	INSTRUCTION FOUR MARKS OF THE CHURCH (+5th pg?)		

1862

L177ES-S.F17	26 JAN	3RD SUNDAY AFTER EPIPHANY	
L178ES-S.F18	02 FEB	PURIFICATION (SUNDAY)	
L179ES-S.F16	16 FEB	SEPTUAGESIMA	
L180ES-L.NER	23 MAR	3RD SUN OF LENT	
L181ES-S.F3b	INSTRUCTION RESURRECTION		

1863

L182ES-L.NER	**24 JUN**	**SAINT JOHN THE BAPTIST (WEDNESDAY)**	**204**

<u>1864</u>

L183ES-LNER	24 JUN	SAINT JOHN THE BAPTIST (FRIDAY)		
L184ES-LNER	10 JUL	8TH SUN AFTER PCOST		
L185ES-LNER	**08 SEP**	**NATIVITY OF BVM (THURSDAY)**		**208**
L186ES-S.F16	INSTRUCTION RENOVATION OF VOWS		6416	
L187ES-S.F8A	RETREAT	INTRO	6418	
L188ES-S.F8B	RELIGIOUS STATE		ditto	
L189ES-S.F8C	POVERTY			
L190ES-S.F8D	CHASTITY			
L191ES-S.F8E	OBEDIENCE(interpolation = '64#18)			
L192ES-S.F8F	TEACHING GIRLS			
L193ES-S.F8G	CHARITY			
L194ES-S.F8H	VENIAL SIN			
L195ES-S.F8I	PASSION OF CHRIST			
L196ES-S.F8J	GLORIA (Heaven)			

<u>1865</u>

L197ES-LNER	**23 JUN**	**SACRED HEART (FRIDAY)**		**162**
L198ES-S.17A	25 DEC	CHRISTMAS (SPANISH)	*NMSRO*	
L199EN-S.17B	25 DEC	CHRISTMAS (ENGLISH)	*NMSRO*	
L200EN-S.F4G	**INSTRUCTION PERSEVERANCE**			**116**

<u>1866</u>

L201ES-LNER	24 JUN	SAINT JOHN THE BAPTIST (SUNDAY)

<u>1867</u>   no sermons

<u>1868</u>

L202ES-S.F19	**03 APR**	**VIERNES DE DOLORES (wk before Good Fri)**	**126**
L203ES-S.F20	12 APR	EASTER	
L204ES-S.F11	27-8 AUG	RETREAT NOTES (not Lamy's hand)	
L205ES-S.F21	25 DEC	CHRISTMAS (FRIDAY)	

<u>1869</u>   no sermons

<u>1870</u>

L206ES-S.F4F	**INSTRUCTION BLESSING OF CAMPOSANTO**	**220**
L207ES-S.F09	INTRO TO RETREAT	
L208ES-S.11A	INSTRUCTION ON OBEDIENCE # 1	
L209ES-S.11B	INSTRUCTION ON OBEDIENCE # 2	

<u>1871</u>   no sermons

<u>1872</u>

L210ES72.#13)	RETREAT: CHARITY
L211ES72.#14)	RELIGIOUS PROFESSION

<u>1873</u>   no sermons

1874

L212ES-S.F12	INSTRUCTION CONCURSUS AT OUR LADY OF LIGHT ACADEMY
L213ES72.#12	RETREAT: OBEDIENCE

<u>1875</u> – all AASF ld 1875 # 17 (49 pp.!!)

L214ES75.17a	ADVANTAGES OF RELIGIOUS LIFE
L215ES75.17b	ADVANTAGES OF RELIGIOUS LIFE
L216ES75.17c	RELIGIOUS LIFE
L217ES75.17d	RETREAT: TEMPTATIONS

Index

A

B

D

E

F

Index of Scripture Citations
OLD TESTAMENT

About the Author

Father Tom Steele was born and brought up in the St. Louis area (at the wrong end of the Santa Fe Trail). Following high school, he joined the Jesuits in 1951, attended St. Louis University (B.A., M.A., Ph.L., S.T.L.), and was ordained a priest in 1964. He came to Albuquerque in order to earn a doctorate in English and American literature at the University of New Mexico and fell in love first with the *santos* of Hispanic New Mexico and eventually with everything New Mexican except the politics.

He recently resigned from the English Department at Regis University in Denver, but he serves as the curator of the Regis collections of santos and Pueblo pottery, teaches New Mexican topics at UNM and lives at Immaculate Conception Parish in Albuquerque.

His hobbies are art, fishing, golf, and ranching, and he claims to be "the best cowboy in Guadalupe County, New Mexico, who will gladly work for nothing – and worth it!" Father Steele has served as a judge at both the New Mexico State Fair and Spanish Market. Father Steele was awarded a 1999 UNM Alumni Zia Award for his contributions to New Mexican cultural research.

Father Steele continues to work on many writing projects at one time, ensuring a constant stream of research and thought on New Mexico and its culture.

Writings by Thomas J. Steele, S.J.

New Mexican Studies

"Sgraffito As a Santero Tradition." co-authored with Charlie Carrillo, *Tradición Revista*,
IV#4 (Winter 1999), pp.27-29.

"The Archbishop Comes Back to Life." *Tradición Revista*, IV#3 (Fall 1999), pp.31-33.

"True Confessions of a Santo Collector: Or Judge Mescall's Gift to Regis." *Tradición
Revista*, IV#2 (Summer 1999), pp 38-40.

"Today's Artists: The Fresh Talent of Jay Seale." *Tradición Revista*, IV#1 (Spring 1999),
pp.57-59.

"Santero del Norte: Carlos Santistevan - The Dean of Denver Santeros". *Tradición
Revista*, III#2 (Summer 1998), pp49-52.

*Seeds of Struggle: Harvest of Faith, The Papers of the Archdiocese of Santa Fe Catholic Cuatro
Centennial Conference - The History of the Catholic Church in New Mexico*, Albuquerque, LPD Press, 1998.

"Remembered Backward, Repeated Forward: J.P. Rael's 'Los Pobladores de Questa,'"
Journal of the Southwest 40 (1998) 87-105.

"Indigenous Voice in Nuevomexicano Anti-Clerical Satire," *Catholic Southwest* 9 (1998)
53-74 (with Enrique Lamadrid).

"Foreword" to Alice Corbin Henderson, *Brothers of Light*. Las Cruces: Yucca Tree
Press, 1998 (orig. 1937)

"Family Spirituality in Traditional Hispanic New Mexico," *Our Saints Among Us: 400
Years of New Mexican Devotional Art*, Albuquerque, LPDPress, 1998.

"The Santos of Colorado and New Mexico". *Tradición Revista*, II#4 (Winter 1997), pp
19-21.

"The Regis Santos: What is a Teaching Collection?" *Tradición Revista*, II#2 (Summer
1997), pp54-55.

"Martínez, Antonio José," pp. 846-47, and "New Mexico," pp. 1038, in *Encyclopedia of
American Catholic History*. Collegeville: Liturgical Press, 1997.

"Anne Evans' Christmas Pilgrimage," *Colorado History* 1 (1997), 57-67.

"Chapels: The Centers of the Hispanic World," pp. 4-7 in *La Capilla de Todos los Santos*
(San Luis: Sangre de Cristo Parish, 1997).

Santos: Sacred Art of Colorado, Albuquerque, LPD Press, 1997.

The Regis Santos: Thirty Years of Collecting 1966- 1996, Co-authored with Barbe Awalt & Paul Rhetts, Albuquerque, LPD Press, 1997.

New Mexican Spanish Religious Oratory: 1800-1900. Albuquerque, University of New Mexico Press, 1997.

"An Old New Mexican Retablo Shows Us a New Subject," *Tradición Revista* I#3 (Fall 1996), pp. 39-41.

"The Early Santo Revival in Albuquerque: Santero Luis Aragon," *Tradición Revista* I#2 (Summer 1996), pp. 45-47.

"Fray Angélico Chávez: In Memoriam," *Book Talk* 25 #3 (June 1996), pp.1-2.

"Alburquerque in 1821: Padre Leyva's Descriptions," *New Mexico Historical Review* 70 (1995), pp. 159-78.

Santos and Saints: The Religious Folk Art of Hispanic New Mexico. Santa Fe: Ancient City Press, 1994.

Folk and Church in Nineteenth-Century New Mexico. Colorado Springs: Hulbert Center for Southwest Studies, The Colorado College, 1993.

"Foreword" to fray Angélico Chávez, *My Penitente Land.* Santa Fe: Museum of New Mexico Press, 1993.

"Church Buildings and Land in Old Albuquerque: In Celebration of the Bicentennial of the Present Church Structure, 1793-1993." Albuquerque: San Felipe Neri Church, 1993.

"The Virgin Mary and Her Images in Spanish Colonial Art." Denver: Denver Art Museum, 1993 (with Mary Armijo).

"Foreward" to Larry Frank, *New Kingdom of the Saints.* Santa Fe: Red Crane Books, 1992.

Hispanic Los Aguelos and Pueblo Tsave-Yohs. Albuquerque: Southwest Hispanic Research Institute, 1992.

"Territorial Documents and Memories: Singing Church History," *New Mexico Historical Review* 67 (1992), pp. 393-413 (with Rowena A. Rivera).

"The Sad Poet of Ranchos de Albuquerque," *Traditions Southwest* 1 #1 (September 1989), pp. 38-40 (with Rowena A. Rivera).

"The View From The Rectory," in E.A. Mares,ed. *Padre Martínez: New Perspecitves* (Taos: Millicent Rogers, 1988), pp. 71-100.

(editor of) *The Life of Bishop Machebeuf.* Denver: Regis College, 1987 (with Ronald S. Brockway).

"The Hispanic Arts in Colorado," in "Hispanic Night at the Center" (January 31, 1987), pp. 3.

"Cofradía," *The World & I* 1 #8 (August 1986), pp. 148-61.

Penitente Self-Government: Brotherhoods and Councils, 1797-1947. Santa Fe: Ancient City Press, 1985 (with Rowena A. Rivera).

"Funciones of a Village," pp. 6-8 in Frederico Vigil, ed., *Funciones: Communal Ceremonies of Hispanic Life.* Albuguerque: Sagrada Arts Studio, 1983.

Works and Days: A History of San Felipe Neri Church, 1867-1895. Albuquerque: Albuquerque Museum, 1983.

"Albuquerque Parish Celebrates Centenary," *The Southern Jesuit* 2 #3 (April 1983), pp. 11-15 (and cover).

"The Naming of Places in Spanish New Mexico," pp. 293-302 in Marta Weigle, ed., *Hispanic Arts and Ethnohistory in the Southwest*. Albuquerque: University of New Mexico Press, 1983.

Diary of the Jesuit Residence of Our Lady of Guadalupe Parish, Conejos, Colorado, December 1871- December 1875. Colorado Springs: Colorado College, 1982 (with Marianne L. Stoller and José B. Fernández).

Santos and Saints: The Religious Folk Art of Hispanic New Mexico. Santa Fe: Ancient City Press, 1982.

"St. Peter: Apostle Transformed Into Trickster," *Arche* 6 (1981), pp. 112-28 (with William J. Hynes).

"The Brief Career of the 'Healer,'" *Albuquerque Journal* "Impact" (November 11, 1980), pp.10-13.

"The Triple Rostro of Arroyo Seco," *Denver Post* "Empire" (April 8, 1979), pp. 23-25.

"The Death Cart: Its Place Among the Santos of New Mexico," *Colorado Magazine* 55 (1979), pp. 1-14 (and cover).

"The Spanish Passion Play in New Mexico and Colorado," *Historical Review* 53 (1978), pp.239-59.

Navajo Ceremonial Practice. Denver: Regis College, 1977 (revised 1985) (with Randolph Lumpp).

"Italian Jesuits and Hispano Penitentes," *Il Giornalino* 5 #1 (February 1978), pp. 11-17.

Holy Week in Tomé: A New Mexico Passion Play. Santa Fe: Sunstone Press, 1976.

"The American Passion Play," *The Jesuit Bulletin* 55 #1 (March 1976), pp. 10-11.

"Peasant Religion: Retablos and Penitentes," pp. 123-139 in José de Onís, ed., *The Hispanic Contribution to the State of Colorado*. Boulder: Westview Press, 1976.

Santos and Saints: Essays and Handbook. Albuquerque: Calvin Horn Press, 1974.

"New Mexico Santero Art," *La Luz* 1 #8 (December 1972), pp. 22-24.

Literary Studies

"Hopkins' Heraclitean Fire," *Victorian Poetry* 35 (1997), 233-35.

Adducere II: The Faculty Lectures at Regis College of Regis University, 1987-1993. Denver: Regis University 1995 (co-editor)

Masterplots II: Poetry. Magill, 1992. (four poetry explications)

A Guidebook to Zen and the Art of Motorcycle Maintenance. New York: William Morrow Publisher, 1990 (with Ronald DiSanto).

Fraser Haps and Mishaps: The Diary of Mary E. Cozens. Denver: Regis College Press, 1990 (with Alice Reich).

"The Games of Life," in Margaret L. McDonald. ed., *Adducere*, Denver: Regis College, 1987. pp 50-56.

"Orality and Literacy in Matter and Form: Ben Franklin's *Way to Wealth*," *Oral Tradition* 2 #1 (January 1987), pp. 273-85.

"The Foundational Pattern of 'God's Grandeur,'" *Hopkins Quarterly* 12 (1985-86), pp. 80-82.

"Vertigo in History: The Threatening Tactility of 'Sinners in the Hands,'" *Early American Literature* 18 (1983-84), pp. 242-56 (with Eugene R. Delay).

"The Figure of Columbia: Phillis Wheatley Plus George Washington," *New England Quarterly* 54 (1981), pp. 264-66.

"Zen and the Art of Motorcycle Maintenance: The Identity of the Erlkonig," *Ariel* 10 #1 (January 1979), pp. 83-93.

"Seminar in Denver Explores Plains Indians' Religious Values," *National Jesuit News* 7 #9 (May 1978), p. 13.

(editor of) A.E. Housman, "Fragment of a Greek Tragedy," *Network* 2 (1974), pp. 18-21.

"Tom and Eva: Mrs. Stowe's Two Dying Christs," *Negro American Literature* 6 (1972), pp. 85-90.

"The Tactile Sensorium of Richard Crashaw," *Seventeenth-Century News*, 30 (1972), pp. 9-10.

"The Oral Patterning of the Cyclops Episode, *Odyssey* IX," *The Classical Bulletin* 48 (1972), pp. 54-56.

"Donne's Holy Sonnet XIV," *The Explicator* 29 (1971), #74.

"The Biblical Meaning of Mather's Bradford," *Bulletin of the Rocky Mountain Modern Language Association* 24 (1970), pp. 147-54.

"Literate and Illiterate Space: The Moral Geography of Cooper's Major American Fiction," *Dissertation Abstracts* 29 (1969), 4507 A.

Approaches to Literature. 5 volumes. Syracuse: L.W. Singer, 1967 (with Julian L. Maline, S.J., and James Berkley).

(translations of some of Martial's *Epigrammata)* in Garry Wills, ed., *Roman Culture: Weapons and the Man.* New York: George Braziller, 1966.

"For Teresa, Dying of Cancer" (poem), *Review for Religious* 24 (1965), pp. 273.

Prose and Poetry for Enjoyment. 5 volumes. Syracuse: L.W. Singer 1965 (with Julian L. Maline, S.J.).

Archbishop Lamy: In His Own Words

In addition to both cloth and soft cover version, the complete sermons of Archbishop Lamy are available on CD-ROM disk. The CD, compatible on both PC and Macintosh platforms, contains the original text of Lamy's sermons as well as translations into English. All 250 of Lamy's sermons, instructions, retreat talks, and other speeches are included, comprising over 250,000 words of original English (from Lamy's Ohio and Kentucky years), Spanish (from his time in New Mexico), and French (from Lamy's French Seminary years). Spellings are regularized so that the texts are completely computer-searchable.

The CD-ROM is available for $29.95 and can be ordered from LPD Press at 505/344-9382 or at www.nmsantos.com.

ALSO FROM LPD PRESS

Seeds of Struggle Harvest of Faith
The Papers of the Archdiocese of Santa Fe
Catholic Cuatro Centennial Conference
The History of the Catholic Church in New Mexico
Edited by Thomas J. Steele, S.J., Barbe Awalt, & Paul Rhetts

Our Saints Among Us: 400 Years of New Mexican Devotional Art
by Barbe Awalt & Paul Rhetts

The Regis Santos: Thirty Years of Collecting 1966-1996
by Thomas J. Steele, S.J., Barbe Awalt, & Paul Rhetts

Santos: Sacred Art of Colorado
edited by Thomas J. Steele, S.J.

Hispanic New Mexican Pottery:
Evidence of Craft Specialization 1790-1890
by Charles M. Carrillo

Charlie Carrillo: Tradition & Soul/Tradición y Alma
by Barbe Awalt & Paul Rhetts

Tradición Revista: The Journal of Traditional & Contemporary
Spanish Colonial Art & Culture
Barbe Awalt & Paul Rhetts, publishers

LPD Press
2400 Rio Grande Blvd. NW PMB 213
Albuquerque, New Mexico 87104-3222
505/344-9382 fax 505/345-5129
email PaulLPD@aol.com   www.nmsantos.com